Rec'd of Miss M. E. Ballard
$1.00 pay for this Magazine
for One Year, commencing
with this No.
            Sam'l Whittamore

ANCIENT ATHENS.

For the Christian Family Magazine.

THE

CHRISTIAN FAMILY MAGAZINE,

OR

PARENTS' AND CHILDREN'S ANNUAL.

EDITED BY

REV. D. NEWELL,

ASSISTED BY AN ASSOCIATION OF CLERGYMEN.

VOL. II.

NEW YORK:
PUBLISHED BY D. NEWELL 132 NASSAU STREET.
LONDON—WILEY & PUTNAM.

1843.

Entered according to the Act of Congress, in the year 1842,
By D. NEWELL,
In the Clerk's Office of the District Court for the Southern District of New York.

Stereotyped by R. C. Valentine,
45 Gold-street.

INDEX TO VOL II.

Advent, The. By W. M. Fahnestock, M. D.	100
Amaranth	50
American Antiquities. By the Editor	196
A Voyager's Adieu. By H. M. Parsons	116
An Omnipresent God. By Mrs. M. L. Gardiner	191
Athens in Ruins. Editorial	112
Autumn Fruit. By the author of "Blind Alice"	4
A Subdued Temper—Example of Roger Sherman	20
Boston, A Trip to. By Rev. A. D. Eddy	239 295
Blue Jay and Bird of Paradise. By H. M. Parsons	204
Brothers and Sisters. By Rev. A. D. Eddy	37
Bible, The	77
Caldeira, Visit to. By H. M. Parsons	271
Child and Hermit	199 244 298
Christian Family Altar. By Rev. F. C. Woodworth	40
Claims of Religion on the Young. Editorial	25
Close of Life. By the Editor	169
Cotton Mather's Rules	18
Death's Doings	49
Description of Whitfield's Preaching. By Miss Francis	44
Destruction of the Richmond Theatre	114
Disappointed Hopes	248
Doubting Christian, To a. By G. W. Baird	220
Duck, The Eider. By Mrs. Sigourney	49
Earthly Glory	99
Family Circle	128
Female Education. By Miss C. Thurston	69 139
Female Biography. By H. M. Parsons	131
Female Influence. By Hon. D. Webster	269
Filial Tribute. By the Editor	30
Filial Obedience. By Rev. Tryon Edwards	65
Forsaken, The. By the Editor	205
Flower in the Icicle. By Mrs. Emma C. Embury	164
Franklin in the Social Circle. By Wm. Wirt	73
Giraffe, The	194
Glimpse of Heaven	120
Good Manners	180
God, The Love of	90
Heart, The Broken. By W. Irving	117
Health—Rules of Diet	41
Human Frame. By Rev. B. H. Draper	176
Horrors of War	135
Hippopotamus, The	229
Illinois	152
Influence of Family Prayer	78
Jonah and his Gourd. By E. W. Chester	88
Kedron	202
Last Day of Adam. By J. W. Bailey	183
Last Day of Eve. By Miss Mary A. Chester	66
Light Literature, Influence of. By the Editor	105
Marriage—Blighted Hopes. By the Editor	5
Maniac and Duellist. By Rev. S. I. Prime	230
Maternal Societies. By the Editor	46
Method, Mrs. Cecil's. By the Editor	144
Memoir of Mrs. Ann S. L. Gilbert. By Mrs. L. H. Sigourney	282
Mount Vesuvius. By G. A. Noble, A. M.	92

INDEX.

My Brother. By Miss Cynthia H. Stow	134
Moral Rubicon of Life. By the Editor	265
Mother, To my	74
Music—Jerusalem, my happy home	51
" Saviour hear us through thy merit	102
" Lord, let my Prayer	152
" Thou sweet gliding Kedron	202
" We give thee joy, young Bride	302
National Relics. By H. M. Parsons	228
Nursery Maxims	75
Not lost, but gone to Heaven. By Mrs. M. St. Leon Loud	162
Ornan, The Threshing-floor of. By E. W. Chester	22
Our Mortal and Immortal Destiny. By the Editor	259
Parting and Return of the Bride. By Mrs. L. H. Sigourney	214
Portfolio, The Youth's	98
Ravages of Time. By A. Lloyd	178
Reflections on the New Year. By the Rev. G. Spring, D. D.	150
Religion	120
Rejected; and the Forsaken. By the Editor	212
Repentance—A German Parable	279
Return, The Bride's. By Miss E. R. Comstock	43
Rich Blessings in Disguise	148
Robber Son. By Rev. S. I. Prime	12
Rules for Family Government	50
Sabbath Scene. By Mrs. M. L. Gardiner	281
Savoyard Orphan's Death. By H. M. Parsons	170
Self Knowledge	192
Serious Counsels to the Young. By Rev. J. Bennett, D. D.	195
Shaft, The Archer's Fatal. By Mrs. L. H. Sigourney	64
Sisterless, The. By J. L. Chester	121
Slanderer, The. By the Editor	101
Song for the Bereaved. By H. M. Parsons	17
Sustain your Minister. By the Editor	155
Teachings of Autumn. By F. W. P. Greenwood	61
Timothy. By Rev. W. B. Sprague, D. D.	215 275
The Brother and Sister. By Mrs. E. C. Embury	221
Tiger Lily	54
Tomb of the Exiled Emperor. By H. M. Parsons	185
Touching Incident	142
True Happiness in the Conjugal Relation. By Rev. A. A. Lipscomb	230 290
True Greatness	96
Value of Parental Government. By Rev. A. A. Lipscomb	171
Valuable Remedies	201
Valuable Maxims	137
Van Rensselaer, Hon. Stephen. Editorial	262
Way to be Happy. By the author of "Blind Alice"	82 122
Widow, The Stricken. By the Editor	55

EMBELLISHMENTS.

Frontispiece—Christian Family Altar. Steel Plate	3	Frost Gage. Colored Engraving	4
		Tiger Lily	54
The Bible my richest treasure	53	The Golden Pear	104
Ancient Athens	103	Morning Glory	154
Devout Meditation	153	Blue Jay and Bird of Paradise	204
The Forsaken	203	Honeysuckle and Humming Bird	254
The Patroon	257		

THE GOLDEN PEAR.

Delicious fruit, thou golden pear,
Thy richest flavor all may share;
Tree of the cottage and the poor
Can palace of the rich have more?
For sweet content as seldom dwells
In palaces as lowly cells.

Oh! I would scorn the mansion fair,
If pomp, and pride, and care were there;
And to the humble cottage flee
Leaving each proud and lofty tree,
For thee—sweet harvest pear, for thee!

THE
CHRISTIAN FAMILY MAGAZINE.

JANUARY, 1843.

Original.

THE INFLUENCE OF LIGHT LITERATURE UPON THE FAMILY CIRCLE.

BY THE EDITOR.

Our country presents one vast field, already ripe for the sickle. What shall be the harvest, and who shall gather it? are questions of momentous interest to the philanthropist and Christian. The tide of emigration will soon swell beyond the Rocky Mountains, and reach the Pacific Ocean. Our 18,000,000 will increase to 100,000,000 long before the sun of a single century shall go down.

In the opening volume of Divine Providence every year presents to the view of the discerning Christian new and important events; while every thing around and in prospect proclaims to the inhabitants of this nation that nothing short of enlarged views, high purposes, unquenchable zeal, and mighty action, can satisfy the claims of humanity and of God.

Much has been said of the alarming crisis which our Republic is fast approaching—of the bold adventure of this age—of the frightful appearance of misrule and innovation, both in the State and Church—and we are not without our apprehension that this nation may, ere long, reach an era that shall cause our millions to grow pale with fear! Already we see enough in the aspect of human affairs all over the globe to elicit the serious inquiry: 'What is the Almighty about to do? what is the controversy which he has with the nations?'

Whatever may be portended by the clouds that are gathering in the political and moral horizon—by the roar of thunder that breaks on the ear from the distant heavens—of one thing we are perfectly satisfied, the CAUSES that have conspired to bring about the evil in prospect have had their origin and progress, if not their maturity, in the family circle; and to this source must the remedy be applied, if the threatened evil is to be averted.

As well might we attempt to purify the deep, while all its tributary streams were full of deadly poison, as to depend upon a thorough work of reform in the State. The work of regeneration must be commenced at the FOUNTAIN, and THEN will the streams be pure! The great fountain of the Church and State, of society, and of nations, is the FAMILY CIRCLE. Around this social sanctuary cluster the dearest hopes of mankind! From this FOUNTAIN flow the bitter waters of strife and misrule, or the streams that give vigor and health to the nations!

If our sacred altars are to stand firm, amidst the combined assaults of the common enemy, help, under God, must come from this source of unlimited strength.

Too long have we boasted of our wealth, intelligence, enterprise, and extent of territory. While with proud self-complacency we have seen this infant nation attaining to the vigor and strength of full-grown manhood, and taking its seat among the kingdoms of the earth, we seem to have forgotten that all the Republics of the ancient world have been overthrown in the wreck of time, and that we stand on a perilous eminence, and without STRONG moral principles and a firm trust in the great God, our foundations must ere long crumble from beneath!

In the material world, great bodies, rolling onward with a tremendous momentum, have been known to fall asunder by their OWN GRAVITY. Nothing short of the strong bonds of INTELLIGENCE and VIRTUE, and the favor of Heaven, can save this nation from falling into the same gulf of licentiousness where other republics perished!

We have no time to descant on this great topic of interest, or to give any extended specification of the numerous agents that are at work at the foundations of our public weal, and which may yet hang over the future a veil of impenetrable sackcloth. In this paper we design to call attention to the alarming influence of light literature upon the youth of our country. This has long been a subject of solicitude with the moralist and philanthropist, and of late has justly awakened the increased interest of some of our most eminent statesmen and divines.

From reports that are entitled to our utmost confidence, we have statistics which are calculated to awaken in the bosom of every benefactor of our race a thrilling interest.

Not less than twelve millions of volumes are annually sent forth from the American press, "one SIXTH part of which are NOVELS and TALES!!" while the proportion of fictitious to solid reading in France is only one SIXTEENTH!! Let the patriot and Christian lay this astounding fact to heart!

The increasing, all-pervading influence of the newspaper press in this country, is certainly without any parallel in the history of the world. We have one thousand weekly, forty semi-weekly, fourteen tri-weekly, and more than one hundred daily papers. These, allowing a subscription list of only two thousand each, make a grand aggregate of about 200,000,000 sheets per year! while, according to the returns of the stamp office of 1836, Great Britain issued less than 37,000,000 for her population of 25,000,000.

While we contemplate the gigantic influence of our three or four thousand Editors, Authors, Compilers, and Publishers, who are sending abroad over the land 3,000,000 of numbers of Periodicals, 12,000,000 of volumes of Books, 200,000,000 of Newspaper sheets, to form the mind and morals, and mould the character and destiny of this country, well may the public guardians of our morals and laws feel CONCERN for the tremendous issue!

Shall this mighty engine contribute to the public weal or wo? This is an inquiry which deserves the most serious consideration of all. Who in the Church and State will not contribute their influence for a PURE, CHRISTIAN LITERATURE? a literature that shall be safe—that shall form the intellectual and moral aliment of the people?

We speak not of the alarming tendency of the 100,000 infidel and impure books, that are daily sending their moral leprosy through the length and breadth of the land: for we fancy ourselves in the Christian Family circle: but we earnestly inquire—what is the influence of light reading upon the rising generation! By light literature, we mean those works of the imagination and of fiction which have no direct tendency to elevate and strengthen the social and moral feelings—which have for their grand aim, AMUSEMENT and EXCITEMENT, rather than intellectual and moral culture; including novels, plays, and romances, with many of our light magazines and annuals.

We pass no unqualified censure upon works of fiction, as such. Many exceptions are found among works of this class; especially those of modern date. Shall we reject Mackenzie's Man of Feeling, Pilgrim's Progress, Paradise Lost, Johnson's Rasselas, H. More's Cœlebs, The Vicar of Wakefield, etc. simply because they do not abound in literal matters of fact? Far from it.—In this sweeping condemnation we should be compelled to include the parables and apologues found in the Sacred Volume. As our first objection, we urge that—

LIGHT LITERATURE GIVES FALSE VIEWS OF HUMAN LIFE. Many writers of novels, romances, and plays are gifted with master minds. They often combine all the graces of style with the most fascinating powers of language—eloquence, wit, humor, pathos, genius, and learning. Consequently, their writings possess an attractiveness scarcely to be resisted by the young. But let it not be forgotten, that all the richness and lustre of the golden chalice or its choice sweets cannot form an antidote for the deadly poison it contains. He who destroyed Paradise, though an angel of light, was a mighty fallen spirit!

INFLUENCE OF LIGHT LITERATURE.

The pictures which light reading contains are too strong, unreal, unearthly. They often represent human life as one glorious holiday, divested of its sorrows and woes—Time as a golden summer, full of shady groves, refreshing sunshine, cooling streams, singing birds, fragrant flowers, delicious fruits, and all that heart can wish.

But alas! how do these gilded day-dreams vanish, when youth is gone, and the heart is made to feel that life is a scene of adversity—that man is made to mourn!

Behold the youth whose taste and principles have been formed under the intoxicating influence of novels and of romantic visions. The heyday of youth, the season of leisure passes away, and he takes the stage of active and responsible manhood—ardently expecting to find in conjugal love unalloyed happiness—in riches and honors durable enjoyment—in society the greetings of warm hearts.

But, perchance, ere he has reached the meridian of life he finds, to his unutterable disappointment, that the companion of his first love possesses not a generous, kindred spirit—that his offspring have caused his heart to bleed with anguish—that his riches and honors have taken to themselves wings and are gone for ever; and his early companions, in the cheerless winter of adversity, like summer birds, have forsaken him. In early life enchanting romance spread out to his view naught but scenes of prosperity. He was never taught to expect that this mortal life is but a pilgrimage—and consequently he saw no necessity for the work of DISCIPLINE for its trials and woes? and what is the sequel?

In the hour of trial and fearful onset, he attempts to drown his sorrows in the intoxicating bowl, plunges into scenes of dissipation and vice, and with a broken heart and ruined family goes to an inglorious grave!

Let the youthful reader be assured—that a character formed under the influence of light reading will be but miserably fitted for the stern duties and trials of this serious life.

2. Light Literature has a direct tendency to lead the young into vain and unsatisfying amusements. Novels not only occasion a distaste for works of intellectual merit, blunt the moral sensibilities, weaken the principles, and still the voice of conscience; but they have an alarming tendency to lead the young from the ways of safety, if not to a returnless distance from the path of Heaven. They make the young not only dissatisfied with the sober and substantial realities of life, but cause them to seek after exciting adventure.

The exciting tales of romantic love, etc. etc., prepare the mind for the more dissipating scenes of the ball chamber and theatre; and these, in their turn, for games of chance and scenes of vice, the very thought of which, a few years before, would have caused the heart to sicken. How many pure-minded young females—how many promising young men—on their death-beds, have dated their first departure from the paths of virtue and peace, and their final overthrow, to the perusal of novels!

3. Light reading is a prodigal waste of time. The longest life is but a vapor when compared with an immortal existence, and not too long to make ample preparation for the eternal world. Take out the years of childhood and of old age—the time of sickness, languishing, and of sleep, and what is allotted to worldly business, and how small a portion is left for meditation, prayer, and works of benevolence! And shall these precious moments be wasted in mere exciting amusement? Great and good men have wept when they lost a day. Queen Elizabeth, when dying, exclaimed, "Millions of worlds for an inch of time!"

Multitudes spend their precious days and nights in the perusal of books that please the fancy, charm the imagination, corrupt the taste, excite the passions; but which have no tendency to improve the heart. To the young, we must say, this is wasting the seed-time and spring of life, upon which hang the dearest hopes of the golden harvest. Life is a probation for eternity—and youth is a probation for manhood.

Light reading is not only a positive waste of time, but it is calculated to vitiate the taste, weaken the moral principles, cause a disrelish for works of intellectual and moral worth, and thus render the heart indifferent to the truths of the Bible and the influence of the Holy Spirit.

We admit the importance of an able, learned, and holy ministry—of wholesome laws, and of their faithful administration—of multiplying schools, and of the universal diffusion of useful knowledge, and yet, do we not perceive that all these rich and invaluable blessings are designed to produce only a LIMITED INFLUENCE, while the foundations of our strength are weakened by the light, corrupting literature of the age?

THIS IS THE TIME FOR UNITED, VIGOROUS ACTION. England, France, and Germany are sending abroad thousands of novels and other works of still more alarming tendency. Many of these works are republished in America as soon as they fall from the foreign press, and are scattered like leaves of autumn over the face of the land, almost without money and without price. And it is PAINFUL to see that so many, in the bosom of the church of God, instead of lifting up a standard against the alarming evil, are giving countenance to this traffic. Such are some of the evil features of the age.

WHAT IS THE REMEDY?—we almost despairingly ask. Let parents, as the guardians of the family circle—let ministers of the Gospel on the walls of the church—let teachers in our colleges, seminaries, and schools, and let every noble and high-minded youth of the age, and every lover of good order and sound morals, SERIOUSLY view the influence which the PRESS, that mighty lever of power, must have upon the character of this age, and upon the destinies of this country.

The increasing popularity of the theatre, ball-chamber, games of chance, &c., can be checked and done away by no legislative enactments or coercive measures. But there is one GLORIOUS, if not SOVEREIGN REMEDY. This is by showing a BETTER WAY. Let our family circles be furnished with able, spirited, useful periodicals and books, that will be FOOD for the mind. Let libraries, lyceums, evening lectures for young and old, become popular in every town and village of the nation. Let our able, gifted, high-minded spirits, who pant after a pure literature, come to the work. It has been said, "this is an age of great events?" But where are the mighty men, like those of the past. And upon whom has fallen the mantle of Edwards, Dwight, M. Henry, Gill, R. Hall, A. Clark, J. Wesley, Cowper, H. More, and Mrs. Hemans.

O, what an inglorious retribution must authors of light and hurtful books at last meet! The author of Don Juan will continue to corrupt the moral feelings, and form a rampart against the Gospel, when the influence of Napoleon, whose arm once shook the globe, and whose ashes are still mightier than many crowned heads of Europe, shall have ceased forever!

Original.

ATHENS IN RUINS.*

EDITORIAL.

Among the celebrated cities of Greece, none is so distinguished for political greatness, military achievements, and progress in the arts and sciences, as the one represented in the engraving of this number.

Athens was situated on the Saronic gulf, about four miles from the sea, and was connected with three harbors by walls of great strength built of hewn stone, and so broad that carriages could pass each other upon them. Its chief ornament was the Acropolis, situated on an elevation in the centre of the city, where painting, sculpture, and architecture accumulated those treasures whose ruins still awaken the admiration of the traveller. Among its splendid edifices was the Parthenon, two hundred and seventeen feet in length, and ninety-eight in breadth, containing a statue of ivory, thirty-nine feet in height,

* See frontispiece.

covered with gold. On the north side of the Acropolis, forming magnificent entrances to the temple of Minerva, were the Propylea and Eryctheum, and other noble structures of white marble, with numerous and imposing monuments of illustrious men. Without the walls was the Temple of Jupiter Olympus, inclosing a circumference of half a mile, its exterior containing one hundred and twenty fluted columns, each sixty feet in height and six in diameter. Three-fourths of a mile to the north of the town was the Academy where Plato taught. The Lyceum, famed for the instructions of Aristotle, was on the opposite side of the Ilissus. Among the political associations connected with Athens are the Pnyx and Areopagus. On the former the deliberations of the people were held, and from the latter the decisions of the tribunal were proclaimed.

But the grandeur of the Parthenon has been mutilated by the barbarian—the Corinthian columns of the temple of Jupiter Olympus have fallen beneath the feet of war—the exquisite sculpture of the Propylea and Erychtheum have been defaced by the Venetian—the groves of her sages have been devastated by the plunderer, and the seats of her judges overthrown by the Mahometan. The stork plumes his wing on a shattered shaft of the Acropolis, and the colonnade of Lysicrates stands an isolated relic of the former magnificence of Athens. Parrhasius, Phidias, and Andronicus Cyrrhestes no longer walk her streets and survey the trophies of their skill. Under the direction of Xenophon and Miltiades she no longer sways the destinies of surrounding states—nor does she longer listen to the appeals of Demosthenes, or the lessons of Solon and Socrates. The victories of Macedon subverted her liberties, and the Ottoman conquest extinguished her ancient greatness. Her last attempt at emancipation, in 1820, resulted in the nomination of Otho to the throne, and the restoration of comparative quiet to the distracted city.

But the Turk yet roams lawlessly among her ruins, while midnight broods on the fallen grandeur of the Acropolis.

From the history of this ruined city let Americans learn that the perpetuity of their institutions depends upon the prevalence of the spirit of the Gospel. No government can long exist while a moral adaptedness to freedom is wanting in the people. The seminal principles of virtuous independence must be planted and cherished in the hearts of our citizens, or the arm of our liberty will be palsied. Corruption follows excess of wealth—political contests accompany national degeneracy—civil discord or foreign invasion is the usual attendant of faction. Facilities for exploits of mercy, and qualities for achievements of patriotism, are possessed by us in greater measure than by any nation who has preceded us. But our energies must be directed to conquests of benevolence—speech and the press must be wielded, to purify and elevate the tone of national morality, or our country will not escape the grave of preceding republics, or attain her high destiny, in acting a conspicuous part in the conversion of the world.

APPALLING SCENE.

DESTRUCTION OF THE RICHMOND THEATRE.

ABOUT thirty years ago, there occurred in the city of Richmond one of the most distressing events that has ever happened in this country. There was a theatre in that city, to which the gay and fashionable people were accustomed to resort. On the night of Dec. 20th, 1811, there were some unusual attractions at the theatre, which drew together a very large audience, in which were some of the most distinguished men, and many of the most beautiful and accomplished women in the state. The performances of the evening had commenced. The actors were strutting upon the stage, in all the mock dignity of kings and queens, lords and ladies, and endeavoring, with pompous display, to personate the characters of men and women, of whose real feelings and manners they knew as little as you do; and the audience was in a rapture of delight,

APPALLING SCENE.

applauding and criticising, laughing and talking, and planning new schemes of pleasure, when suddenly the awful cry of "FIRE! FIRE!" fell upon their ears. O, what an awful moment was that! and how soon were all the vanities of the theatre forgotten! The passages leading from the building were few and narrow, and in the general rush, were so crowded as almost to preclude to many all chance of escape. In a little time, the whole of the interior of the house was on fire, and one and another were heard to utter their last piercing cries of anguish, as they fell into the flames and died. Others were crushed to death in the narrow passages, and some were maimed and wounded as they leaped from the windows. The governor of the state, and nearly one hundred persons, of the first families in Virginia, perished! One lady succeeded in reaching an open window; but as she looked down upon the pavement, she drew back, afraid to leap. The flames were rapidly advancing towards her, and she again sought the window, and again drew back. There appeared no way of escape, and in an agony of despair, she shrieked for help. She was heard and recognised by some of her friends, on the outside of the building. They ran to the spot, stretched out their arms towards her, and urged her to throw herself into them; but the height appeared too great, and her courage failed. They entreated her, by every motive they could suggest, to trust them. They assured her they could save her, that many had thus been saved, and that there was no time for delay. As one and another part of the building fell with a fearful crash into the flames, or the piercing shrieks of some unhappy victim sounded in her ears, she would step upon the window sill; but as she contemplated the distance to the ground, she would shrink back, afraid to venture. In this state she remained, halting between two opinions, dreading the danger that was approaching, and afraid to trust the friends who were entreating her to commit herself to them, till the flames burst through the floor beneath her, and, with one cry of despair, she disappeared for ever."

This lady was in danger from the flames, which could destroy the body; but the sinner is in danger from those fiercer flames, which destroy the soul. She refused to hear entreaties and to trust the help of earthly friends, who might fail to save her; but the sinner shuts his ears against the calls and warnings of the Son of God, and refuses to trust the arm of an Almighty Saviour. God is now calling. "Turn ye, turn ye from your evil ways, for why will ye die?" He is pleading with you. "Come, let us reason together, saith the Lord; though your sins be as scarlet, they shall be white as snow; though they be red like crimson, they shall be as wool." And he is mourning over you, and saying, "How can I give thee up, Ephraim?' O, beware, "that you refuse not him that speaketh," or the time may come when he "will laugh at your calamity, and mock when your fear cometh." Selected.

Original.

A VOYAGER'S ADIEU.

BY HENRY M. PARSONS.

Childe Harold bade his native land,
 In numbers wild, good night,
Nor wished again to view the strand
 That linger'd in his sight.
But sweet the voice of hope that brings
 A promise made before,
That I shall cease my wanderings,
 And hail my home, once more.

Land, where the hill and mountain stand,
 With forest verdure crown'd,
Where valleys deep and rich expand,
 And spreading plains abound,
I see no heights save yonder sky,
 No depths besides the sea—
I hear the night bird scream, and sigh
 Good night, my land, to thee.

Land of the free! no servile chain
　Is laid upon thy neck—
The children of thy broad domain
　Bow at no tyrant's beck.
The spirit knows its empire there,
　And o'er the realms of mind
Sweeps like a bird in upper air
　With pinions unconfin'd.

Land, where affection loves to bind
　A wreath for wintry hours—
Where he who seeks, is sure to find
　Its sweetest, choicest flowers.
Full many are the loved I leave
　Behind yon beacon light—
O where is he who would not grieve
　To bid such friends good night?

The shades of eve are deepening fast
　Upon the trackless main,
But morning's beams will soon be cast
　O'er all its waste again.
If man must cherish idle fears
　When he is forced to roam,
Who then would break away for years
　From all the joys of home?

Often the thoughts may homeward hie,
　Often the tear may swell,
Sometimes the heart may breathe a sigh
　That it has sighed farewell.
But never should it brood o'er ills
　That may its lov'd betide—
There is a POWER who kindly wills—
　What should man ask beside?

THE BROKEN HEART.

BY WASHINGTON IRVING.

It is a common practice with those who have outlived the susceptibility of early feeling, or have been brought up in the gay heartlessness of dissipated life, to laugh at tales of romantic passion as mere fictions of novelists and poets. My observations on human nature have induced me to think otherwise. They have convinced me, that however the surface of the character may be chilled and frozen by the cares of the world, or cultivated into mere smiles by the arts of society, still there are dormant fires lurking in the depths of the coldest bosom, which, when once enkindled, become impetuous, and are sometimes desolating in their effects. Shall I confess it!—I believe in broken hearts, and the possibility of dying of disappointed love. I do not, however, consider it a malady often fatal to my own sex; but I firmly believe that it withers down many a lovely woman into an early grave.

Man is the creature of interest and ambition. His nature leads him forth into the struggle and bustle of the world. Love is but the embellishment of his early life, or a song piped in the intervals of the acts. He seeks for fame, for fortune, for space in the world's thought, and dominion over his fellow-men. But a woman's whole life is a history of the affections. The heart is her world: it is there her ambition strives for empire; it is there her avarice seeks for hidden treasures. She sends forth her sympathies on adventure; she embarks her whole soul in the traffic of affection; and if shipwrecked, her case is hopeless—for it is a bankruptcy of the heart.

To a man the disappointment of love may occasion some bitter pangs: it wounds some feelings of tenderness—it blasts some prospects of felicity; but he is an active being—he may dissipate his thoughts in the whirl of varied occupation, or may plunge into the tide of pleasure; or, if the scene of disappointment be too full of painful associations, he can shift his abode at will, and taking as it were the wings of the morning, can "fly to the uttermost parts of the earth, and be at rest."

But woman's is comparatively a fixed, a secluded, and a meditative life. She is more the companion of her own thoughts and feelings; and if they are turned to ministers of sorrow, where shall she look for consolation? Her lot is to be wooed and won; and if unhappy in her love, her heart is like some fortress that has been captured. and sacked, and abandoned, and left desolate !

How many bright eyes grow dim—how many soft cheeks grow pale—how many lovely forms fade away into the tomb, and none can tell the cause that blighted their loveliness! As the dove will clasp its wings to its side, and cover and conceal the arrow that is preying on its vitals, so it is the nature of woman to hide from the world the pangs of wounded affection. The love of a delicate female is always shy and silent. Even when fortunate, she scarcely breathes it to herself; but when otherwise, she buries it in the recesses of her bosom, and there lets it cower and brood among the ruins of her peace. With her the desire of the heart has failed. The great charm of existence is at an end. She neglects all the cheerful exercises which gladden the spirits, quicken the pulses, and send the tide of life in healthful currents through the veins. Her rest is broken—the sweet refreshment of sleep is poisoned by melancholy dreams—"dry sorrow drinks her blood," until her enfeebled frame sinks under the slightest external injury. Look for her after a little while, and you will find friendship weeping over her untimely grave, and wondering that one who but lately glowed with all the radiance of health and beauty, should so speedily be brought down to " darkness and the worm." You will be told of some wintry chill, some casual indisposition, that laid her low;—but no one knows of the mental malady that previously sapped her strength, and made her so easy a prey to the spoiler.

She is like some tender tree, the pride and beauty of the grove; graceful in its form, bright in its foliage, but with the worm preying at its heart. We find it suddenly withering, when it should be most fresh and luxuriant. We see it drooping its branches to the earth, and shedding leaf by leaf; until, wasted and perished away, it falls even in the stillness of the forest; and, as we muse over the beautiful ruin, we strive in vain to recollect the blast or thunderbolt that could have smitten it with decay.

I have seen many instances of women running to waste

and self-neglect, and disappearing gradually from the earth, almost as if they had been exhaled to heaven; and have repeatedly fancied that I could trace their death through the various declensions of consumption, cold, debility, languor, melancholy, until I reached the first symptoms of disappointed love.
Selected.

GLIMPSE OF HEAVEN.

Our world is in shadow; but man is higher than his place. He gazes forth, and spreads abroad the pinions of his soul; and when the sixty minutes, which we call sixty years, have done striking, he springs aloft, and kindles as he rises, and the ashes of his plumage fall behind him, and the disembodied soul comes along, with nought of earth about it, and pure as a tone, into the ether. But there it sees amid its shadowed life the mountains of the world to come, standing in the golden morning light of a sun, which never rises here below. So the dweller near the north pole, in the long night, when no sun rises, sees at noon a golden dawn on the highest mountain, and he thinks of his long summer, when the sun never sets.
Selected.

RELIGION.

How sweetly on yon tranquil stream
　The setting sun imprints his ray;
Which back reflects the saffron beam,
　And glows when it has passed away.

More sweetly far, when death draws nigh,
　Religion casts her soothing light,
Sheds on the spirit's opening eye
　Her hues immortal pure and bright.

Original.

THE SISTERLESS.

BY J. L. CHESTER, ESQ., NEW YORK.

Sweet sister! art thou dead? I seem to feel
   Thy gentle presence near me while I sit
Within the room where I was wont to steal
   Beside thy dying couch. Blest visions flit
Before me as the sorrowing tear I shed—
Surely, sweet sister, thou canst not be dead!

Thy form is absent—I no longer see
   Thy gentle face, and love-expressing eye,
Whose fondest glance was often turned on me,
   Ev'n in thy hours of deepest agony;
And yet, canst thou be dead, when day and night
I see that eye in all its meteor light?

I know thy lip no longer meeteth mine
   In those long kisses of ecstatic love—
Those lips, more rosy than the richest wine,
   Have found another object far above;
And yet, I fancy oft, at eve's still hour,
I feel thy kiss in all its blissful power.

I see thee in the slumberous hour of night,
   When sleep hath wrapped me in her dreamy wing—
I see thee in a vision blest and bright,
   And press thy hand, and hear thee sweetly sing;
Surely, sweet sister, thou canst not be dead,
When such blest visions on my sleep are shed!

I have no sister now! Oh! blame me not,
   If from mine eye I cannot keep the tear;
A sister's love can never be forgot,
   And she to my lone heart was doubly dear.
I have no sister now! Oh! let me weep,
And o'er her grave my lonely vigils keep.

Oh! blame me not, if my o'erburdened heart
   Be almost bursting in its wild excess:
Alas! it is a dreadful lot to part
   For ever with a sister's fond caress,

To feel no more her kiss upon my cheek—
Nor meet her glancing eye—nor hear her speak.

Alas! I am a lonely being now—
  Shut out for ever from a sister's love:
My young heart hath been early taught to bow,
  And mourn its loss as doth the widowed dove.
Forgive me, then, if on my youthful face
  The hand of sorrow leaveth many a trace.

Forgive me, if my voice no more is heard
  To breathe the merry tones of former days;
And blame me not if grief should tinge each word—
  And oh! forbear within my heart to gaze;
For lowly I have been constrained to bow—
Alas! alas! I have no sister now!

Original.
THE WAY TO BE HAPPY.

MRS. GRANT'S STORY.

BY THE AUTHOR OF "BLIND ALICE," ETC.

My boy, my beautiful and brave and gentle boy, was twelve years old, my twin daughters nine, and my youngest darling, also a daughter five, when a malignant sore throat appeared in our neighborhood. Never shall I forget the cautious tenderness with which my husband told me this. Having done so, he added, "Now, my dear Eliza, it seems to me our duty to remove our children from the reach of this plague."

"Oh yes!" I exclaimed, "let us go at once; come, my dear husband, we cannot go too quickly."

He caught my hand as I was hurrying away, and said, "to-morrow morning all shall be ready for you and the children to set out. You cannot well go before."

"I and the children—and when will you come?" "When the pestilence has passed away I will come for you."

* Continued from page 82.

"And you will remain here till then?" His looks answered me, and I reseated myself, saying, firmly, "Then I remain with you."

"Not so, Eliza," said Mr. Grant, "you will not, I am sure, do so when you have thought a moment. Remember that we are neither of us our own. We have been bought with a price, and are God's servants to perform that which he appoints to us. He has constituted me a Shepherd of souls, and given me this people in charge. I cannot leave them when they most need my care. I must stay to strengthen and cheer the dying, and to comfort the mourner. But your children are especially trusted to your care, and you have no right to indulge even your generous affection towards me to the neglect of this duty. Do your duty, my love, and leave me to do mine, free from care on your account, and we may hope that God will bless us, and restore us to each other."

Long, long hours, I prayed and struggled, ere I could yield my will in this matter to what I yet felt was the will of God— ere I could leave my dearest and best earthly friend in His hands; but I did at last yield—I did leave him, and, I did it with a calm and peaceful mind. I had at last been brought to feel that God's will was not only wiser and holier, but kinder, more tender towards those I loved than my will, and I now truly desired that His will should be done. I knew it would be done, I believed He would hear my prayer that I should be prepared for it, and I was calm.

I went with my children the next morning to a place about twenty miles distant, and my husband stayed with his people. I heard from him and wrote to him daily. For three weeks he was in the midst of the pestilence, watching by the dying and burying the dead—yet he escaped. God was his shield. The pestilence had abated, and we were anticipating a speedy and joyous reunion, when my boy sickened. In a few hours he was seriously ill, and the physician who saw him declared his disease to be scarlet fever. Again I passed the night watches by his bed, and they were lonely watches, for he who had, in his former illness, shared and soothed my cares was afar off—yet I was happier than I had been then. Then, the utmost I could do, you may remember, was to be still. Now, I could say from my heart, as my husband then said, "Thy will, not mine, be done." His will was done. In three days I had closed my boy's eyes and seen him laid in his coffin. He was beautiful even then, more beautiful indeed than ever, but it was a beauty not of this earth. Young as he was, he had learned to love, and striven to imitate his Saviour, and as I sat beside his lifeless body, unwilling to shut from my sight that which I had so long loved to look upon, I knew that he was with my parents, an angel in heaven; and though I sorrowed that my precious gift was taken from me, I felt that my Father was wise and good, and I did not desire to resist His will. My husband arrived some hours after his son's death, and we sorrowed and rejoiced together—sorrowed for our own loss, and rejoiced in the assurance of his happiness, and the consolation of our Heavenly Father's loving kindness and tender mercy.

From our boy's yet unburied remains, we were called to the sick bed of his sisters—the twins. They had been seized with the same symptoms, and they too died. I wept over my loved and lovely ones, but I did not refuse to be comforted, for I knew that they too had been taken by our Father, and that this also He had done in love. He had preserved my husband amidst many dangers, and thankfulness and joy mingled with my mourning.

Our youngest child was still spared to us. She had the disease which had been so fatal to her brother and sisters very slightly, and as soon as she recovered, we returned to our home. We missed there the pleasant faces of our children, and their sweet voices, but we thought how their faces shone in the light of heaven, and how their voices mingled with those of angels in their songs of praise, and we blessed God and were happy.

It was two years after this that I began to perceive marks of ill health in my husband. It would take me very long, and tire you perhaps, were I to attempt to tell you half my feelings and thoughts then. All my other losses had been as nothing to the fear that I should lose him. My kind heavenly Father saw this, and he dealt very gently with me. For eighteen months after we both saw, from the nature of his disease, that separation was inevitable, He still delayed the moment of our parting. During all this time, my dear husband had been able to strengthen and comfort me, and I seemed to approach with him so near the heavenly world, that, when at length he left me, I felt that he had only gone home to our Father a little while before me, and I turned to my earthly duties, satisfied that, when what He had given me to do was finished, God would take me where my heart and my treasures already were.

I had still one daughter left, and I thought it was one of my first duties to make some provision for her support. I have told you already that the property left by my father was lost through the unfaithfulness of an agent; and my husband's salary ceased of course with his life. By the advice of friends, I sold our furniture—books—every thing which would bring money, and bought an annuity for my daughter's life—that is, I paid it to a company, who agreed, in return, to pay her a certain sum every year she lived. They would have given more if it had been for my life, for I was in feeble health, and they thought I could not live long, while my child was strong and healthy; but I wanted it for her, not for myself. For the next seven years we boarded in the country, living very plainly and frugally, but happily. My child had shown from her birth the most gentle, thoughtful, and loving nature I ever knew. She had been much with her father during his illness, and her religious feelings had been deeply and permanently influenced by his teachings and example. I never saw her angry. The toys and sports of children never interested her much; but she loved to sit at my feet and talk of her brother and sisters and father—of her remembrance of them on earth—of what she supposed to be their employments and their enjoyments in heaven—and of her hope that we should all, through the grace of God, be reunited there. This was so pleasant to me, that, perhaps, I encouraged it too much. Had I checked it, and sent her out to play with others of her age, it may be that her health would have continued strong, and this gift of God have been longer left with me. But I can hardly regret the loss, which was to her such perfect gain. She was nearly seventeen when she left earth for heaven, with blessings and praise to God in her heart and on her lips. She had been my pleasant companion for many years, and our separation was painful, yet I felt sure that it was best for both, or our holy Father would not have decreed it; and as I pressed my last kiss upon the last lips from which I should ever hear the tender name, "mother," I felt, that, though the joys of earth were all taken from me, God had given me instead the peace of heaven.

That peace, my dear children, is enduring—it has never been taken away—blessed be God!—I know it shall never be taken away—and while I have that, I want nothing. I am happier, far happier, than when I was surrounded with all earthly enjoyments, but wanted that. I have endured much suffering, since my daughter's death, from illness, and have been now for many months the inhabitant of an alms-house— but why should these things move me? I know that my Father, my heavenly Father, orders them all—that he is, by these means, bringing me nearer to himself and to those whom he has already taken home to heaven. When I had the tenderest earthly friends, and riches and health, I was often disappointed and dissatisfied, as I have often told you, for I had many unreasonable and selfish wishes. My Father saw, that, like a child absorbed with its toys, I was absorbed with his gifts—forgetting him, the Giver. He knew that these gifts could never make me as happy as He designed me to be, and gently, tenderly, He took them back, soothing and supporting me all the time, till, like a subdued child, I lay in His arms, desiring no gift that could tempt me thence. I can have no dissatisfaction, no disappointment, while I desire only that His will should be done; for in every thing that happens, I see that desire fulfilled. And I receive from Him many pleasant proofs of his love, such as the friendly interest which your dear father and mother have taken in me ever since they met me here, and your visit to me this afternoon.

And now, William, is your question answered? Do you think a person can be happy, who has lost his property and his friends?

William thought he could.

"I hope, my dear boy, that you will have that happiness, that only true happiness, which you will discover sooner or later, that no fortune or friends, no earthly blessing can bestow, which is to be found, not in God's gifts, but in Him—not in the gratification of our wishes, but in the surrender of all our wishes to Him—in having no will but His will."

Mrs. Grant ceased speaking, but William and Kate remained quiet, as if still listening. There was much of what she had said not very well understood by Kate, perhaps even William did not take in all its meaning, but they understood enough to feel that she was one who loved God, and desired to please Him—that she was a good woman, and therefore a happy one. All love goodness, even those who are not very good themselves; and William and Kate loved Mrs. Grant; and when, after a few minutes' silence, she asked, in a cheerful tone, of what they were thinking, Kate answered at once, "I was wishing that you would go home with us, and live at our house."

Mrs. Sedley looked at her friend with a smile, as she asked, "And what are your thoughts, William?"

"I think, mother," said William, "that if I had Mrs. Grant to live with us, and talk so to us every day, I should not be so impatient as I am now."

"My dear friend, you cannot resist this," said Mrs. Sedley.

Tears were streaming down Mrs. Grant's cheeks, but they were not sorrowful tears, for she was smiling through them. Looking up for a moment, her lips moved in prayer; then turning to Mrs. Sedley, she said, "No, my dear friend, I cannot, nor do I wish to resist it. If I can aid you in leading these children to our heavenly Father, I shall be doing His will, and can only bless His goodness in providing for me so pleasant a resting place on my way to Him."

It has been nearly a year since Mrs. Grant removed to Mr. Sedley's house. Mr. and Mrs. Sedley regard her as an honored mother; their children call her "grandmother," and love and reverence her as such. Kate is never so well pleased as when sitting with her, or waiting upon her; and William has already learned from her to bear disappointments more patiently than he formerly did. Mrs. Grant loves them tenderly, and cherishes their kind feelings as tokens of her Father's love. She is happy, yet scarcely happier than in the almshouse, for outward circumstances are of little moment to one who has the "PEACE OF HEAVEN" in her heart.

THE FAMILY CIRCLE.—THE HOPES AND FEARS OF HOME.

O, THE HOPES of Home! What a vision of bright and lovely things do these words summon around us! How many sparkling eyes and smiling faces peep over the circle of our thoughts, and claim our notice! There would be no such thing as home, were it not that hopes hang within its bowers. Cold and cheerless as the world may be, the heart is solaced by the bland whispers of Hope's syren voice. Her radiant imaginings, though they may lie in the future, still entrance the spirit, and forbid utter abandonment. Her song, prophetic only of good, glides sweetly down into the heart's depths, and calls up there echoes all its own. The young and lovely bride, as she enters her new-chosen home, wreathes round its altars her hopes; and what freshness, what fragrance is there in them! Years are before her,—years which are to link yet closer the bands of sacred union with one most beloved. On every side—along the path that they are to tread hand in hand together, buds of promise and blossoms that open gently, yet radiant with life's best hues, throw out their allurements, and hide the thorns that may wound the unwary. She looks and smiles; no raven pinion of doubt shadows that hour; it is all full of expectation. Her heart has made its election, and the time is reached to which the past has been summoning her spirit; childhood's home she has left, or rather has exchanged for a husband's abode—the home of her heart. But are there no FEARS, too ?—is there no bird of ill omen to utter its startling note upon the ear of that soul, ready to drown itself in the circling eddies of present and future happiness? There may be such, and yet they seem but fancies that are not worth regarding. They come and they go, but they break not the golden chain of assurance on the faith that has been plighted; for they hold no connection in the thoughts with a want of fealty to that claim. She doubts not that he will be true, as she knows herself to be; and she, if hers to stay its approach, will see no cloud gather over the sunshine of that abode. The trembling is of one, if trembling there may be, who feels that no love can entirely shield from harm, and that some dart may be speeding to its high mark, to bring down the soul's idol, or to cut in twain the silken cord which years would bind in links of more perfect strength.

The mother, too!—what hopes ride buoyant on the heaving swell of that bosom! Light as the little paper ships which the child sets afloat, and often, too, as frail, they glisten in the sunbeam, mock the efforts to seize on them of the hand that sent them forth, and tremble with every breath that freshens over the stream on which they have been launched. The merest pebble cast on the surface, where in the watery mirror it is imaged, may agitate the slightly constructed bark; and so, too, with the tranquil stream down which are gliding the mother's hopes—it may be disturbed, the little vessel freighted with unnumbered cravings of her spirit may be reached by the movement which as it extends gathers force, and the expectations that have cheered her, may sink beneath the increasing tide. Fears will sometimes scud over the sky of the brightened day, and becloud the landscape; for the same bosom of maternal tenderness that feels a warmer glow of hopeful thoughts as it catches a ray of gratified delight from the dawn of that hour when the eye of a young immortal first opens upon life and its eventful scenes,—cannot help feeling, too, the uncertainty press there of its continuance long to bless parental hope. Ay, gaze on that family circle, stand there within the sacred precincts of yonder home, and watch the group that cluster on that spot, and say if there is not the weaving and twining of hopes and fears; say if every morning and every evening hour does not bear testimony to many a castle reared in air, which will fade in a moment, as topples down at one blow the child's architecture, which he calls his house—his palace. Still there is in the hopes of home a purer influence than flows from any other earthly ones; and though fears cling round them, and too often weigh them down, yet well is it to cherish and prize them while their greenness and freshness may last; we need them, and a kind providence has vouchsafed them to us. The spirit that rules the domain of this inner circle of sympathies and loving offices, must be one of Hope; the fears that flit over the field are needful to attemper the heart to the realities of life, and prepare it for its appropriate allotments of discipline below the skies. The bird that leaps from bough to bough, luring on the seeker; the rainbow after which the deceived eagerness of childhood chases; the spring that gushes up, and then sinks again into the deep bosom of the earth,—these are true images of the hopes and fears of home. Day begins the alternations, and night closes them only to renew them again in the dreamy fancies of the slumberer on his bed. They wrap about us like the drapery in which we are clad—every fold, every hem of our social existence hides its hope; there is not a nook or corner of the hallowed domicil but renders back an echo of what we long for, what we hope may be. The bright-eyed little warbler, whose tones of voice are music dear as earth can give, breathes hope with the first note the unpractised lips may utter. The aged grandame or hoary sire, notch down on their calendar hopes and fears; and the blooming sister, or the manlier brother, grasp the hand and join in the fraternal embrace with hope painted on the cheek, catching at the heart-strings, and only struggling with fear because things so much beloved cannot for ever endure. These all are part of that wise discipline by which infinite Wisdom tries his creatures; feelings which spring from that constitution, and those adaptations, by which we are rendered capable of discharging the parts of rational and immortal beings, in training for a home beyond the skies. The hope that has its birth below, and which looks out from the bounds of Time to grasp upon the revelations of Eternity, may too be the dearest hope of Home. Its beams may gild the little worlds which sit down, and rise up together beneath their own canopied heavens, whose morning and evening incense ascends in truest devotion to the Giver of all good, and who bind in one loving embrace of pious faith, the spirits of feeble strength or of riper years. To that world, that home where fear has no place, where hope is turned to perfect happiness, may we all turn our most ardent gaze. God only can brighten for ever the hopes, and God only can for ever quell the fears of Home.

MENTOR.

Original.

FEMALE BIOGRAPHY—CYNTHIA H. STOWE.

BY HENRY M. PARSONS, NEW YORK.

THE greatest utility of Biography is the transfer to the mind of the pattern of virtue. Hence those are worthiest of historic notice whose lives best exemplify correct and elevated principle. Biography consists too often of the exploits of heroism, the achievements of patriotism, and the labors of genius and science, and too seldom of religious worth, shedding light and gladness in the humbler walks of society. There are few who have not known, in the circle of their association, one superior to the rest of their acquaintance, in cultivated intellect, and warm and pious thoughts. Such, in the remembrance of the writer, was Cynthia H. Stow, whom he first met at a May-day festival, in the bloom of ripened girlhood,

"Like Proserpine gathering flowers,
Herself a fairer flower."

Three years had passed. Daylight broke upon a stormy sea. The winds howled in mournful tones around the tempest-tossed steamer, filling the hearts of most with ill-defined but fearful forebodings. He who has slept upon the bosom of the great deep, rocked to repose by the lullaby of its gentle gales, who has mused upon the deck when the soft breeze of midnight fanned his cheek, can for these have but dim conceptions of the majesty of the ocean, when danger threatens in every gust, and rides upon the crest of each succeeding wave. They felt it, however, on the ill-starred Home, in that hour when hope of deliverance had fled, and the certainty of a watery grave was imprinted upon every mind. Instinctively, then, did the half-obliterated record of past thoughts and feelings sweep in rapid, yet distinct outline before their mental perception, and visions of another world divide their reflections between the fear of death and the anticipation of eternal realities. But in that group who clung to the railing of the vessel there was one in whose form and countenance were seen the lineaments of youthful beauty, whose heart acquired fresh joy as every wave that broke upon the bark weakened the dividing line between her spirit and her God. Confiding in the promises of Him "who rides upon the whirlwind and directs the storm," a calm, like the slumber of innocence, was diffused over her mind, while a hope, full of immortality, possessed her soul. And when a mountain billow bore off that fair and lovely girl, it was but the messenger of Heaven to introduce Cynthia H. Stowe to the paradise above. What matters it that her remains are pillowed on the sands of Ocracoke, since in the morning of the resurrection they shall be restored in renewed loveliness and clothed with immortal perfection.

Cynthia possessed beauty in an eminent degree, but without that vanity which too frequently accompanies it. The graces of her person formed no subject of self-congratulation, and yet those very graces became important agents in the promotion of truth, for they drew around her a circle of admirers over whom she sought and exerted an extended and hallowed influence. How lovely the charms of form and feature when we discover in them but the outward shadowing of inward beauty!

Cynthia was distinguished for the variety and compass of her ornamental accomplishments. But she was far from priding herself that these were the theme of remark, nor did she suffer a desire to please to usurp the nobler purpose to be useful. While she was fertile in dispelling ennui from the social circle, she was equally fertile in directing amusement in the channels of utility. Never should ornamental education become a primary object of pursuit with woman, thus detracting from her dignity, and limiting her paramount and commanding responsibilities.

Cynthia was pre-eminent for a strong and refined intellect. Some of the productions of her pen are gems of rare and surpassing excellence. One of these, a poem addressed to a beloved brother, on the eve of her embarcation on the Home, is subjoined to this article, because reflecting such credit upon her understanding and heart. Fond of reading, she yet rejected a large proportion of the periodical literature of the day, preferring the standard works of her own and earlier times, and the volume of revelation, that mine of inexhaustible treasure. She was characterized for a classical purity of taste, and a remarkable correctness of judgment in matters of literature. She thought for herself, and her conversation was unusually intellectual and instructive. Her desire of improvement was ardent, but she cherished no undue estimate of mental attainments, regarding them as no equivalent for that meek and quiet spirit which alone is acceptable with God. Too few of her sex endowed with superior faculties and rich in intellectual stores are conscious that these, without the superadded graces of piety, are like the rivers of Damascus, whose waters are unwholesome and bitter. Conscience must be enlightened and quickened, the fiery passions of the heart must be controlled, and the affections elevated to the Almighty, or the character is unfitted for the duties of this life and the retributions of another.

Cynthia was a CHRISTIAN, and reflected, in the varied relations of society, the image of the Redeemer, to whom she had dedicated her all. She seemed to hold intimate communion with the Author of her being and hopes, to feel a child-like affiance in his promises, a uniform adoration of his perfections, and an ever fresh remembrance of his goodness. She derived her knowledge of the Deity not alone from revelation, but nature, in whose ample volume she read the wisdom, power, and boundless love of the Creator. She saw Him in the lofty mountain, the humble valley, the quiet streamlet, and the rushing river. She heard Him in the gentle breeze, the swelling tempest, the resounding ocean, and the startling thunder. She traced his handiwork in the gorgeous firmament of heaven, as well as in the delicately painted flower of the earth. Like the friend of Grenville Mellen, "she had mind as well as heart in her religion."

Daughter of beauty! have you a tear of penitence for sin, and a smile of joy for mercy and forgiveness through the Savior, whether you worship in a temple reared by the hand of Nature, or in the narrow limits of a closet, your intercourse with Heaven will cheer and invigorate your spirit, and prepare you for works of duty and benevolence which breathe alike the sublimity of truth and the beauty of holiness.

Original.

TO MY BROTHER.

BY THE LATE CYNTHIA H. STOWE.

When the last rays, at twilight's hour,
Fall gently o'er the drooping flower—
When mists are gathering on the hill,

Nor sound is heard save mountain rill:
Then hear the echo, whispering near,
In softest accents to thine ear—
  I love thee, dearest brother!

When silence reigns through earth and sea;
When glows the star of memory;
When music wakes her thrilling tone,
And Autumn winds around thee moan;
Their accents hear, and oh, rejoice!
For hark! there comes a well known voice—
  I love thee, dearest brother!

When fancy lifts her radiant wing,
And morning birds around thee sing;
When joy lights up thy beaming eye,
And love's enchantment too is nigh;
When calm, blue waters round thee flow,
Then hear thy sister, breathing low—
  I love thee, dearest brother!

Should disappointment's withering breath
Consign thy brightest hopes to death;
Should friendship's trust, in boyhood made,
In after years prove faith betrayed;
Then to thy sister yet return,
For oh! her heart will fondly burn
  To clasp thee, dearest brother

Should sorrow cloud thy coming years,
And bathe thy prospects all in tears,
Remember that the rainbow's hue
Is bright mid clouds and sunshine too;
Remember, though we're doom'd to part,
There lives one kind and faithful heart
  That loves her dearest brother!

HORRORS OF WAR—CONFLAGRATION OF MOSCOW.

The French entered Moscow on the 14th September, 1812, but they possessed only a heap of smoking ruins. A degree of mystery hangs over the conflagration of this ancient city: whether it was occasioned by the inhabitants, or in consequence of the defence made by them, and is the bombardment of the French, is yet doubtful. The fact, however, is certain, and the grand effects of the destruction are of the most consoling nature. It is impossible, however, to contemplate without horror, an event which deprived 200,000 persons of their homes and possessions, and consigned to the agonizing tortures of the flames many thousands of persons, including a large number of sick and wounded soldiers, who had bled in the defence of their country.

The retreat of the French from Moscow exhibits a picture of disaster and human misery dreadful and horrific, almost beyond example. It is stated that the cold, from the 6th of November, was so intense that in a few days more than 30,000 horses perished: the cavalry was dismounted, and the baggage, without the means of conveyance. From the 9th to the 18th of November, Bonaparte lost, without counting the killed and wounded, 11 generals, 243 officers, 34,000 rank and file in prisoners, 250 pieces of cannon, and four standards, besides baggage, &c. The total loss to France and her allies in this campaign has been estimated at 400,000 men killed, disabled, and prisoners, and $30,000,000 of property in equipments, &c. &c.

The loss of the Russians in soldiers killed, wounded, and prisoners has been stated at 130,000, to which must be added 70,000 persons burnt and destroyed in various ways at Moscow; the loss of Russian property cannot be less than $540,000,000. Severe as these sacrifices appear to be, the safety and independence of Russia have been established; and we cannot sufficiently admire the patriotism and the courage of all ranks, from the prince to the peasant, in their united determination, not only to resist, but to vanquish the common enemy.

Oh! when will the time come that the knowledge of the Lord shall cover the earth, and men shall learn war no more! Hasten, O Lord, this golden age!

VALUABLE MAXIMS

A MAN who does not really deserve a character for truth, probity, good manners, and good morals, at his first setting out in the world, may impose, and shine like a meteor for a very short time, but will very soon vanish, and be extinguished with contempt. People easily pardon in young men the common irregularities of the senses; but they do not forgive the least vice of the heart.

Advice is seldom welcome, and those who want it the most, always like it the least.

Envy is one of the meanest and most tormenting of all passions, as there is hardly a person existing that has not given uneasiness to an envious breast; for the envious man cannot be happy while he beholds others so.

A great action will always meet with the approbation of mankind; and the inward pleasure which it produces, is not to be expressed.

Humanity is the peculiar characteristic of great minds; little vicious minds abound with anger and revenge, and are incapable of feeling the exalted pleasure of forgiving their enemies.

The ignorant and the weak only are idle: those who have acquired a good stock of knowledge, always desire to increase it. Knowledge is like power in this respect—those who have the most, are most desirous of having more. Idleness is only the refuge of weak minds, and the holy-day of fools.

Modesty is a commendable quality, and generally accompanies true merit; it engages and captivates the mind; for nothing is more shocking and disgustful than presumption and impudence. A man is despised, who is always commending himself, and who is the hero of his own story. Indeed, it is next to impossible for any one to speak his own praise without injury to himself.

Not to perform our promise, is a folly, a dishonor, and a crime. It is a folly, because no one will rely on us afterwards; and it is a dishonor and a crime, because truth is the first duty of religion and morality: and whoever is not possessed of truth, cannot be supposed to have any one good quality, and must be held in detestation by all good men.

A man who tells nothing, or who tells all, will equally have nothing told him.

If a fool knows a secret, he tells it because he is a fool; if a knave knows one, he tells it wherever it is his interest to tell it; but youth are very apt to tell what secrets they know, from the vanity of having been trusted. Trust none of these when you can help it.

Knowledge may give weight, but accomplishments only give lustre; and many more people see than weigh.

Take care always to form your establishment so much within your income as to leave a sufficient fund for unexpected contingencies, and a prudent liberality. There is hardly a year in any man's life, in which a small sum of ready money may not be employed to great advantage. Selected.

Original.
FEMALE EDUCATION.
BY MISS C. THURSTON.
NO. III.

IN the education of the young, teachers, next to parents, exert a powerful influence, and like them are involved in fearful responsibilities, still it is a fact too well known to be contradicted, that teachers are often but illy qualified for their business, and not aware of the duties devolving upon them. In the learned professions, and in the mechanic arts, education for the particular employment is deemed necessary, but to form the mind is thought so simple and easy, that no preparatory course is required. "Any person may become a TEACHER without any definite preparation, and without any test of skill or experience." Teaching is hardly regarded as a profession, but as an employment which serves as preparatory to some other business. Persons engage in it from convenience, or interest, or because they imagine it easier or more honorable than manual labor; and so great is the lack of parental discrimination, that patronage is extended to all. Much more anxiety is manifested for the qualifications of a mechanic, than a teacher; indeed, it would seem that the fashion of a dress or the shaping of a shoe was regarded as more important, than the formation of the character, the training of the undying spirit! Money is freely expended for the adornment of the body, but in the adornment of the mind, the utmost parsimony is practised. This is particularly true as respects females. In the education of sons, parents often are willing to expend something, but for the education of daughters, little or no provision is made. In explaining the cause of this apparent partiality, we are driven to the conclusion, that it arises from low and incorrect ideas respecting the profession of woman. It is not that parents love their daughters less, and are unwilling to provide for their future comfort and respectability, but it arises from a mistaken view of their own obligations, and of the great end of education. If it be true that woman is, and must be, a teacher, and that she is instrumental in forming the character of each succeeding generation, then parents are bound to educate their daughters for the station which they may be called to occupy. In this age of improvement and intelligence, the sphere of woman is greatly enlarged, and increasing opportunities are afforded her for imparting to others the blessings she enjoys. Not only in the domestic circle, and in the cottage of poverty, but in the Sabbath school, in the various institutions of learning with which our country abounds, and among the distant heathen, may she exert her influence. Who is better fitted to form the mind and manners of her own sex, than the intelligent and pious female? Endowed with strong sensibilities and indomitable perseverance, with warmth of heart and energy of purpose, she seems by nature formed to be a teacher, and experience proves that to woman the training of the youthful mind is best committed. Let her, then, spurning the soft indulgences of luxurious life, instead of sinking into listlessness and insignificance, consecrate all her energies to the great work for which Nature has designed her. Already may she see in advance a long train of illustrious females, renowned not like Zenobia or Semiramis, for military prowess, but whose glory, like that of Hannah More and Isabella Graham, is to have elevated the character of her own sex, by promoting the cause of thorough Christian education. Let teachers of this character be greatly increased, and let the Christian public awake to the importance of sustaining such, and discriminate between the fashionable teacher who attracts the admiration of the passing crowd, and those who patiently labor to train their pupils for the duties of earth and the glories of Heaven.

Some, who are in other respects judicious persons, seem greatly to misjudge on the subject of female education; and if through our instrumentality they can be led to more correct and enlarged views, our labor will not have been in vain. Earnestly would we entreat them to consider the inconsistency of professing to desire for their children a heavenly inheritance, while they place them under such influences as have a direct tendency to make them enamored with the things of time. "The children of this world are wiser in their generation than the children of light." It is not wonderful that those whose hopes all centre here, and who, though having tried the pleasures of earth, and found themselves disappointed and deceived, yet, captivated by things below, desire nothing better for their children; but it is wonderful that those who have had a glimpse of their heavenly inheritance, should seek for their beloved offspring only the paltry things of earth; that having drunk of the pure streams of celestial joy, they should direct them to the bitter fountains of earthly pleasure.

Parents HAVE what they most desire for their children; and this desire will manifest itself in the selection of teachers, as well as in the manner in which themselves give instruction. The gay, the worldly, who desire nothing better for their daughters than an alliance with rank or fortune, will of course be most anxious that they should acquire external accomplishments; the airs and graces of fashionable life; and will, therefore, select teachers in accordance with this wish. Such parents, however, seem practically to have embraced the Mahometan doctrine, that "woman has no soul;" and that THEY should pursue such a course does not seem so strange, but that believers in the Christian religion should pursue the same course is unspeakably strange.

It is much to be lamented, that in this land of light there should be schools, where woman is trained to be a mere butterfly of a day, an ephemeral being, fitted merely to "allure and shine;" where right principles are not inculcated, and youth is left to habits of insubordination, indolence, pride, and selfish gratification. A pious father, who had placed his daughter in a fashionable seminary, intending to qualify her for a teacher, too late discovered his error; for when offered the situation of assistant, she refused, having there learned that "only POOR PEOPLE worked for a living." Notwithstanding the influence of such institutions, wise and Christian people patronise them, and wonder that their children are not every thing they should be.

Who has not marked the haughty air of the young miss just returned from a boarding-school, her disinclination to useful employments—her dislike to the occupations of the kitchen— her contempt for those whom she supposes her inferiors—her supreme devotion to self, and utter disregard of the feelings and wishes of her parents! Alas! at what an expense has she learned to dress and dance, to play a few fashionable airs upon the piano, and to give the names of a few things in bad French or Italian! It is a remark of a noble lady of the last age, that "a girl cannot acquire the polished air of a person of fashion, without imbibing too much of the spirit of the world;" and parents who seek this portion for their children, do it at the risk of their souls. Such have what they desire, but the fruit, that at a distance looked fair and beautiful, is like the apples of Sodom, "full of ashes and bitterness."

Moral laws are as fixed as the laws of nature. "Whatsoever a man soweth, that shall he also reap," is as true in the culture of mind, as in the culture of the earth—the end will follow the means. If parents commit the education of their children to teachers who are destitute of moral principle, ignorant of themselves and of the nature of mind; vain, conceited, and artificial in their manners; teachers ignorant of the word of God—insensible to their own accountability—drawing all their motives to action from the things of time; and who, incapable of exercising salutary discipline, inspire the worst of passions to effect the object for which they labor; they need not complain if their daughters return from school proud and ignorant, ungrateful and irreverent, indolent and conceited. Modern fashionable education cannot produce reverence to parents, respect to superiors, and a desire to contribute to the happiness of others, because the very spirit encouraged is one of selfishness and vanity. It cannot make the discreet and useful woman, because the discipline of mind, and the culture of the heart, form no part of the system; nor is it reasonable to expect that those who have been trained to consult their own ease, and seek their own gratification—those who have been taught to worship at the shrine of fashion, and to despise the simple pleasures of domestic life, will become affectionate, devoted wives, or faithful, self-denying mothers. An affectation of politeness that may be assumed at certain times and places may have been acquired, but "true Christian good-nature," which is the "soul of politeness," and which is "compounded of kindness, forbearance, and self-denial;" which "seeketh not her own;" cannot be the result of modern fashionable education. By such a course no suitable preparation is made for the pressing responsibilities of this life, and far is it from leading to a preparation for the life to come.

TOUCHING INCIDENT.

When Mr. Monroe was Minister from the United States at Paris, and when General La Fayette was confined in the prison at Olmutz, by the Emperor of Austria, information was brought him that Madame La Fayette, the General's wife, was thrown into prison, and no doubt in a few days would follow the fate of her mother and grandmother at the guillotine. Mr. Monroe alone could save her; and, as Paris was then in the hands of the mob, it could only be accomplished by arousing the sympathies of the people. The destruction of life had been such in every state of society where opulence was perceptible, that, to avoid certain death, all luxuries and splendor were laid aside; and the wealthy, instead of riding in their equipages, either walked or rode in the miserable vehicles of the city.

It therefore created a great sensation when the splendid equipage of the American Minister's carriage appeared at the gate of the prison, and his lady informed the keeper that she had come to see the wife of General La Fayette. Such a call at such a time was like electricity—like life from the dead. The news spread in all directions, and before Mrs. Monroe drove from the prison thousands had collected round her carriage, and the feelings elicited by the meeting of two such females in such a situation, arrested the axe of the executioner, and eventually set the captive free. The feelings of Colonel Monroe cannot be realized during the absence of his wife. He could not accompany her, as that would have counteracted the feeling he knew must be awakened to save the prisoner. When Mrs. Monroe met Madame La Fayette she was in a state of perfect phrensy, supposing that she was led out to execution; and when she found herself embraced by the lady of the American Minister, within the walls of that gloomy prison where, but a few days previously, had been led forth to execution her mother and grandmother, it was a long time before she could realize her situation. Mrs. Monroe assured her she should be saved, and that her husband had determined to risk all, if it should become necessary, to accomplish her deliverance.

Original.

MRS. CECIL'S METHOD.

FAMILY CULTURE AND DISCIPLINE.

BY THE EDITOR.

In a previous number we gave a narrative of the Cecil Family; of the "Stricken Widow," and of the empire which death at last obtained over that extraordinary family.

Mrs. Cecil had been educated by parents who well knew the value of religious culture. She was brought, early in life, to a saving knowledge of the truth, and when she became a mother she devoted herself afresh to the service and kingdom of God.

Mrs. Cecil felt that her children were immortal beings—candidates for endless bliss or wo.

She labored and prayed to KEEP this impression constantly on her mind. She also made the subject of her influence and responsibility a theme of fasting and prayer—for she looked upon her offspring as her "prisoners of hope;" and felt deeply that every thing pertaining to their future character and destiny, by the Divine blessing, depended upon parental vigilance and fidelity.

EARLY IMPRESSIONS. Aware of the vital importance of early impressions, and the rapidity with which the young mind opens, at the earliest dawn of reason, Mrs. Cecil began to instruct her children to fear God, and keep his commandments—to hate sin as the worst of all evil ; to be open, ingenuous, and sincere in all their actions—because the eye of God was upon them!

Among the early lessons taught by this extraordinary mother was, that life is but a vapor—that everything on this side of the grave is of small importance compared with the favor of God, an interest in the Saviour, and in the incorruptible glories of the righteous in the world to come. The only school-room of her children until they were six years of age was her NURSERY. There twice every day they recited their lessons. As soon as they could speak they began to commit to memory the Lord's prayer, the commandments, the Apostles' creed, etc.— As soon as they could read, they were taught the most striking historical parts of the Bible, and at an early age began to recite the New Testament in course, and were required to answer questions from each portion as they thus passed through the whole Bible. This exercise was never remitted in their education.

They also read, daily in course, the books which SHE selected for them, her children being required to give a careful narrative of what their lesson contained.

THE FAMILY ALTAR. At family worship each member of the household was present, and all were provided with books. A portion was read and explained, and oftentimes enforced with great tenderness and effect—after these remarks, the children were called on to give the most important parts of the Scripture which had been read, and then they were expected to ask questions. After the Bible was read, all joined in a song of praise to God, and the throne of grace was addressed.

If any one of the children had manifested a bad temper, or broken the commandments of their parents, it was the custom of Mrs. Cecil to retire and pray with and for the offending child—thus her offspring were afraid to do wrong.

Mrs. Cecil early taught her children their state by nature; their proneness to sin, the way of salvation; the necessity of repentance and a holy life. She taught them not only the nature and duty of prayer, but the LANGUAGE of prayer.

TABLE TALK. When the social group were gathered around the breakfast-table, the children recited a portion of the Bible in course, and each in his turn was required to give an explanation of what he recited.

At the dinner-table, some fragments of Scripture or sacred history, or some doctrine or duty, or some chapter from the arts, sciences, or biography, etc.. was the topic of conversation.

GOVERNMENT. Mrs. Cecil strove to make her children feel a sense of their accountableness to God and to their parents.

She seemed to act upon the principle, that to govern her children well, she must not only govern herself, but must be under subjection to the authority of God. She strove to maintain GOD's authority rather than her own.

If any child had done wrong, the mother appeared to be grieved, not because the child had displeased the parent, so much as because he had offended the great God. The rod was seldom used in Mrs. Cecil's family, nor was it ever spared when it was the best method of bringing the child to feel his wrong.

If a child had failed in getting his lesson, he was perhaps deprived of his dinner or tea, or not permitted to join the family in a ride, or was denied some other recreation.

A SACRED REGARD FOR TRUTH was deemed of fundamental importance by Mrs. Cecil. The slightest departure from a full, simple, undisguised statement of facts, was always looked upon with alarm, and was viewed as a barrier in the way of all moral elevation and future usefulness in the world. If the child who grows up to manhood without a serious regard for truth and filial obedience, is ever converted and made a useful member of society, it must be by a miracle of God's grace!

I will only add, Mrs. Cecil and her companion were never weary in the work of educating their offspring for the duties of life and the destinies of eternity. Both felt that their work was not one of limited moment; that its results would reach onward beyond the grave and judgment into an immeasurable life to come. And what were the fruits of their fidelity, and labors, and prayers, and perseverance? They were richly crowned, even in this life, with a rich reward. Their children were all made subjects of divine grace, and went to an early grave from the fellowship of the church of God. From the example of these parents, and the results of their success, let all parents, especially mothers, be encouraged to zeal and fidelity in their momentous work.

When the illustrious sculptors of the Grecian and Italian schools had completed their works of exquisite beauty and skill, after the unwearied labor of many years, their names were proclaimed immortal.

"The sculptor upon his dead marble, ought not to surpass in patience us, who fashion the living image, and whose work is upon the fleshly tables of the heart. Can we keep too strongly in view the imperishable nature, the priceless value of those for whom we toil? In every child, there is an endless history. Compare the annals of the most boasted nation, with the story of one unending existence. Has not our Saviour already shown the result, in his parallel between the gain of the whole world, and the loss of one soul? Assyria stretched out its colossal limbs, and sank ignobly, like the vaunting champion on the plains of Elah. Egypt came up proudly, with temple, and labyrinth, and pyramid, but fell manacled at the feet of the Turk. Greece, so long the light of the world, deserted by poet and philosopher, fled, pale as her own sculpture, from the same brutal foe. Rome thundered, and fell. She struggled indeed, and was centuries in dying. But is she not dead? Can the mummy in the Vatican, from its gilded sarcophagus, be indeed that Rome before whom the world trembled?"

"The story of these empires fills many pages. The little child reads them, and is wearied. But when their ancient features shall have faded from the map of nations, and the tomes that recorded their triumphs and their fate blacken in the last flame, where shall be the soul of that little child? Mother! WHERE?"

"Will it not, then, have but just begun its eternal duration? Will not its history be studied by archangels? Proud Philosophy perchance viewed it as a noteless thing, an atom. Doth God, the Father of the spirit, thus regard it?

"Mothers of the four millions of children who are yet to be educated in this Western World, to whom our country looks, as her defence and glory, Mothers, of four millions of immortal beings, have you any time to lose? any right to loiter in your great work?"

Original.

RICH BLESSINGS IN DISGUISE.

Few persons duly realize the benefits to be derived from the trials and disappointments incident to human life. Many look upon afflictions with dread, and deprecate them as they would the assaults of a foe. The trials of life are not joyous, but grievous—it is their CONSEQUENCES which sweeten the bitterest cup. When we consider the advantages which are the result, and examine the rich shade of the picture, can we call them misfortunes?

Afflictions are intended as disciplinary or remedial. Man was formed by the Creator for the enjoyment of pure and lasting pleasure. He is gifted with a soul which was kindled into existence by the breath of Jehovah, and which is susceptible of boundless happiness. The angel of mercy points to the abodes of the righteous, and bids us seek there our enjoyment; holds out to us an overflowing cup, and bids us drink of the waters from the pure fountain of life. He promises the unalloyed and enduring happiness prepared for the pure in heart. He holds in prospect a diadem glittering with transcendent radiance, reflecting the glories and splendors of Heaven. These are viewed at a distance. Frail mortals, caught with the glitter of earth, and fascinated with its pomp, we stoop to satisfy the desires of the immortal mind with its vain emoluments and transitory joys. Guardian angels call after us, but we are too deeply immured in earthly scenes to heed the invitation!

Afflictions should teach us how evanescent and unstable are worldly enjoyments.

Look at the man who is hoarding up earthly treasures. Mammon is the shrine at which he bows. A blast sweeps by. His prospects are blighted. In one night his possessions are destroyed by the devouring element. Thus, by sad experience, he learns that nothing earthly is enduring, and he is directed to lay up his treasure where "moth doth not corrupt and thieves do not break through and steal."

Look at the VOTARY of PLEASURE as he whirls in the giddy circles of dissipation. Behold the cup is dashed from his lips and he becomes the victim of a disease which feeds upon his vitals and drinks his life blood. Amidst languishing and suffering he learns, that earth's pleasures have their poison too. He writhes in agony under the pangs of remorse for mis-spent time, having neglected the invitations of the Gospel. And, like the dying malefactor on the cross, at life's latest hour he raises his streaming eyes to Heaven for mercy. His prayer is heard—his pardon sealed, and e'er the lamp of life goes out, he receives the consoling assurance that his spirit, purified from its pollutions by the blood of the atonement, shall find rest in the mansions prepared for the pure in heart. Look at the MERCHANT deeply immured in the ensnaring business of life. He has no time for reflecting upon subjects pertaining to the future. His vessel floats upon the ocean, laden with the treasures of foreign nations. The tempest gathers, and that ship which recently, careered proudly over the deep, and was hailed almost within its destined port, becomes a wreck, and his priceless treasures lie deep among the pebbles of the ocean. He learns that every thing on earth is transitory while he is pointed to more enduring riches. Behold the student searching for intellectual wealth. But while he trims the midnight lamp his intellectual powers give way, reason is dethroned and delirium usurps its place. After months of darkness reason again returns, and he learns that the wisdom of the world is foolishness with God.

Look at the CHRISTIAN MOTHER. To-day her affections are entwined around her tender offspring. She clings to it with an inordinate attachment as the object upon which are centred her fondest hopes. To-morrow the fondly cherished being is torn from her embrace. In the bitterness of her affliction she turns to the sacred volume for consolation, and finds upon its page—"Thou shalt have no other gods before me." She bows with resignation under the stroke and with a chastened spirit kisses the rod. She looks forward to the time when that which she once called her own, shall be restored, without the fear of separation. The fiery ordeal through which she has been called to pass, she now views as a "light affliction, which through grace shall work out for her a far more exceeding and external weight of glory."

Look at the FAIR ONE who has pledged herself to him who has her sincerest affections. The heart like a deep fountain gushes towards him with pure and generous emotions.

While her spirit faints, she recalls the assurance that "Earth hath no sorrows which Heaven cannot heal."

With the penitence of a devout and humble suppliant she now kneels at the altar which before she never approached. She prays with the fervor and earnestness of one clinging to the last hope. And though many days pass ere she receives the consolation she seeks, yet the moment finally dawns, and it bursts in upon her with a flood of light and glory indiscribable. Hers is the joy of a new born soul.

Virtues which bloom not beneath the radiant sun of prosperity, flourish in the darkness of adversity. Now she lives not for herself, but is actively engaged for the good of others.

REFLECTIONS ON THE NEW YEAR.

BY REV. G. SPRING, D.D.

CAN it be that another year has fled? With all its joys and trials, all its sins and duties, all its instructions and privileges—is it fled? Yes, it is gone. It has terminated the lives of millions, and, like an irresistible current, has borne them on to the grave and to the judgment. It has gone—like a dream of the night, it has gone!

Amid the rapids of time, there are few objects a man observes with less care and distinctness than himself. To one standing on the shore, the current appears to pass by with inconceivable swiftness; but to one who is himself gliding down the stream, the face of this vast extent of waters is unruffled, and all around him is a dead calm. It is only by looking toward the shore, by discerning here and there a distant landmark, by casting his eye back upon the scenery that is retiring from his view, that he sees he is going forward. And how fast! The tall pine that stands alone on the mountain's brow, casts its shade far down the valley; while the huge promontory throws its shadow almost immeasurably on the plain below. It is but a few years, and I was greeting life's opening day. But yesterday, I thought myself approaching its meridian. To-day I look for those meridian splendors, and they are either wholly vanished, or just descending behind the evening cloud. I cannot expect to weather the storms of this tempestuous clime much longer. A few more billows on these dangerous seas, perhaps a few days of fair weather is the most I can look for, before I am either shipwrecked, or reach my desired haven.

Why fly these years so rapidly? It is in anticipation rather than retrospect, that men put too high an estimate upon earthly things. I have been wandering to-day in the grave-yard. I have trodden softly on the place of my fathers' sepulchres. I have been playing with the willow and the cypress that weep over their dust. The generations of men DWELL HERE. Yes, here they are. Those whom I have loved, and still love, and hope to love, are here. THE FASHION OF THIS WORLD PASSETH AWAY. The fair fabric of earthly good is built upon the sand. It rocks and falls under the first stroke of the tempest. MAN, AT HIS BEST ESTATE, IS ALTOGETHER VANITY. It is well that it is so. Were it otherwise, we should put far off the evil day, and live as if we flattered ourselves with immortality on the earth. When the Duke of Venice showed Charles the Fifth the treasury of St. Mark, and the glory of his princely palace, instead of admiring them, he remarked, "These are the things that make men so loath to die." Selected.

ILLINOIS. L. M.

1. Lord, let my pray'r like in-cense rise, And when I lift my hands to thee, As in the eve'-ning sa-cri-fice, Look down from heav'n, well pleas'd on me.

2. Set thou a watch to keep my tongue,
Let not my heart to sin incline;
Save me from men who practice wrong;
Let me not share their mirth and wine.

3. But let the righteous, when I stray,
Smite me in love; his strokes are kind;
His mild reproofs like oil allay
The wounds they make, and heal the mind.

MORNING GLORY.

JOY CONVOLVULUS.

Sweet flowers will fade, and one by one
    Did each its scent or beauty loose;
Now were the **rose's** blushes gone,
    And faded now the tulip's hues.

Fair, fragile, and inconstant friends!
    A summer past they all were gone;
And as the oak tree upward tends,
    It stands deserted and alone:

And the two friends so closely twine,
    The one supports—the one adorns:
The oak need not for youth repine,
    Nor the frail ivy fear the storms.

Thus let our friendship ever be
    Founded on qualities which last;
That it may live on sympathy,
    When beauty and when youth are past.

Painted by Stonehouse.   Engraved by A.L. Dick.

DEVOUT MEDITATION.

THE CHRISTIAN FAMILY MAGAZINE,
AND
ANNUAL.

SUSTAIN YOUR MINISTER.

BY THE EDITOR.

The pulpit is a consecrated place; it is the grand watch-tower of the church. Ministers of the gospel occupy a station of immeasurable importance; their trust is one of tremendous responsibility, for to them is committed the care of immortal souls.

So important was the trust of the Roman sentinel, that it was death, death inevitable, for him to be found asleep on his guard. But how much more important and sacred are the interests which the watchmen in Zion are called to guard and defend! If they are unfaithful, if they sound not the trump of alarm on the approach of evil, it is at the peril of the church—it is at the peril of their own souls.

Ministers of the gospel are styled, "ambassadors for Christ." Men sent on an embassy to negotiate a treaty of peace between contending kingdoms, are mere worms sent to their fellow-worms. But ambassadors sent forth under the sanctions of the Son of God bear commissions of fearful interest, of weighty responsibility.

The archangel who burns brightest in glory, and stands nearest the throne of God, can be invested with no higher honor than to bear the trust of an ambassador from the Court of Heaven to this revolted and apostate world. Every devoted servant of the Lord Jesus is an ambassador for Christ. "Now, we are ambassadors for Christ; as though God did beseech you by us, we pray you in Christ's stead, be ye reconciled to God." What are the temporal interests of a kingdom, compared with the weighty responsibilities which are intrusted to him who is sent to negotiate a treaty of peace with ruined men? The interests of the former are finite and temporary; of the latter, infinite in their bearing, and eternal in their duration. The one will perish in the wreck of nature and conflagration of worlds, while the other will be as indestructible and lasting as the throne of the Eternal!

If such is the work of gospel ministers, such the amazing interests intrusted to them by the Head of the Church, may we not most earnestly plead that they be sustained?

Far be it from us to bespeak for the ministers of Christ, as MEN, any special honor or favor, which is not due to others of equal rank in society. The respect due to them arises from the sacred office they bear, and the fearful consequences which would follow, should that ministry be despised which God has ordained as the grand instrument of redeeming the world. "He that heareth you heareth me, and he that despiseth you despiseth me, and he that despiseth me despiseth him that sent me."

Cast your eye over those lands where the pulpit has lost its power, where the gospel and sabbath have long ceased to exert their life-giving influences upon the souls of men, and you behold a night of intellectual and moral darkness.

Would you, then, honor the great God our Saviour, whose interests his ministers are appointed to plead and defend—would you behold the growth of grace in the church—would you promote the salvation of those who are dead in trespasses, you will delight to honor the gospel ministry set over you in the Lord.

1. One important method of sustaining your minister, is by connecting your personal influence with his great plans of usefulness. How cheering it must be to the devoted servant of Christ, to feel assured that his people are heartily united with

him in his plans and labors to build up the Redeemer's kingdom!

While in his closet and study, and in his public administrations, he sees the pleasure of the Lord prosper in the work of his hands, as well as in the hour of severe labor and trial, nothing can cheer and animate his soul more than to feel that he is not ALONE; that in sympathy and effort his people are united with him.

The influence of a FEW thus joined together in the church, will be greater than that of MANY, very many, whose plans and energies are divided and distracted.

The motto, "UNITED WE STAND, DIVIDED WE FALL" is of great practical importance in the church as well as state.

In the successful issue of battle, much, it is true, must depend on the skill of the GENERAL; but in the hour of perilous onset, what can HE do, if single-handed and alone, but to retreat or fall? So the minister of Christ, surrounded by a scattered, divided people, can do nothing. Palsied will be his arm, powerless will be his efforts, and the enemy of all righteousness will prevail.

2. Sustain your minister in his fidelity. His commission is from no earthly prince; it is from Heaven. As a man of God, he must be faithful, though it be at the risk of interest, reputation, and life. Should he be time-serving, or shun to declare the whole counsel of God, he may peril the dearest interests of the church; he may see perishing men slumber over their immortal welfare, and at the bar of the Judge he may be condemned as a traitor.

We commend the skilful surgeon when called to administer relief in cases of life or death, though he administer harsh medicine, or use the probe, saw, or knife; and shall we not honor and sustain the minister of Christ, in the full discharge of his trust, while he presents the only remedy which the gospel provides for the maladies of the immortal soul?

If ministers are uncompromising in their fidelity, they will often enkindle the rage of the natural heart. This should occasion no alarm in the bosom of the church; this often only proves that truth has found an avenue to the conscience, and by the grace of God it may reach the heart and be instrumental in the salvation of the soul. May not one important reason why the empire of sin remains comparatively so unbroken in our midst, be owing to the want of higher moral courage in the church? For the honor of the Saviour, for the purity and enlargement of Zion, for the safety of our children, and for the good of perishing sinners, the servants of Christ must be sustained in their fidelity.

3. Cheer your minister by your presence in the house of God, and at the stated meetings of the church. Give him your warm sympathies and kind offices; administer to his necessities of your good things; yet while you leave him to preach to naked walls and empty pews, you will greatly lessen his usefulness, if not break his heart and send him to an untimely grave. This is strong language, but the truth is stronger. Few things are more comforting and inspiring to a public speaker, than a crowded house.

If your minister possesses the spirit of his holy office, he has chosen his subject and prepared his message with much anxiety and prayer. He has adapted his discourse to the present wants of his people; but when he enters the house of God, and finds most of those ABSENT for whose benefit he has brought his message, well may his heart faint within him, and he complain in his closet, "Lord, who hath believed our report?" How can those fair-weather, half-day hearers, expect to receive extensive, saving benefit, though placed under the administration of the most able, faithful, and successful gospel ministry?

4. Shield the character of your minister from the assaults of the wicked. It may be taken for granted, if he is a faithful and devoted follower of his Master, that he will be persecuted for the gospel's sake. The most able and successful men have ever borne the severest shafts of the common enemy.

Amidst these assaults let the church give her united influence for the cause of truth and righteousness, and the shafts of the enemy will fall powerless at her feet. We ask for those who bring the gospel into disrepute, no sheltering influence, though they bear the commission of the sacred office.

How often might a few words, from some influential members of the church, when the character or motives of the minister were misunderstood, misrepresented, or impugned, have resulted in immeasurable good. How guarded ought parents and members of the church to be, in all their words and actions, lest through their influence they cause the gospel to be dishonored.

How often has an unguarded, imprudent remark, destroyed the good impressions of a sermon on some awakened mind! A disrespectful conversation has, doubtless, not unfrequently resulted in the dismission of a devoted minister of the gospel. A sneer from a parent may prejudice the mind of a child against his pastor, and prove a strong barrier against the gospel forever.

5. Sustain your pastor by administering to his temporal wants of your abundance. In no age of the church have the ministers of Christ been characterized for their affluence. The divine preacher and Saviour of the world was so poor, that "he had not where to lay his head." Is it strange, then, that his disciples and servants should be characterized for their dependance on the church for a sustenance?

In this enlightened age, few things are more affecting than to see ministers of the gospel, who by their office are cut off from the means of procuring their own subsistence, and who give their labor and lives for the spiritual benefit of their people, placed in circumstances of want and pecuniary embarrassment. We are told that ministers must not preach for MONEY; we answer, they must have money for preaching. Some—too many in the ministry, are so poor, that, were this a day of miracles, and had they the faith of Elijah, they might be fed by "ravens." Yet no duty of the church is more clearly taught, both in the Old and New Testament, than that of providing ample support for the servants of Christ. See the provision which God made for them under the Jewish dispensation. Read also the strong language which the apostle uses on this subject, 1 Cor. chap. 9, etc.

While we drop a kind word of admonition on this delicate and important subject, we cannot forbear saying, that most of the churches of our respective denominations, evince a most noble and praiseworthy example of kindness and liberality in the support of their ministers.

Those annual and occasional presents which many churches are accustomed to make to their ministers, are of great importance, not, perhaps, so much on account of their pecuniary value, as for the salutary influence they secure, as tokens of respectful remembrance, and as pledges of a continuance of that social union of hearts so much to be desired between pastors and their people.

And what an additional influence might ministers have over the youth and children of their charge, were they in the habit annually of making some such expression of their respect for their ministers! Let youth, let families and congregations who have not been accustomed to such efforts, make the experiment; and if they receive no rich blessing in their basket and store, this may be the means of binding, not only their minister, but the gospel closer to their heart, and in the life to come they may reap a rich reward.

6. Sustain your minister by your prayers. The ablest divines, men who possessed the profoundest learning and erudition, have felt the need, not only of high moral feelings and the graces of the Spirit, but of all the helps which God has instituted in the church to secure success in their responsible work. Even the chiefest of the apostles could often break forth in the strong language of dependance, "Brethren, pray for us." When Aaron and Hur held up the hands of Moses, the God of battles gave success to his people; but when in the prolonged and sanguinary struggle they became faint and weary, Amalek prevailed.

When the people of God humble themselves, and unitedly invoke the Divine benediction upon the efforts of his servants —when they hang all their hopes of success and Heaven on the Cross of Christ, it is then that God delights to bless the efforts of his ministers, and is pleased to enlarge the borders of his kingdom.

Can it be doubted that the reason why ministers are often unsuccessful in their work, and why pastors are so frequently removed from their charge, is referable to the neglect of united, importunate prayer in the church?

Some of our readers will remember the pertinent answer which an able and godly minister gave to one of his people, on his making the following interrogations. "Sir, do you, of late, preach with that success with which once you did?" The clergyman said he was alarmed at the query which he had expressed, and declared there was one reason which might be given, but which prudence perhaps would dictate best to withhold. The inquirer earnestly requested his pastor to make known to him that reason; when, to his great astonishment, he declared, that HE HAD LOST HIS PRAYER-BOOK. "Lost your prayer-book, sir! I never knew that you used a prayer-book." The pastor, with emotion and tears, replied—"My church is my PRAYER-BOOK. They, I fear, have ceased to offer up united and strong cries to God for my success as formerly. I CANNOT PREACH!"

We doubt not that many of the servants of Christ, in this day of darkness and rebuke, when the thousand harps of Zion are on the willows, and languishing and discouragement have taken hold on them, like a strong man armed, are ready to say with emotion—I have lost my prayer-book!

Let the time come when each member of the church of God in the closet, around the family altar, as well as in the stated assemblies of the church, shall intercede at the Throne of Grace for the divine blessing to descend upon their pastor, and who can tell how benign would be the result? Nothing would contribute more strongly to honor and exalt the holy office of the gospel ministry in the family circle, and prepare the mind of our youth and children for the reception of the truth which the servants of Christ present, than the offering up to God of daily, united prayer for the pastor.

Let that golden age of the church return which our fathers saw, when the combined energies of God's people shall be connected with the great plans of their minister; when the congregation shall warmly sustain him in his fidelity—shall cheer and animate him by the presence of their family groups in the house of God; when all shall deem his character most sacred, and shield it from the assaults of the enemy; when his temporal wants shall be supplied by the liberality of his people, and the church, like the heart of one man, shall hold up his hands by their cries to God for his success. Ah, when this period shall again be enjoyed by the church, what a rich revenue of praise will be brought to the glory of God in the salvation of the world!

Original.

NOT LOST, BUT GONE TO HEAVEN.*

BY MRS. M. ST. LEON LOUD, PHILADELPHIA.

A MOTHER bent o'er her sleeping boy,
And in her eye was the light of joy;
For unto her had the boon been given,
To rear a plant for the bowers of Heaven.
But the fount grew troubled within her heart,
And I saw the smile from her lip depart,
When she thought of the paths where his feet might stray—
Of travels sore on the world's highway—
Of the tempter's wiles for the young heart spread—
And of storms that beat on the pilgrim's head;
Of pain and sorrow, perchance of sin,
Ere that blest haven his soul might win;
And her warm tears fell like a summer shower,
On the folded leaves of a fair young flower.

* "I rather rejoice than mourn for the death of an infant," said a mother who had lost several lovely and interesting children. "They are taken away from the evil to come."

NOT LOST, BUT GONE TO HEAVEN.

Pure as a wreath of the new-fall'n snow,
'Mid its golden curls was that baby brow;
Dark lashes droop'd o'er his deep blue eye,
Like the grass-fring'd bank where spring violets lie
While his dimpled cheek and his dewy lips
Were bright as the rose which the wild-bee sips.
She gazed with pride on her noble child,
But oh! her heart with its fears grew wild,
When she thought of him as a care-worn man,
With guilt on his haggard brow, and wan;
With a furrowed cheek, and an earthward eye,
And a heart that had treasured no hopes on high;
An aged man who had lived in vain,
And her tears fell fast as the summer rain.

Closely she bends o'er her treasure now,
A shade is dimming that bright young brow;
For the angel that watch'd o'er his slumbering
Gave place to one with a darker wing,
And he pass'd away at the touch of death,
Like a flow'ret chill'd by the hoar-frost's breath.
Then the mother knelt by her only son,
And murmured, "Father, thy will be done!
In mercy thou takest the sinless home,
From the blight of the evil days to come."
And though her tears fell like summer rain,
They were not wrung from a heart in pain;
For she sung in a sweet and melting tone
Her last farewell to the spirit-flown.

Farewell, farewell, my child!
Like a pure dove thy spirit hath departed,
  With snowy pinions plumed for upward flight
To cloudless skies; I weep not broken-hearted,
  For thou art dwelling in eternal light,
      My loved, my undefiled.

Oh! early call'd and blest!
Not thine to run the race with footsteps weary,
  And life's dark travel-stains upon thy soul;
Nor manhood's strife—nor age uncheer'd and dreary:
  Thou at the starting-point didst win the goal,
      And sink to peaceful rest.

THE FLOWER IN THE ICICLE.

Cold is my bosom now,
Where bird-like thou didst nestle; sad and lonely
In its deep silence is my home-bower made;
By day and night I dream of thee, thee only,
And oft they tell me that there is a shade
Of sorrow on my brow.

Yet not for thee I mourn,
Sweet flower of earthly promise, early smitten!
'Tis but the moving of deep thoughts that swell
A mother's yearning heart, who, childless written,
Longs for a mansion where her lost ones dwell,
In the bright spirit-bourne.

For thee—joy! joy! The wild
And fearful clouds life's pathway overshading,
Bursting full oft in tempest—and the grief
Of the young heart whose glowing hopes are fading,
E'en as the hues of morning fair and brief—
Thou hast escaped, my child!

And where pure waters swell
From living fountains, peacefully thou'rt straying
'Mong kindred angels, in thy native skies;
Whilst I in patient hope still linger, praying
That soon thy hand may wipe my weeping eyes—
'Till then, beloved, farewell!

~~~~~~~~~~~~

Original.

THE FLOWER IN THE ICICLE.

BY MRS. EMMA C. EMBURY, BROOKLYN, N. Y.

"This our life, exempt from public haunt,
Finds tongues in trees, books in the running brooks,
Sermons in stones, and good in every thing."

It was the morning of a day in early spring,—a heavy rain had fallen during the night, congealing as it fell upon the leafless branches and brown stalks of the garden shrubs, while a heavy, lowering sky, still overhung the melancholy landscape, threatening continued gloom and tempest. The appearance of nature, sombre as was her garb, was sadly in unison with the feelings of her who had now looked on this desolated scene. It was the anniversary of the death of a beloved child; and the bereaved mother, though years had passed since that fair blossom was blighted, ever spent the returning day in sadness and despondency. It had been the first deep, heart-piercing grief she was called to bear. It came upon her like a thunderbolt falling from a cloudless sky; for never had earth looked brighter,—never had the atmosphere she breathed seemed so redolent of happiness,—never had the shadow of sorrow's dusky form been so entirely hidden from her view, as at the moment when the dread fiat went forth, and the messenger of death sped upon his fearful errand. The child, too, was the fairest, and, it may be, though the mother knew it not till then, the best-beloved of the little flock; for the remembrance of a buried sister had enstamped the image of the loved and lost upon her bright beauty, and the love which had heretofore been wasted at the grave of early friendship, now poured its fulness in the fathomless channel of maternal affection. But death came! His touch was gentle and his voice was low, yet his breath chilled the warm heart, and checked the bounding pulse of beautiful childhood. The mother, with breaking heart but unmurmuring lip, gave the fair creature to the grave, strong in her faith that the arms of Him who said "Suffer little children to come unto me," would now enfold her treasure with a love passing the love of a mother's heart. Yet the scenes of that dark and miserable day would recur to her on that melancholy anniversary, and memory, too faithful to her trust, sent forth, from her haunted cell, shadow after shadow, to pass before the mental vision of the mournful one.

"Aye, thus," said the mother, as she looked out upon the frozen earth, "even thus has my heart been desolated. In the spring of life,—when the buds of hope were promising such rich blossoms of future happiness,—then came the cold blast from the valley of the shadow of death; and, even as the rain has frozen upon yon unopened leaves, so, it seems to me, that tears have congealed upon my every future hope. Yes, joys are still left, but they bud and blossom amid griefs,—hopes still remain, but they are enshrined in sorrow's crystal drops.

>'Life's flowers for me
>But wreathe a cup of trembling.'

"I am like one who sits at an Egyptian feast. The banquet is spread,—the vessels of gold and of silver glitter upon the board,—the wine sparkles in every cup,—the garlands are fresh and fragrant on the brows of the revellers around me. But there is one veiled and silent figure who tastes not of the viands,—who joins not in the mirthful song,—who heeds not the merry laugh which echoes round. It is the fearful form of Death,—the skeleton at the banquet,—veiled and garlanded, to hide him from the eyes of those who would be recklessly gay, but not the less ghastly and heart-chilling! I cannot forget that the King of Terrors has silenced the music of my life, and dimmed the sunshine of my heart. I cannot forget, even in the midst of peace, that his footsteps may again cross the threshold,—that his shadow may again darken my quiet home. From the brightest sunshine I see the deepest shadow ever cast—in the midst of summer's richest verdure I behold the dead and withered branch—in the sweetest strains of joy—I can detect the under-tone of sadness. No: life can never be to me what once it was.

>A shadow lies upon my path, which nought can chase away,
> Save the great Sun of Righteousness, with healing in its ray;
>A shadow from the mountain dark o'er which my feet must tread,
> To meet again my loved of yore,—my treasures of the dead."

While the mourner thus sat indulging her desponding fancies, a bright-haired, sunny-faced boy, of some five summers, bounded into the room, and throwing himself into his mother's arms, in the sweet abandonment of childish affection, held up before her a branch of the newly-budded and fragrant lilac, enshrined in transparent crystal, exclaiming—"Look, mother, look how beautiful! God has made a FLOWER WITHIN AN ICICLE!"

It was a simple, childlike, but beautiful thought; and, as the mother gazed on his innocent brow, she felt how full of wisdom are the teachings of childhood. Tears gushed from her eyes, as she remembered her own vain repinings, while gazing on the object which had excited so much joy in the heart of her happier boy. To HER it had seemed the similitude of sorrowful remembrance, binding every flower of life in an icy chain. To HIM it was only another proof of the goodness and power of God,—a new pleasure, evanescent but full of innocent enjoyment,—another gem added to his accumulating treasures of knowledge.

"Heaven lies around us in our infancy."

The lessons of wisdom are often learned from infant lips; and the sinlessness of childhood has often, ere now, softened the indurated heart of sinful manhood. The mother wept no more; she dwelt no longer on the mournful fancies which had so saddened her spirit. Henceforth she resolved to see the rainbow in the stormy cloud,—the fruit in the unsightly bud, —THE FLOWER WITHIN THE ICICLE.

Years passed away, and worldly cares came upon her. The wealth which men prize even beyond their immortal souls, had been hers from childhood, but now a sudden and unlooked for blast of evil fortune swept it away forever. She was no longer the daughter of luxury, whose foot trod daintily the earth, and whose brow the winds of heaven visited not too roughly. Poverty had come "like an armed man," and the "pride and pomp, and circumstance" of riches were at an end. It was a sore and bitter trial to her whose life had been like a fairy-tale. It was a trial, not for her own sake, but for the sake of those dear children, whom she would fain, in her blind affection, have surrounded with those manifold appliances of enjoyment which had impressed their influence upon her own youthful mind. But she had been schooled to better feelings; she believed that God knew best, and she uttered no murmur at his decree. Toil became her portion, and she shrunk not from her duties even though the world withdrew its smiles, and turned its back upon honest poverty, while it fawned with sickening servility upon those who, lacking the moral courage to be poor, had exercised the villain, daring to become rich. She purchased her daily bread by the labor of her own hands, and felt no shame. Her children grew up amid privations, but they also grew up amid those lowly plants of true virtue which flourish best on the rugged and sandy soil of humble life. The rank weeds which the sunshine of prosperity so soon brings out in the heart, and whose growth can scarce be repressed by all the watchfulness of affection, had little cherishing within their bosoms. When in after-life the mother, from a situation of comparative comfort, regarded the noble and excellent character of those children, whose better nature had been so admirably developed by the painful but salutary teachings of necessity, she felt that even amid the chill of poverty and worldly scorn she had found THE FLOWER WITHIN THE ICICLE.

Yes, the life of that sorrowing mother was like the course of some Alpine traveller;—sometimes her feet pressed a soft, green sward, and crushed out the fragrance of those odoriferous herbs which are ever sweetest when trampled upon;—sometimes she trod a rough and rugged mountain pass, leaving the track of her footsteps in blood upon the jagged rocks;—sometimes she basked in the soft and genial sunshine which calls the violet from its leafy covert and wakens the melody of bee and bird;—sometimes she sat chilled and wearied beneath the cold, dark shadow of an overhanging cliff, whose brow seemed to frown dismay into her soul;—sometimes the murmur of a gentle mountain stream came to her with lulling melody;—sometimes the dull and muffled thunder of the dreadful avalanche thrilled her inmost heart with the surprise of sudden fear;—sometimes amid the stern rocks, whose stony bosoms seemed as if they could give out no kindly blessing to the wayfarer, she found hidden clefts where the birds had built their nests, where the wild-flower bloomed in unsuspected beauty, and where pools of sweet water had gathered to refresh the wearied one;—sometimes in the green and cultivated valley, where the hand of man was busy and his heart was throbbing with active life, she was condemned to eat only of the bitter herb, and to quench her thirst in the muddy fountain. Yet, while treading this varied and chequered path, her course was ever UPWARD;—" EXCELSIÒR" was written upon her heart as she went on and on towards that better world, where rest awaited her;—and when Death met her in the way,—when she sank down upon the topmost height, still bearing in heart the FLOWER WITHIN THE ICICLE, one beam of heavenly joy piercing the opening portals of the Eternal city, dissolved the icy band, and left her to enjoy, in a mansion above, the perfect sweetness of the expanding flower.

Original.
THE CLOSE OF LIFE.

DEATH is fitly styled the King of Terrors. To the devout Christian, death is the end of sin and sorrow. In the church, in his deepest trials, in his last sickness, in his triumphant departure; God is his Father, the Lord Jesus is his Saviour, the Holy Spirit is his Sanctifier and Comforter, and Heaven is his destined home. Death is the hour of his release from bondage. At the termination of this mortal life, his soul enters upon the scenes of ineffable bliss and eternal glory!

Not so with the sinner. To him death is the period of all hope and joy. He has wasted life in the pursuit of trifles. If he has attained riches, honors, and power, he dies as poor as a beggar, for he has lost his soul! What a loss!—no tongue can tell, no pencil delineate, no imagination conceive—it is the loss of Heaven. The fool sports on the edge of the giddy precipice, and plunges the awful verge. The maniac casts himself into the fiery volcano and sinks from sight. But the sinner, with the voice of reason and conscience, and the spirit of God sounding their alarm in his ears, throws away life, and wakes at death—at the bar of the Judge, to a sense of his loss!

Editor.

Original.

THE SAVOYARD ORPHAN'S DEATH.

BY HENRY M. PARSONS.

The snow was falling, and the wintry wind
Sighed through the city's now deserted streets,
As late at night, the Pastor wrapped his cloak
Closely around him, and went forth to bear
A Christian message to the couch of death.

In an unlighted lane
He entered a small room, and stood beside
A pale, young girl, whose sunken eye
Welcom'd that good man to her lowly home,
While in a voice, mellowed by suffering,
Her artless tale, fell like a plaintive strain:—

I was born in a valley of distant Savoy,
'Neath the cliffs where the hunter pursues the chamois,
But my parents deserted the vineyards they drest,
For the hopes which were flung o'er the land of the West.

My beautiful brother grew sick on the wave,
And the love that we bore him his life could not save—
The heart of my mother was crush'd when he died,
And her, too, we buried beneath the dark tide.

The night that succeeded my father grew wild,
But imprinted one kiss on the lips of his child,
Ere he leaped in the foam of the billowy crest,
Where he sleeps till the trumpet shall call home the blest.

My heart would have broken while stricken with grief,
If the friend who had smitten had not brought relief;
But I thought of the counsels of those who were gone,
And I plead not in vain with the All-wise One.

Since I trod on these shores, nearly three years have fled,
During which the kind Shepherd my footsteps has led;
And though clad in the garb of the lowliest poor,
And fed with coarse food, I have sighed not for more.

'Come away,' 'come away,' thus the angels invite,
'Let the band sundered here, round the throne re-unite'—
'I will come,' 'I will come,' for the gloom of the grave
Breaks away at the voice of The Mighty to save.

She ceased, folded her hands upon her breast,
And slept.
   The Pastor kiss'd her white, cold brow,
And kneeling by the sleeper, bless'd that grace
Which wrought so richly in the orphan's heart,
And gave such peaceful transit to the skies.

Original.

VALUE OF PARENTAL GOVERNMENT.

BY REV. A. A. LIPSCOMB, ALABAMA.

IF amid the ruins of the fall there remains any thing beautiful and noble in human nature, it is found in the affections. The glory of the original creation, though faded, yet lingers around them; and as withered roses retain their former fragrance, the affections still exhibit their primeval power. The development of intellect—its energy and scope depend upon circumstances, and consequently different individuals manifest different degrees of ability. Physical obstacles often restrain mind. Tact can find no sphere of action; talent lies hidden in a napkin; and genius, the sublimest form of intellect, is prostrated beneath misfortune. The heart is exempted from such laws. All possess strong affections; all carry a flame within, that the pure breath of Heaven has kindled; and all, under wise moral culture, may realize the abiding blessedness that flows from well-regulated feelings. Every thing in the universe exists for the heart. If imagination dwell amid its bright creations—if it constitute the connecting link between the physical and moral world—it is exercised for the heart. If memory intercept the flight of time to the sepulchre of ages, and perpetuate the duration of departed days; if reason judge and decide, it is for the heart. The pleasures of life are the pleasures of the heart. The home of Christianity is the heart.

Heaven has ordained that the domestic constitution should be the chief sphere in which the affections should be exercised. That constitution was established amid the loveliness of Eden. Social perfection was an element of original purity. If sin has marred it, Jehovah has mercifully continued its pristine laws. The Saviour always paid great respect to it. His social character was perfect. Had he been a Cicero, his simple eloquence would never have won childhood to his arms. Had he been a Pharisee, the home of poverty had ne'er been cheered by his presence. Had he been a Stoic, the grave of Lazarus had ne'er been moistened with his tears. Had he been inimical to social pleasure, the marriage feast would not have been honored by his attendance. Nothing could more fully show the estimate he placed upon it, than the fact, that the operations of his benign religion are called by social terms. What is Christianity but UNION, FELLOWSHIP, INTERCOURSE with Heaven? What is the special, the most tender designation of God, but "OUR FATHER, WHO ART IN HEAVEN?" The domestic constitution, family organization, is the foundation of all social character. Our first ideas and our earliest feelings are identified therewith. Providence has designed that our education should commence and advance within the sacred enclosure of home. The natural longing for society is here to be gratified, and the powerful principle of imitation brought into action. Few things are more obvious, than the importance of family government.

The necessity of law and government, as a general, social provision, is too apparent to require illustration. A band of pirates cannot exist without regulations. A tribe of savages is compelled to have its rules. As man progresses in civilization, law is felt to be more and more essential. Every step in refinement brings new relations, augments social power, and increases the endearments of home; hence, government is more particularly needed in the highest forms of civilization. The science of jurisprudence has been more slowly matured than any other, because, the maturity of civilization brings such a variety of social circumstances and incidental connections, all requiring the protection of law. For the same reason that government is needed anywhere, it is needed in the household. Here there are relations; here are rights; and hence, the spirit of law must be sacredly enthroned around the fireside, and the strong sanctions of Jehovah annexed to it.

The nature of domestic government is determined by the relations that exist in the social circle, and the benevolent objects that are to be secured. Its elements are authority and love. The will of parents is ever to be SUPREME. Jehovah has invested them with sovereignty. To honor that sovereignty, one of the commandments of the Decalogue was given. If the splendor of miracles accompanied the solemn enthronement of that law amid the chosen nation, such sublime manifestations applied to this portion of the sacred code, as much as to any other. So clearly is this sovereignty the dictate of nature, as well as the announcement of revelation, that in all ages it has received the sanction of intelligence and the support of virtue. No child has a right to dispute this authority. It is measurably absolute; from it there can be no appeal. Such a power is obviously liable to great abuse, but is there no check? is there no wise principle to direct it? All nature is a system of well-balanced forces. Astronomy teaches that the centripetal and centrifugal laws govern each other. So in the moral world; one sentiment acts upon opposite sentiments. Parental authority is to be regulated by affection. A spirit of harshness, selfishness, and tyranny is to be subdued. No man is fit for the paternal office, who loves the sceptre for its own sake. If the father ordain family rules, and execute them from day to day, tenderness is to be his predominant feeling. Let it be otherwise, and his authority will soon fall into contempt. Individuals are more under the influence of emotion and affection, than thought and principle. It is especially the case in the family group. Heaven has ordained that love and authority should be united in this patriarchal empire. If it were otherwise, sad results would follow. Power without affection would be tyranny; affection without power would be weakness. Both should be associated. Fear and love, the two master passions of the heart, will thus be addressed. Reverence and regard will be called into action. The wisdom of the domestic arrangements will reveal itself, and every instinct of the bosom will hallow the authority of the fireside.

To ensure the beneficial consequences of family government, parents must be under the dominion of moral principle. The idea of mere relation is not sufficient to enforce their will. It must be based on elevated sentiment. The minds of children also must be early imbued with the same spirit. Every thing indicates that moral culture should be commenced at the very dawn of conscience and affection. Providence has so arranged it, that the depravity of the heart is held in abeyance for a season, that the lessons of Christianity may be taught. Another law of our nature, that law by which habits of evil are formed slowly, points to the same duty. Parents must never trust to instinct in their children. The possession of reason and sentiment, evinces that this was never designed. Let parents cultivate the moral sense of their children, and strive to lead them to act from principle, in all their conduct towards them, and they will find their authority resting on a permanent foundation. Let them be ever harmonious in the exercise of parental power; if the father and the mother exhibit any want of union, judicious government is at an end; discord will prevail, and peace will depart.

Such an administration of family government will be productive of the highest good. Intercourse with the world will be anticipated, and the growth of depravity arrested. The active spirit of childhood will find appropriate exercise, and the heart be early consecrated by the descending glory of the Holy Ghost. The social nature will receive a right direction. An important part of domestic education is secured, when a proper social character is developed; and this will be readily accomplished if a correct discipline be maintained at home. Could this essential portion of human acquirements be obtained any where else, it might be of less moment; but the law of Heaven is, that it should be realized beneath the paternal eye.

The neglect of domestic government is a violation of one of the first and holiest institutions. No one can thus act with impunity. These infringements of the divine economy are visited with punishment in THIS world. As if Justice could not wait for the day of future retribution, it avenges the truth and wisdom of Jehovah at once. Its cloudy pavilion rests over such a home; its dark curse abides upon it. The garlands around its bowers wither, and the bloom of its beauty dies forever. Uninstructed and unsanctified, the children of such families go forth into the world without a benediction upon their heads, or a light upon their path. Passion is their master. They live for selfish gratification; they die, and experience only a sadder retribution. Earth disdains their memory; Heaven has no blessing for their graves.

The influence of woman is to be constantly recognised in all efforts to advance social order and happiness. We should never have been placed under her tuition, at so tender an age and impressible a season, had she not been peculiarly fitted to direct the first aspirations of the mind, and govern the wayward impulses of the passions. Her position is the proof of her power; her name, the seal of her commission. If the ills of life press more heavily upon her than upon us, she is partly recompensed by the agency she exerts in moulding human character, and by the delightful exercise of her affections upon those who, in after time, gather flowers for her shrine. Could any thing be wanting to show her elevated place in the scale of creation, the conduct of the adorable Redeemer would exhibit it, for some of his sublimest miracles were wrought for her benefit. One of the last acts of his life was to acknowledge his obligations to the beloved Mary, and commit her to the care of the affectionate Apostle.

Let Christianity preside over the domestic circle—let her

name be reverenced and her power here be felt—let wisdom and prudence always be observed by parents, and respect and affection maintained by children, and Heaven will never want for an image in this dark and evil world. Death may invade such a home, but it will be but another form of life. Memory will receive the departed as sense resigns them; and as one species of the American oak retains its leaves after they have withered, so will memory cling to them after they have perished beneath the stroke of the great Destroyer.

THE HUMAN FRAME.

BY REV. B. H. DRAPER.

The human frame affords an astonishing display of the wisdom of the adorable Creator.

How wonderful is the eye! Where could it have been placed more suitably for the guidance of the whole body? How surprising are the faculties of hearing and smelling! And where, since all sounds and odors ascend, could these organs have been placed more advantageously?

The human heart, which receives the blood every instant, and throws it out again as often to every part of the system, is placed in the middle of the body. Was it placed there by blind chance? He who can believe it, may believe any thing. Who keeps it beating, at the rate of a hundred thousand strokes every twenty-four hours? Who has provided for the protection of this prime mover of the human frame, by the covering of the arms, and the strong range of bones we call ribs—and which, at the same time, secure for it room to play in? Who has encircled the delicate brain by the hard cranium? And who has given it so beautiful a covering of hair? Who, but He "who is mighty in counsel, and excellent in working?"

I met a person a few days since who had but one arm, as, by an accident among the machinery of a foundry, he had lost the other; but this one was exceedingly useful to him. I have a friend who, a few years since, lost one of his eyes; but he has not much missed it, as the other has been all that was essential to his welfare. If God had given but one arm, and one eye, and if this had been lost, all would have been lost; but how bountiful, and what a display is it of his wisdom, that he has given two arms and two eyes!

What a wonderful instrument is the arm! At once strong and light, and capable of performing every useful motion; with what facility, and how gracefully, does it bend inwardly and outwardly, upward and downward, and in whatever direction its owner pleases! And what has it done? It has performed innumerable works of skill and utility. It has built large and beautiful structures and cities. It has framed the noble vessel in which we can sail round the world in which we live. It has tastefully adorned very many parts of the globe committed to its care.

How beautifully does the skin cover the whole body! It is a fine net-work, woven with divine skill by God's own hand.

The formation of the teeth is a display of the wisdom of the adorable Creator. The foremost are thin and sharp, to cut the food asunder; and the hindermost broad and strong, to grind it in pieces.

How wonderful is the sense of tasting! How surprising the gift of speech, by which we make known our wants, and the inmost sentiments of our hearts!

But it would occupy a long duration, and fill no small volume, to relate all the wonders which are evident in the human frame.

How ought those noble faculties which he has created, and which he every moment preserves, to be devoted to his service!

Selected

Original.
RAVAGES OF TIME.

BY A. LLOYD.

Contemplate the ravages of time. How vast the theme! how extended the field! How can mortals grasp the amplitude of duration! What is time? A moment—an hour—an age!

When he commenced his course, the morning stars sang together, and all the sons of God shouted for joy. Time advancing, brings forth from his treasury and develops the various changes and vicissitudes which occur; thus exhibiting to short-sighted mortals the mysterious purposes of the Infinite, the Eternal One.

Who that contemplates the mighty empires and kingdoms which once flourished where Apollo sheds his orient beams, would have imagined the time would ever come when so few vestiges of their magnificent cities, splendid temples, gorgeous palaces, and cloud-capped towers, with all their thousand forms of power and wealth, would remain?

Babylon, where once was concentrated the wisdom and power of the world, is no more. Even her place cannot be found. The contemplative traveller sits down amid the vast and magnificent ruins of Balbec or Palmyra. Struck with remains of superior architecture, evidences of great advancement in the arts—he asks, Who reared these majestic columns?—who inhabited this city?—for what purpose was it built? The desert winds bring no reply.

Approach the land of fable and mythology. Upon the banks of its deified river you behold the remains of cities once the pride and glory of the world. View her massy temples—her mighty pyramids—her towering obelisks—her dark labyrinths! On every hand you perceive the marks of gigantic minds, and the labors of extraordinary mechanism. Enter Thebes, famous in fable for her hundred gates, her million of troops, and her ten thousand chariots. Examine her majestic temple. Filled with wonder, you exclaim—" Was this mighty structure erected merely for the worship of a bird?" For what purpose were the vast pyramids constructed? Even fable scarce ventures to turn aside the curtain which conceals this. Contrasting these remnants of antiquity with the meager race that cling around their ruins, how sensibly do we perceive the ravages of time!

The glory of Tyre has departed, leaving scarce a vestige of her power and grandeur. Her merchants are no longer princes. Where once stood her festive halls and commercial marts, the fisherman spreads his net beside his miserable hut. Carthage, her foster-child, Rome's rival, is no more. Classic soil of Greece—birthplace of heroes—school of statesmen, philosophers, and orators—mother of the muses—land of liberty, patriotism, and genius—how has the scythe of time prostrated all save the mementoes of your greatness! How has fallen the imperial city of the Cæsars, once the mistress of the world! The iron firmness of Roman integrity and virtue was relaxed by her luxury, wealth, and dissipation. Her orators, poets, and heroes, have passed away. The Augustan age has expired!

Our own continent exhibits striking evidences of the ravages of time. We see in the antiquities of this hemisphere, proofs that a powerful and enlightened people once flourished here. Who they were?—what revolutions they have undergone?—are questions which could only have been answered in the light of the past.

Oblivion has engulfed them and their works, except here and there a small remnant saved from universal wreck. This is a faint picture of the ruins of time. But may it not be that those who succeed us shall contemplate greater changes and revolutions? The existing governments of Europe may then have passed away. What great changes have occurred! Babylon, Tyre, Egypt, Greece, Carthage, Rome, all flitted their brief hour, and are gone. And who can say that this infant republic, just commencing its career of glory, having become greater than the nations that preceded her, shall not share their fate? Far be it from any American to wish or desire to dwell upon so mournful a catastrophe. Rather let every bosom heave with warm aspirations for the perpetuity of our civil and religious institutions.

GOOD MANNERS.

PROPRIETY of behavior in company is necessary to every gentleman; for, without good manners, he can neither be acceptable to his friends, nor agreeable in conversation to strangers.

The three sources of ill-manners are pride, ill-nature, and want of sense; so that every person who is already endowed with humility, good-nature, and good sense, will learn good manners with little or no teaching.

A writer, who had great knowledge of mankind, has defined good manners as THE ART OF MAKING THOSE PEOPLE EASY WITH WHOM WE CONVERSE; and his definition cannot be mended. The ill qualities above mentioned all tend naturally to make people uneasy. Pride assumes all the conversation to itself, and makes the company insignificant. Ill-nature makes offensive reflections; and folly makes no distinction of persons and occasions. Good manners are, therefore, in part negative: let a sensible person but refrain from pride and ill-nature, and his conversation will give satisfaction.

So far as good manners are positive, and related to good-breeding, there are many established forms, which are to be learned by experience and conversation in society. But there is one plain rule, worth all the rest added together; that a person who pretends to the character and behavior of a gentleman, should do every thing with GENTLENESS; with an easy, quiet, friendly manner, which doubles the value of every word and action. A forward, noisy, importunate, overbearing way of talking, is the very quintessence of ill-breeding: and hasty contradiction, unseasonable interruption of persons in their discourse, especially of elders or superiors, loud laughter, winkings, grimaces, and affected contortions of the body, are not only of low extraction in themselves, but are the natural symptoms of self-sufficiency and impudence.

It is a sign of great ignorance to talk much to other people, of things in which they have no interest; and to be speaking familiarly by name of distant persons, to those who have no knowledge of them. It shows that the ideas are comprehended within a very narrow sphere, and that the memory has but few objects.

If you speak of any thing remarkable in its way, many inconsiderate people have a practice of telling you something of the same kind, which they think much more remarkable. If persons in the company are commended for what they do, they will be instantly telling you of somebody else whom they know, who does it much better; and thus a modest person, who meant to entertain, is disappointed and confounded by another's rudeness. True gentility, when improved by good sense, avoids every appearance of self-importance; and polite humility takes every opportunity of giving importance to the company; of which it may be truly said, as it was of worldly wealth, "it is better to give than to receive." In our commerce with mankind, we are always to consider, that THEIR affairs are of more importance to THEM, than ours are; and we should treat them on this principle, unless we are occasionally questioned, and directed to ourselves by the turn of the conversation. Discretion will always fix on some subject in which the company have a common share. He that speaks only of such subjects as are familiar to himself, treats his company as the stork did the fox, presenting an entertainment to him in a deep pitcher, out of which no creature could feed but a long-billed fowl.

The rules I have laid down are such as take place chiefly in our conversation with strangers: among friends and acquaintance, where there is freedom and pleasantry, daily practice will be attended with less reserve. But here let me give you warning, that too great familiarity, especially if attended with roughness and importunity, is always dangerous to friendship, which must be treated with some degree of tenderness and delicacy, if you wish it to be lasting. You are to keep your friend by the same behavior that first won his esteem: and observe this, as a maxim verified by daily experience—that men advance themselves more commonly by the lesser arts of discretion, than by the more valuable endowments of wit and science; which, without discretion to recommend them, are often left to disappointment and beggary.

We are apt to look upon good manners as a lighter sort of qualification, lying without the system of morality and Christian duty; which a man may possess or not possess, and yet be a very good man. But there is no foundation for such an opinion: the apostle Paul has plainly comprehended it in his well-known description of CHARITY, which signifies the FRIENDSHIP OF CHRISTIANS, and is extended to so many cases, that no man can practise that virtue, and be guilty of ill manners. Show me the man, who in his conversation discovers no signs that he is PUFFED UP with pride; who never behaves himself UNSEEMLY, or with impropriety; who neither ENVIES nor censures; who is KIND and PATIENT toward his friends; who SEEKETH NOT HIS OWN, but considers others rather than himself, and gives them the preference; I say, that man is not only all that we intend by a gentleman, but much more; he really is, what all artificial courtesy affects to be, a philanthropist, a friend to mankind; whose company will delight while it improves, and whose good will rarely be evil spoken of. Christianity, therefore, is the best foundation of what we call good manners; and of two persons, who have equal knowledge of the world, he that is the best Christian will be the best gentleman.

It is an express and admirable distinction of a gentleman, that in the ordinary affairs of life he is extremely slow to take offence.   Selected.

[Original.]

THE LAST DAY OF ADAM.

BY J. W. BAILEY.

It was sunset. The clouds that hung about the western horizon were still bathed in the gorgeous hues of the departed luminary. The gentle breath of the evening wind—sweet with the perfume of a thousand flowers—brought a refreshing coolness after the sultry heat of the day; and the deep stillness that was gradually stealing over all things awakened in the mind calm and holy feelings. On a soft couch, beneath the shadow of a tent, over which a cypress waved its mournful head, lay the venerable form of Adam—majestic even in the hour of death. Around him stood the representatives of many generations, that had risen up to fill the earth, awaiting with sad hearts the departure of that spirit that once bore the "image of God." A faint smile passed over the features of the dying man as he was raised up to gaze for the last time upon the fair and beautiful earth, that had owned him for its lord. The rustling of the leaves among the tall trees—the faint murmurings of a gentle stream that wound its course amid the spicy groves—and the sweet notes of a solitary bird, that rose upon the air, soft and clear, filled his mind with visions of the past. Memory recalled the hour when first he stood in Eden's lovely bowers, and heard the loud chorus of "the morning stars," that "sang together" for joy. The faint streams of light, that were fast fading from the sky, seemed like the bright wings of angels, that once came in messages of peace and love to earth, seeking again their home in Heaven. The fair form of Eve appeared once more to stand before him, beautiful as in that hour when first he received her from the hands of the Creator, and called her his own. Then the "voice of the Lord God walking in the garden" struck upon his ear—and he wept. The words of that fearful curse, which shall be re-echoed through all the long ages of eternity, were again repeated. The "tree of life" waved its majestic head above him, around which turned the "flaming sword of the cherubims,"—and he felt anew the anguish that wrung his heart when he was driven forth from the garden by the command of the Almighty. But, the same voice that had uttered the words of condemnation, spoke of One who should bring peace and joy to men,—and hope enlivened his heart, as when the promise was first given. He knew that the path to the grave, dark and dreary as it was, would reveal to him the avenues that lead to the regions of light and love.

From these thoughts he was awakened by the low voice of prayer, and by a cloud of incense that ascended up toward the Throne on High. It was the hour of evening sacrifice. All bowed down and worshipped. In that sad and silent hour was uttered the last prayer of Adam, ere his spirit was borne by guardian angels to its home in Heaven.

Visions of the past had floated before his mind, and now the dim shadows of the future rose before him, dark and gloomy. He saw the race of man, ignorant and guilty. Nature put on her loveliest robes, and decked herself fairer than a queen,—the rich bounties of the great Giver were strewn thickly around,—Heaven and earth called for songs of praise and gratitude, yet no heart was raised to Him whom angels adore. Conscience warned and threatened,—the angry voice of God was heard in the low mutterings of the distant thunder,—the "still small voice of the Spirit" whispered in every breeze, but man heard them not. Wrath and judgment were fast gathered up against the day of vengeance. That day came. "The windows of Heaven were opened, and the fountains of the great deep broken up," and all perished,—all, save the small remnant who had proved faithful to the Most High. Peace and mercy descended again to earth. There was seen the bright star that shone in the east, the harbinger of a glorious day. With prophetic eye the history of man was traced through the long vista of years that ended in the destruction of the "last enemy." The lips of Adam moved in prayer and thanks to Him who had revealed some of the counsels of eternity. His eyes closed—a peaceful smile stole over his countenance—all was still—and the father of mankind was not.

Original.

TOMB OF THE EXILED EMPEROR.

BY HENRY M. PARSONS.

On a lovely morning in May, the rugged outline of St. Helena was descried darkly pictured upon the horizon at the distance of thirty-five or forty miles. In a few hours the sombre tints which the island presented in the distance, were exchanged for the dark brown of a nearer view. The stranger familiar with the history of him whose exile, residence and burial at St. Helena, have given it renown, naturally indulges, while approaching it, reflections upon that eminent but singularly unfortunate man. Proximity to the rocks diverts the thoughts into conjecture of the feelings of Napoleon when he gazed for the first time upon their frowning heights. One could easily believe that the gloomy features of these repulsive walls must have imparted a darker coloring to his spirit. The ambitious schemes which might have swelled his bosom and gilded his passage across the ocean, must have given place to sterner visions thronging confusedly before him. His doom, with its lonely haunts and lonely hours, must have pressed with a sickening weight upon his heart. How must the exile have yearned for the social endearments of the land where he had builded his fame!

A landing is easily effected beneath a cliff at the southwest of Jamestown, under a fort and battery, projecting from the rock a hundred feet above. At this jetty, Bonaparte landed in the twilight of the evening, and, accompanied by his escort, proceeded to his lodgings, the government castle, a little distance from the bridge, overlooking on the east and south a rich and beautiful garden, on the west extended barracks, and on the north a rampart formed by a wall stretching across the valley, surmounted by a battery and ornamented with trees. From his lodgings the emperor proceeded on the following day to Longwood, and never after revisited the town. From the landing place there is a causeway a quarter of a mile in extent, hewn from the rock; passing this by a gate beneath a massive archway you enter an open square, beyond which the town extends in a direct line up the defile, terminating in a botanical garden.

The private residences are generally of two stories, and built of the stone of which the island consists, their fronts stuccoed and painted. To many of them, pleasant verandahs are attached, opening into gardens of tropical trees and flowers.

From what appears on a cursory examination of the geological features of St. Helena, there is decisive evidence that the island was originated by earthquakes occasioned by a contrary cause than that by which they are ordinarily produced. From the appearance of the rocks, the convulsions which threw them into their present forms, must have been caused by the bursting in of water upon mineral fire, an agency which will occasion violent shocks and sudden explosions. Some of the mountains have been precipitated into the valleys, and now exhibit at their bases remains of decomposed substances originally produced on the surface of the globe. Others seem to have been swallowed in the bosom of the earth, leaving behind them frightful chasms and tremendous precipices. The mountains are conical or hemispherical, whose strata are in one place perpendicular, and in another horizontal. Among the minerals of the island are beautiful agate, jasper, and chalcedony; but the localities of these are not numerous or extensive.

To the visitor entering upon an excursion to the central parts of the island, the ascent of the mountain on the left of James' valley is beguiled by rich prospects of the town beneath, the shipping, and country seats opening in the distance through lengthened defiles. Half an hour's ride conveys him into a region of plants and flowers that flourish in countless variety amid perpetual spring. The road thence for a mile winds along the brow of a mountain and disappears in a grove of pines upon its summit. Descending from this eminence, you approach in a few moments a landscape where nature exhibits her rugged and repulsive features in strong contrast with her beautiful and attractive. Twelve or thirteen hundred feet below yawns a frightful chasm, whose sides are discolored with ferruginous particles washed by rains from the mountains above. At the head of this gorge is seen, embosomed in a lovely glen, the tomb of the illustrious but ill-fated Napoleon. Above and beyond it Hut's gate and the house in which Count Montholon lived, rise from an Eden of shrubbery relieved against retreating mountains. The ridge just left stretches in a semicircle to Hut's gate, beyond which the road continues a mile to Longwood. From this spot that plantation appears an elevated plain between two mountain passes, through which you obtain views of the ocean. To the imperial captive, the entire prospect, though studded with oases, must have been destitute of beauty, hemmed in by barren cliffs, and as it was to him, by an interdicted main.

Diverging from the road, the descent is by a steep and narrow carriage-way, shaded by evergreens, to the grave of the exiled emperor :

> "High is his tomb—the ocean flood
>   Far, far below by storms is curled—
> As round him heaved, while high he stood,
>   A stormy and unstable world.
>
> The only, the perpetual dirge
>   That's heard here, is the sea-bird's cry—
> The mournful murmur of the surge,
>   The cloud's deep voice, the wind's low sigh."

After the remains of the great man were thrice incoffined, the sarcophagus was chained to iron bars extending across an excavation of the rock, and covered with cement to its surface but a few inches beneath a rich alluvial soil. Three uninscribed slabs of shaded marble marked the tomb, at whose head and foot geraniums and tulips were in blossom, the whole enclosed by an iron railing, eight by fourteen feet in length. With one exception, all the original willows are decayed, but slips from them were planted among cypress, fir, and other trees, and have attained considerable size. Directly across the outer enclosure from the head of the grave, the spring at which the sleeper was often refreshed bubbles through a fissure in the rock, half hidden among mountain moss. Furnished with beautiful bouquets, you leave this lovely retreat, and resuming your ride, continue round the amphitheatre to Longwood.

From the gate at the entrance to the grounds, you pass through an avenue partially shaded, to the residence in which Napoleon lived and died. It occupies the highest point of land on the plantation, and commands, among other views, one of Deadwood, where soldiers were stationed to intimidate the hero. The farm-house, now occupied by a threshing machine, is one story in height, built of stone, stuccoed, and painted yellow. From the small piazza in front, passing through a diminutive billiard-room, a small apartment is entered, crowded into half its original size by the machinery of the mill. This was used by its distinguished occupant as a sitting-room. Between two windows, opening towards the west, was placed the bed in which the emperor expired. It is with difficulty that an eye-witness can divest himself of the idea that it has always worn its present aspect. As far as practicable the room, and indeed every part of the building, should have been kept in the condition in which its tenant left it. Thus might visitors have gathered impressions of the sources of comfort available by the exile, honorable to the British government. The dining-room is a dark and dismal cell, furnished with the only fire-place of which the house can boast. A well-lighted and airy apartment adjoining this, in the eastern wing, was fitted up for the royal captive's library.

This, with the valet rooms, compose the entire wing. At the south of the dining-room is an antique porch and a paved court, across which were the dressing, bathing, and bed rooms of the emperor. They are mere stables for horses. Indignant at the marks of shameful degradation everywhere apparent, the traveller retraces his steps to the piazza, and after a walk of three minutes, reaches the new house which Napoleon would neither occupy or enter. If the spot just left is an accusing spirit, this is a redeeming one. The edifice is of stone, one story, enclosing a hollow square. It is neatly stuccoed, and painted yellow, with a roof of slate. The rooms for Bonaparte and the family of Count Montholon, are spacious and elegant. The northern front is occupied by a fine verandah, opening into a garden redolent with beauty and fragrance. The entire grounds are tastefully arranged, and exhibit a choice selection of plants and flowers. Were princes to seek a voluntary exile, they could choose no lovelier spot than this.

The return route is usually by Diana's peak, which is twenty-two hundred feet high, commanding a prospect of the entire island. Continuing along a ridge of mountains, with views of the ocean in the distance, and rich meadow lands around, more strikingly interesting as contrasted with the gloomy hills, and passing "Fairy Land," "Lot's Wife," a massive lava pillar thrown by some freak of nature high above the neighboring rocks, and "Plantation House," the residence of the governor, the descent of "Ladder Hill" again restores the pilgrim to the island tombs, to the bustle of the world, but with feelings chastened by his reflections over the ashes of the mighty emperor, before whom nations once trembled.

We cannot dismiss this brief narrative of our visit to the grave of Napoleon, without subjoining some deeply thrilling facts respecting his death-bed, derived from the FEUILLE RELIGIEUSE DU CANTON DE VAUD, a French periodical of acknowledged excellence.

"The French Abbe Bonavita went from Paris, through Belgium and England, to St. Helena, in order to become the emperor's chaplain. In Belgium, he became acquainted with an Englishman, a zealous supporter of the Bible Society. They travelled together to London, and had much intercourse during the Abbe's stay in that city. The English gentleman availed himself of the opportunity to intrust to the Abbe a splendidly bound Bible, of a beautiful edition, begging him to present it to the unhappy exile. He thankfully undertook the commission, saying that he was sure the emperor would highly value the present. This proved to be the fact. Persons fully entitled to credit, who attended Napoleon's dying bed, have declared that he assiduously read the Holy Scriptures; and that, in the pangs of his severe malady, he often, with strong emotion, uttered the great name of Jesus. It may be even said that he 'confessed Christ before men.' In a familiar but solemn conversation, he exclaimed, with expressive accent and emphatic brevity, which had an electric effect, 'I know men; and I tell you that Jesus was not a man. His religion is a self-existent mystery, and it proceeded from a mind not human. There is in it a deep peculiarity of character, "INDIVIDUALITE," which has produced a succession of doctrines and maxims till then unknown. Jesus borrowed nothing from human knowledge. Only in himself are found completely the example or the imitation of his life. Neither was he a philosopher; for his proofs were miracles, and his disciples from the very first adored him. In fact, science and philosophy are powerless to salvation; and the sole object of Jesus, in coming into the world, was to unveil the mysteries of Heaven and the laws of mind. Alexander, Cæsar, Charlemagne, and I, have founded empires; but on what have we rested the creations of our genius? Upon force. Only Jesus has founded an empire upon love; and, at this moment, millions of men would die for him. It was not a day, nor a battle, that won the victory over the world for the Christian. No; it was a long war, a fight of three centuries; begun by the apostles, and continued by their successors, and the flow of generations that followed. In that war, all the kings and powers of the earth were on one side; on the other side, I see no army, but a mysterious force, and a few men, scattered here and there through all parts of the world, and who had no rallying point but their faith in the mysteries of the cross. I die before my time, and my body will be put in the ground, and become the food of worms. Such is the fate of the great Napoleon! What an abyss between my deep wretchedness, and Christ's eternal kingdom, proclaimed, loved, adored, and spreading through the world! Was that dying? Was it not rather to live? THE DEATH OF CHRIST IS THE DEATH OF GOD.' With these words Napoleon ceased; but Gen. Bertrand making no reply, he added, 'If you do not understand that Christ is God, I have been wrong in calling you General.'"

Original
AN OMNIPRESENT GOD.

BY MRS. M. L. GARDINER, SAG HARBOR, L. I.

Through nature's wide and vast domain,
In every part a God I see;
In suns and stars, in hill and plain,
In stormy clouds and rolling sea.
I see him ride on whirlwinds dire,
That o'er the skies in terror sweep;
And wrap in night yon orb of fire,
While trembling millions stand and weep.

I see him in the moon's soft light,
That plays upon a thousand streams;
In every gem that decks the night,
And guides the pilgrim by its beams.
I see him in the wide-spread lake,
Whose gloomy forests girt the shore;
In wilds untrod, and tangled brake,
Where deadly monsters prowl and roar.

I see him in the flowery spring,
When wild-birds tune their sweetest notes;
And to my ear their music bring,
In every gentle breeze that floats.

I see him in the flocks that feed
In quiet round the forest glade ;
The lambs that gambol o'er the mead,
At early dawn, or twilight shade.

I see him in the rolling spheres,
That round in endless circles run ;
And feel him in the weight of years,
That show my wanderings nearly done.
Where'er I look, through boundless space,
In heaven or earth, on sea or air ;
In every part my God I trace,
And see his footsteps printed there.

Original.

SELF-KNOWLEDGE.

A CHARACTERISTIC of the ancients is seen in their comprising in a few words matter sufficient to fill volumes. One of the most laconic and expressive of these was inscribed on the walls of the temple at Delphi, "KNOW THYSELF." If we search all the books within our reach, containing the lore of generations, nowhere can we find more salutary counsel, more important advice, in so short a sentence.

"Know thyself," examine the secret workings of the heart, search the hidden springs of nature, lay open the inexhaustible treasures of the mind—"know thyself" as a human being, possessing its frailties—as an immortal being, stamped with the impress of the Deity.

A knowledge of our organic constitution—its wonderful mechanism, its nicely constructed parts, the adaptedness of each of its constituent parts to the harmony of the whole, its delicate fibres, its arteries, its innumerable nerves—is calculated to fill the mind with admiration and astonishment. The beating pulse, the throbbing heart, proclaim the truth which fell from the lips of Israel's king—" I am fearfully and wonderfully made."

To know ourselves as immortal beings, destined to survive the pangs of expiring nature; the relation we sustain to that eternity which is before us, to that God who is to judge us, is to possess that knowledge which schoolmen of former times fruitlessly endeavored to grasp with their gigantic minds. Philosophy in vain unfurled the banner of reason, and with torches lighted at her altar, sought with sacrilegious effort to discover this knowledge. Futile were the attempts of the sages of antiquity to seize, with the palsied hand of nature, this priceless jewel, discovered alone by Heaven's unerring light.

Philosophy cannot reach it. Reason cannot discover it. If obtained at all, it must be secured by a close investigation of our principles of action—by a perception of our moral destitution, and, above all, by the light of Heaven, beaming from the page of inspiration.

The importance of self-knowledge none will question—few endeavor to obtain it. What inconsistency marks our conduct in this respect! That knowledge, which should have the pre-eminence in our minds, is seldom regarded, while too much time is thrown away on things of minor importance. Should we spend our days and nights in the acquisition of that knowledge, by which we may hope to see our names enrolled on the annals of fame—or descry, with the eye of Herschell, the orbs of Heaven—or, with the intellect of Franklin, draw the lightning from the threatening clouds—yet ignorant of ourselves, our knowledge will be like the light of the meteor that shoots across the heavens, and suddenly disappears, leaving the soul deeper in obscurity and confusion.

Destitute of self-knowledge, with any and every other attainment, we are ignorant of that noble principle which binds us to the skies, and which, by divine illumination, can teach us to aspire to those immortal wreaths of glory which the envy of wicked men and fallen spirits can never pluck from the brow.

P. D. O.

THE GIRAFFE.

This singular animal is eighteen feet high, of a light fawn color, marked with dark spots. The tail is terminated by a tuft of long dark hair. It inhabits Central Africa. The shoulders are so high that it gives the fore legs the appearance of being as long again as the hind ones. The neck is very long and slender. Its head is beautiful, and resembles that of a horse, and its eye soft and animated. In its native country, the giraffe subsists upon the twigs of trees, particularly those of the Mimosa genus. It can with difficulty take food from the ground. Its gait, when it walks, is neither awkward nor unpleasing; but when it trots, its long neck, swaying backward and forward, presents a most singular picture.

SERIOUS COUNSELS TO THE YOUNG.

BY REV. J. BENNETT, D. D.

1. NEVER think you are too young to be converted, and forgiven, and saved, and given up to God, while you know that you are not too young to sicken, to die, to be judged, to go to heaven or hell.

2. Never take up with any thing short of true religion—the entire change of the heart by the power of the Holy Ghost—the true and full forgiveness of all your sins by faith in the blood of Jesus Christ. For only this religion will do you good.

3. Never be satisfied with HAVING religion—seek to ABOUND IN IT. Not merely to be alive, but lively; for, if religion is worth any thing, the more you have of it the better; seek to have as much of God's image as can possibly be enjoyed upon earth.

4. Let me remind you that for this purpose you should study your own easily besetting sin, especially the sins of your youth—be warned against them—watch against them—strain all your efforts to oppose and destroy them, and ask by the grace of God to keep yourselves unspotted from the world.

5. For this purpose form a rule, lay down a plan for life, laying out every day as it ought to be spent, and as you will wish you had spent it when you come to die; for this purpose read daily the Holy Scriptures—consult experienced Christians—ask them how they would advise you to conduct yourself.

6. Seek to live not for yourselves, but to live usefully as well as safely. Do as much good as you can in the world, and as you are young, and have an influence upon the young, seek to win them to the knowledge, and love, and service of Christ. It is a sad thing to leave the world before we have done any good in it. Exert yourselves, then; and, if you have a short race to run, you will be a quick seizer of the crown. If you leave your friends soon upon earth, it will be to depart and to be with Christ, which is far better. This is the consummation of the felicity of true Christians, to be with him where he is that they may behold his glory.

AMERICAN ANTIQUITIES.

BY THE EDITOR.

All the ancient empires in the world have been celebrated in history, poetry, and song, for their relics. Late developments are lifting the pall of oblivion from the face of our mighty ruins—ruins which are filling the mind with astonishment, and which are adding a new and most deeply interesting chapter to the Ancient History of America, and to the wonders of the world!

Foreign travellers have long tauntingly said, America presents none of those magnificent antiquities which everywhere abound in the old world.

But let the traveller, the antiquarian stand amidst the vast catacombs of the mighty dead—survey our ruined cities, ivy-mantled towers, and moss-covered turrets. Let him tell us who reared those lofty mounds and vast depositories of the dead in the west; who built those dilapidated temples, altars, and cities in the south, and he becomes dumb with astonishment!

We design to give our readers, in several numbers of the Magazine, a MINIATURE view of American antiquities. Few of all the ruins which cover palace, and temple, and tower with the dark wave of oblivion, have more justly awakened public interest, than those which skirt Central America, and which were lately explored by the intrepid Stephens and Catherwood of New York. We have place in this number to give a single sketch only, of the field of relics in Copan, lying near the Isthmus of Darien.

"The wall of Copan is of cut stone, well laid, and in a good state of preservation. We ascended by large stone steps, in some places perfect, and in others thrown down by trees which had grown up between the crevices, and reached a terrace, the form of which it was impossible to make out, from the density of the forest in which it was enveloped. Our guide cleared a way with his machete, and we passed, as it lay half buried in the earth, a large fragment of stone, elaborately sculptured, and came to the angle of a structure with steps on the sides, in form and appearance, so far as the trees would enable us to make it out, like the sides of a pyramid. Diverging from the base, and working our way through the thick woods, we came upon a square stone column, about fourteen feet high and three feet on each side, sculptured in very bold relief, and on all four of the sides, from the base to the top. The front was the figure of a man curiously and richly dressed, and the face, evidently a portrait, solemn, stern, and well fitted to excite terror. The back was of a different design, unlike any thing we had ever seen before, and the sides were covered with hieroglyphics. This our guide called an 'Idol;' and before it, at a distance of three feet, was a large block of stone, also sculptured with figures and emblematical devices, which he called an altar. The sight of this unexpected monument put at rest at once and forever, in our minds, all uncertainty in regard to the character of American antiquities, and gave us the assurance that the objects we were in search of were interesting, not only as the remains of an unknown people, but as works of art, proving, like newly-discovered historical records, that the people who once occupied the Continent of America were not savages. With an interest perhaps stronger than we had ever felt in wandering among the ruins of Egypt, we followed our guide, who, sometimes missing his way, with a constant and vigorous use of his machete, conducted us through the thick forest, among half-buried fragments, to fourteen monuments of the same character and appearance, some with more elegant designs, and some in workmanship equal to the finest monuments of the Egyptians; one displaced from its pedestal by enormous roots; another locked in the close embrace of branches of trees, and almost lifted out of the earth; another hurled to the ground, and bound down by huge vines and creepers; and one standing, with its altar before it, in a grove of trees which grew around it, seemingly to shade and shroud it as a sacred thing; in the solemn stillness of the woods, it seemed a divinity mourning over a fallen people.

"We ascended a flight of stone steps, and reached a broad terrace a hundred feet high, overlooking the river. The whole terrace was covered with trees, and even at this height from the ground were two gigantic Ceibas, or wild cotton trees of India, above twenty feet in circumference, extending their half-naked roots fifty or a hundred feet around, binding down the ruins, and shading them with their wide-spreading branches. We sat down on the very edge of the wall, and strove in vain to penetrate the mystery by which we were surrounded.

Architecture, sculpture, and painting, all the arts which embellish life, had flourished in this overgrown forest; orators, warriors, and statesmen, beauty, ambition, and glory, had lived and passed away, and none knew that such things had been, or could tell of their past existence. Books, the records of knowledge, are silent on this theme. The city was desolate. No remnant of this race hangs round the ruins, with traditions handed down from father to son, and from generation to generation. The city lay before us like a shattered bark in the midst of the ocean, her masts gone, her name effaced, her crew perished, and none to tell whence she came, to whom she belonged, how long on her voyage, or what caused her destruction; her lost people to be traced only by some fancied resemblance in the construction of the vessel, and, perhaps, never to be known at all.

"The extent of the ruins along the river Copan, as ascertained by monuments still found, is more than two miles. There is one monument on the opposite side of the river, at the distance of a mile, on the top of a mountain two thousand feet high. Whether the city ever crossed the river, and extended to that monument, it is impossible to say. I believe not. At the rear is an unexplored forest, in which there may be ruins. There are no remains of palaces or private buildings, and the principal part is that which stands on the bank of the river, and may, perhaps, with propriety be called the temple.

THE CHILD AND THE HERMIT.

TRANSLATED FROM THE GERMAN.

Far away from his leafy hut, and with no thought of returning to it, we were told that the "child became happy and joyful;" yet, did he afterwards find himself stretched on his little bed, not knowing how, nor when, he came there. He rubbed his soft blue eyes, and looked around for the dragon-fly—but she was not to be seen.

Then the child arose, and went out of his lonely dwelling, thinking that he should surely find her among his favorite flowers. He spoke to the beautiful full-blown rose, "whose cup was all filled, and whose leaves were all wet" with the sparkling morning dew, but the lovely flower contented herself with offering her fragrance in silence.

The child was astonished, and a sad and strange thought passed across his infant mind, that the rose was proud of her beauty, and would not deign to converse with a simple child. So he went, with gentle steps, towards the meek violet, and asked her to tell him if she had seen his pretty dragon-fly. He went gently, because he knew the violet was a modest flower, loving to hide herself from the world, under the leaves and grass, and he feared that he might crush her with his little foot, if he did not walk cautiously and lightly.

He found the violet, and, in a plaintive voice, he asked for his old play-fellow. The sweet flower suffered him to sit by her side, and poured forth all her delightful perfume, but, like the rose, she answered not.

Then a tear dimmed the child's eye, and he felt grieved that his dear flowers would not speak to him. But he loved them still, and his gentle spirit formed excuses for them. "They are enjoying the first rays of the glorious sun," he said, "and they cannot speak to me now."

So he listened to the cheerful songs of the birds, and watched the lark rising slowly and steadily towards the azure sky. "She will return to the earth, as she did yesterday," he softly whispered, "her hymn of joy will cease for a moment, and she will then give me some tidings of my friend the dragon-fly." Meanwhile the lark carolled sweetly, still soaring upward. The child longed to ascend with her, for the earth seemed lonely to him now. Yet all was fair and blooming. The woods and groves were decked in their brightest green. The insects were dancing in the perfumed air, and indeed "seemed glad to be alive."

The river shone like a sheet of silver amid the distant hills, and flowing rapidly down their sides, came gently murmuring at his feet. The little fish were sporting in the cool stream, their scales sparkling like tiny stars, as they rose now and then to the surface of the waters, whereon the sunbeams played joyously.

A lamb and a kid skipped merrily across the grassy carpet, on which the child was seated, and they came to his call, and ate the green herbage out of his hand, which he had plucked for them—for his heart was full of kindly feelings, and he loved to do good. He was just going to question these pretty animals respecting the dragon-fly, when—O! joyful sight! the beautiful insect flew towards him, and poised itself gracefully on a delicate lily which grew beside him. The child clapped his hands with delight, and greeted his old friend in a happy voice. But—how strange! The dragon-fly continued to flutter round about the fair lily, sometimes resting in its beauteous cup—sometimes spreading her gossamer wings as though she would again leave the child, who loved her so much.

Again he hailed his winged favorite, but she heeded him not. He stretched out his pretty hand, hoping she would settle upon it—but no!—she merely fluttered around him for a minute, and then flew away into the green wood. The child followed her until his little feet could go no further: and at last he sank down beside a streamlet, and wept. He wept—because his beloved dragon-fly had forsaken him; and as the tears slowly trickled down his pallid cheeks,—for he was weary and faint,—he thought there was nothing now to love him. But HE loved every thing, and felt glad to see the birds, and flowers, and insects, all, so happy, though his own gentle mind was sad. So the child lay beside the brook, listening to its soft murmurs, his pretty head resting on his arm—and he fell asleep from weariness and sorrow.

VALUABLE REMEDIES.

HEADACHE.—Bathe the forehead and temples with a mixture of hartshorn and strong vinegar, equal parts, and snuff a little of it up the nose. Sick headache must be cured by an emetic, as it proceeds from a foul stomach.

SORE MOUTH.—Mix together honey and white borax, equal parts, and with a linen rag tied to the end of a skewer, rub the mouth well three or four times a day.

SORE THROAT.—Take twenty drops of spirits of turpentine on loaf sugar every night, till cured. Black currant jelly hastens the cure.

BILIOUS COMPLAINTS.—Take forty drops of Balsam of Peru on loaf sugar, or in a glass of water, every day at eleven o'clock.

INABILITY TO SLEEP.—Take a grain or two of camphor at bedtime: this is a surer and safer remedy than laudanum.

NIGHT SWEATS.—Drink a gill or more of warm water, at night in bed.

KEDRON. 10s.

1. Thou sweet gliding Ke-dron, by thy sil-ver stream, Our Sav-iour would lin-ger in moonlight's soft beam, And by thy bright wa-ters till mid--night would stay, And lose in thy mur-murs the toils of the day.

2. How damp were the vapors that fell on his head!
How hard was his pillow, how humble his bed!
The angels, astonish'd, grew sad at the sight,
And followed their Master with solemn delight.

3 O garden of Olivet, thou dear honor'd spot,
The fame of thy wonders shall ne'er be forgot;
The theme most transporting to seraphs above;
The triumph of sorrow,—the triumph of love!

4 Come, saints, and adore him; come, bow at his feet
O, give him the glory, the praise that is meet;
Let joyful hosannahs unceasing arise,
And join the full chorus, that gladdens the skies.

THE BLUE-JAY AND BIRD OF PARADISE.

Drawn by W. Perring.   Engraved by A.L. Dick.

THE FORSAKEN.

THE CHRISTIAN FAMILY MAGAZINE,

AND

ANNUAL.

THE FORSAKEN.

BY THE EDITOR.

> "FORGOTTEN?—all that fancy wrote
> Upon my breast or brain—
> The dreams of life—are all forgot;
> The hues of joy or pain
> Have faded at the touch of grief:
> Forgotten all—SAVE THOU,
> Whose thought, like summer's latest leaf,
> Clings to a wither'd bough."

How seldom does unalloyed friendship, sincere, mutual love, cast its healing leaves and bring forth its benign and ripened fruit around our social path!

If ministering angels ever hover around the scenes of interest that transpire on earth—if ever they shed tears of sympathy on this fallen world; it must be for that lovely, fair one, who, wooed by kindness and friendship, and won by professions of love and pledges of constancy, after all, is forsaken and left amidst the wreck of long cherished hopes, by HIM who vowed to be faithful unto death.

The man who can sport with the miseries of the unfortunate; who can trifle with the sorrows of the widow and orphan; who can riot in affluence and luxury, while those who gave him birth are suffering for the necessaries of life; can lay no claim to the ordinary feelings of humanity.

VOL. II.—NO. V.

But there is a darker picture of fallen nature than this, seen in the character of the man, who, year after year, lays siege to the most sacred prize which woman can give—who, by all that can allure, fascinate, and bind the affections, takes the citadel of woman's heart—and then, yes, then, wantonly and without a cause—with treachery and perfidy, leaves her to pine away amid the blighted hopes of THE FORSAKEN!

The steel engraving in this number, is designed to represent the affecting, tragical scene contained in the following tale.

Alice Summers was the daughter of a respectable planter, who resided in one of the rich glades of the Middle States. Mr. Summers was characterized for his industry, uprightness, and usefulness in the sphere in which he moved. The little group with which Heaven had blessed him, had been reared with the most unslumbering care. They were early taught to place a true estimate on solid, substantial accomplishments—to more anxiously secure a life of honor and usefulness, than make a show in the fashionable world.

In this happy circle there was one whose natural endowments, whose gentle, winning deportment, had secured the esteem and confidence of all who knew her. Though born amidst the scenes of humble life, it was early discovered that Alice was a treasure of no ordinary value—that, like the unwrought diamond, she needed only the polish of education and refined society, to discover her extraordinary worth.

To prepare her for greater usefulness, she was placed in a genteel boarding-school, in a distant town. Here she became acquainted with young Hamilton, the son of a wealthy merchant of that place. Not many weeks had elapsed, before the attentions of Hamilton forced upon Alice the conviction that he had marked her as the object of his special favor.

But with all that was commanding in his person, manly bearing and ample prospects in life, her heart shrunk at the thought of giving the least response to his attentions; and, so far as would comport with propriety, she retired from his influence.

But Hamilton soon manifested that his heart was fixed, by addressing to her a letter disclosing his feelings and asking the favor of a SPECIAL interview. In reply, Alice thanked him for his marks of condescension and respect, and begged him to accept her friendly salutations; while she assured him, it was her duty to say, in the most positive language, that she MUST decline his proposal.

The time of her leaving school was at hand—previous to this, Hamilton in person paid his respects to Alice, and asked, permission to accompany her to her native place. She respectfully but firmly declined; giving as the reason for this—her youth, humble birth, and the plans of usefulness which Providence had marked out for her in life.

Finding all prospect of success at an end, Hamilton rose and took a most affectionate and expressive adieu!

On the following day she took leave of her schoolmates and started for her native place. It was on one of those balmy days in spring, when all nature is decked in her gayest attire—the groves were covered with a white mantle of promise and were vocal with the melody of happy birds, and every scene conspired to raise her gentle spirit, in devout gratitude, up to Nature's God.

The scenes which transpired while Alice was abroad, in spite of all her resolution and firmness of purpose, had not only kindled a fire in Hamilton's bosom that one day was to be aroused to a flame, but had made a deep impression on her own gentle heart.

On the second day of her journey, Alice arrived at the parental mansion, and soon engaged in the duties for which she had spent a year to qualify herself; and she strove to wear off all impressions of the past.

After two years had elapsed, in which the gloom of the grave had covered the hopes of young Hamilton most unexpectedly, on a fourth of July, the parties met at the capitol of the State; and mutually seemed impressed with the thought that an invisible Providence might design something eventful by their meeting, beyond what had been anticipated by either.

Hamilton, in an interview, found, to his great satisfaction, that he was received by Miss Summers with a good degree of cordiality, and trusted that the lapse of time had produced a favorable change in the feelings of Alice.

This encouraged him to disclose his whole heart to her. He frankly declared that the richest boon he could enjoy was the participation of her friendship—and the apprehension that this was impracticable, had long, not only thrown an air of gloom over his mind, but had covered the future with dark and painful forebodings—that since they had parted, weeks had lingered like months, and months like years.

He told her of the ample estate he was to inherit; of the life of quietude and leisure that seemed allotted to him, if one invaluable prize could be secured, and that, her heart.

The amiable girl listened with emotion to his tale of love, though it was with some effort that she concealed her feelings. After a long pause, Alice frankly confessed, that from an early acquaintance with him, she had entertained much respect for his character; that while she had shared his friendship, she had not been altogether without an answering chord in her own bosom; while a sense of duty from the first, had dictaed the course she had pursued. She said from her childhood, that she had been taught never to allow her inclinations and interests to give an improper bias to her judgment and sense of duty. She had felt averse to leave the humble walks of a planter's daughter, and be raised to the station of eminence which he was destined to fill. And now, on their parting, lest her feelings should lead her astray, she dared not give him a word of encouragement as to his proposals, until her parents were consulted—should they approve of her receiving his proffered friendship, she would cheerfully yield to their better judgment—should they advise her otherwise, she should, at her earliest convenience, send to his address a blank letter.

Hamilton thanked her for this promise, and drew from his pocket a costly jewel and placed it upon her finger as a token of his imperishable love and said he would calmly abide the issue and then bade her a most affectionate farewell!

Some time having elapsed and no unfavorable signal having been received, he addressed Alice and obtained her consent to see her at her father's house; after a few months she gave him her hand; and the nuptials were fixed one year from that day. From that time she devoted herself entirely to Hamilton. If love ever was without romance and affectation; if it ever was warm, uniform and sincere, it was in the case of Alice Summers.

At the instance of Hamilton, Alice returned to the Seminary to complete her education; where she often received his visits and all possible tokens of his esteem.

A short time prior to the day appointed for their marriage—after Alice had returned to her father's house and had made preparations for the full consummation of their union; on his last visit, the devoted and confiding girl thought she discovered that all was not well—that a change had come over his feelings—that the ardor of his attachment had abated.

But on more mature reflection she thought the cause of his apparent distance might be referable to the sudden death of his father—or, it might result in some measure from his late appointment to an office of trust in the State. So conscientious and reserved had been her conduct; so marked and prolonged had been Hamilton's affection for her, that she thought it not possible at that late day, that his love could prove false!

Time rolled on, events ripened fast, and the day came when Hamilton was expected to visit the Glade. But hope was deferred—that sun went down, in all its golden glory—and the morning—the long expected morning of their union was about to dawn. The stricken girl retired to her chamber but not to rest! The first sweet notes of the nightingale awakened in her bosom a faint gleam of hope, that all might yet be well; but while sleep departed from her, the croaking of the raven and the hooting of the midnight owl, in the deep woods of the glen, sent a chill to her anxious heart; and seemed to betoken that all was lost! Thus passed the watches of the night away, until the song of the merry lark told that the light of an eventful morning had dawned. The village clock struck twelve but no chariot wheels of Hamilton were heard! What had before been suspense, had now become most painful incertitude!

The Bridal hour was now passed and the guests had left the place. Mrs. Summers and daughters retired to the drawing-room to compose their perturbation and seek the Divine benediction on Hamilton, if, indeed he might still survive the dead—when suddenly a post chaise drove up to the house—a stranger alighted and pealed loudly at the door of the cottage. A letter was hastily sent to Alice, bearing the insignia of Hamilton—she took the fatal epistle—seeing no death seal, the truth, with almost prophetic certainty, was forced upon her mind, that the league of love was broken! That she was FORSAKEN!

She opened the letter—while silence and suspense, like that which intervenes between successive shocks of an earthquake, reigned in their midst; and her eye fell on this sentence—

"Once Dearest Alice,   I must bid you an affectionate adieu—Within a short time, my heart has been wedded to another and"—   *   *   *   *

The letter fell—it fell like the blade from the hand of Abraham, when the unearthly voice broke the silence that reigned around the altar of sacrifice upon which Isaac was laid!—And, with one loud, long wail, she sank into her mother's arms—and with her glassy eye raised towards Heaven she continued the most wild, hysteric sobs and screams—calling on God to forgive him, who had struck the fatal blow, until her spirit died away!!!

All hearts quailed at the sight and great fear was entertained lest the shock had proved fatal. But alas! she again revived—she opened her eyes, but the world, how changed!—its mortal glory had all departed!

It soon became apparent that the shock had shattered her intellect. Her intervals of reason were like those fitful gleams of sunshine that fall through the gathering tempest—like those midnight flashes of lightning that brighten through the surrounding gloom, only to discover the disorder of the elements!

In spite of the most skillful medical treatment and the gushing tenderness of her friends, the mild lustre disappeared from her eye; disease, like a greedy canker-worm began its prey on the core of her heart, and it was manifest to all, that there was no rest for her broken spirit, this side of Heaven!

A little before her death she revived, and dictated a letter to Hamilton, in which she alluded to the unobtrusiveness, sincerity and depth of her love for him. She said that her heart was not won, by the glare of his honors or equipage; or by the proffers of a life of affluence and leisure, but from a sense of duty and from an attachment, that even THEN, had scarcely become extinct in her bosom. She meekly forgave his wrong, and hoped that Heaven would hold back the bolts of retributive justice, and prayed that they might, when the drama of life should be ended, be so happy as to meet in the realms of glory, where Christ the Savior would prove to them a friend, that sticketh closer than a brother. In a few days the hectic flush appeared; and she sank by a rapid decline to the tomb!

Her loss was greatly bewailed—her death threw an air of gloom over the inhabitants of the Glade and neighboring villages.

Hundreds attended her funeral and lamented her death. The burial took place on one of those sombre, touching-days in Autumn, when no dark clouds mantled the Heavens—When nature puts on her gorgeous yet melancholy livery—When the aspect of forest and field sends home upon the soul the thought,

> " That leaves the greenest will decay,
> And flowers the brightest fade away,
> When autumn winds are sweeping:
> And be the household e'er so fair,
> The hand of death will soon be there,
> And turn the scene to weeping.

The concourse assembled in the village church. The pastor opened the solemnities by reading that appropriate hymn—

> "What is life? 'Tis but a vapour,
> Soon it vanishes away!
> Life is but a dying taper,
> Oh, my soul, why wish to stay!"

But so great was the emotion manifested by the congregation, that the choir, having struck the first notes, paused and took their seats.

Fervent prayer was offered up to God, when it became apparent that the intended sermon could not be delivered—for Death, in the allwise, though inscrutable providence of God, was the PREACHER!

The remains of Alice were laid beneath a cypress in the church-yard to await the morning of the Resurrection!

Many friends and neighbors returned to the desolate house, and strove to soothe the afflicted family, whose sorrow was too deep for tears—for it was manifest to all, that a heavy shaft had broken the rock!

THE REJECTED.

PART II.

The grave had but just closed over the mortal remains of the lovely Alice, before fame with her thousand tongues told this melancholy catastrophy in the native town of Hamilton. The public heralds spread the intelligence far and wide and it soon reached the eye of Mary Leavens who had become the object of Hamilton's late ambition.

With all the reputation and influence of the Hamilton family, so great had become the excitement, occasioned by the treacherous and heartless conduct of this young man, that many of his friends forsook him, and he soon became an outcast from the best circles in society.

This, Hamilton bore with some degree of fortitude, while one GREEN SPOT remained amidst the general desolation that threatened to bury in a common grave all his hopes. As the storm raged, Hamilton flew to the family in whose bosom lived Mary, the object of his ambition, and to whom he had already plighted his faith and hand. He assured her that the inglorious shafts, which were aimed against his reputation, were levelled by the malice of designing men, and with tears begged her not to be moved by the floating rumors of the day—as time which outlives malice would most assuredly overthrow the illusion and establish his character. But a few weeks elapsed before what had been denominated calumny assumed the triumphant front of truth—Mary was a prize that could be won only by the most honorable and manly course of conduct. She assured Hamilton that his character would be submitted to the ordeal of truth and justice. Should it abide that test unscathed; all the malice and rage of the world combined could never shake her faith, or abate her confidence in him.

To ascertain the truth or falsity of the reports in circulation, a despatch was sent to the Glade. The result of this investigation, confirmed the truth of all that had been reported against the character of Hamilton. The next day, Mary firmly and forever rejected him. She declared to him, that she could never, never think of connecting her future hopes and destinies with a man who was capable of such treachery, as had been developed in his conduct towards the amiable Alice Summers, whose blood must cry to Heaven from the ground!

Hamilton, with a heavy heart left the house. For a while, he retired to the depths of solitude. His nights were disturbed with the dreams of by-gone days, and his footsteps seemed haunted with the shadowy form of Alice!

Thus rejected and cut off from society, he soon ran to waste and self neglect; gave himself up to luxury and dissipation; squandered his estate; and before he reached the manhood of life, bowed under the weight of infirmity and seemed forsaken, like some castle in Feudal times left to crumble down in solitude.

Original.

PARTING AND RETURN OF THE BRIDE.

BY MRS. L. H. SIGOURNEY.

From her parent's home, in her beauty's bloom
    Went forth the youthful bride,
A holy smile on her trusting brow,
    And her chosen by her side.

Dear was that home, in its fond array,
    And those vales in their verdant pride—
Yet she shed no tear as she turned away,
    For her chosen was by her side.

And her dwelling she rendered fair,
    With the might of a woman's love;
With the hope that doth bud in the secret heart,
    And the faith that hath rest above.

Again, to her parent's house she came,
    To her native stream, and dale,
The holy smile on her brow the same,
    But that brow was deadly pale.

No word to to the living group she spake,
    Nor soothed the friend who wept,
For on her arm was a snow white babe,
    And the same long sleep they slept.

They made them a bed, in the church-yard green
    Ere the autumn-leaf was sere,
And the riven turf as it droop'd that day,
    Was freshen'd by sorrow's tear.

Yet they bare away as a gift of love,
    The glimpse from a purer sky,
Of the Mother and Babe, in the bliss above,
    Where the beautiful cannot die.

The young mother, to whom these stanzas allude, and who was buried in the same coffin with her first-born babe, left to her lamenting relatives, the strongest consolation, of which such an affliction could admit, the evidence of a christian's life, and of that faith in a Savior, which disarms death of its sting."

Original.

TIMOTHY.

INFLUENCE OF EARLY MORAL INSTRUCTION.

BY REV. WM. B. SPRAGUE, D. D.

The character of Timothy, if not among the most STRIKING characters of scripture, is one of great interest; and the secret of it is seen in this single record, that "from a child, he knew the Holy Scriptures."

In contemplating this, the first thing that strikes us, is young Timothy's knowledge—the SCRIPTURES, or the WRITINGS as the word signifies. The world is full of writings, but these are THE writings by way of eminence—writings which throw all others into the shade, their grand peculiarity is, that they were dictated by inspiration, and bear the stamp of infinite wisdom, goodness and truth. The evidence by which their divine authority is proved, is manifold; and to every person who examines it with a docile spirit, is abundantly conclusive. All other books sustain the same relation to the Bible that the halos round the sun do to the sun itself—they derive from it all their lustre. Every other book might be blotted out of existence, and yet if the Bible were left, every thing ESSENTIAL would remain; but if the Bible were to be annihilated, and all other books to remain, a darkness that could be felt would soon gather over the nations, and mankind would grope to the grave in ignorance of every thing that involves their highest interests.

But the Apostle speaks of the scriptures of the old Testament, with which Timothy had been made acquainted, not only as THE scriptures, but as the "HOLY" scriptures. They are holy in respect to their AUTHOR, for they were dictated by the Holy Spirit. "Holy men of God spake, as they were moved by the Holy Ghost." They are holy in respect to their CHARACTER—their doctrines are according to godliness; and their precepts forbid what is wrong, and require what is right. They are holy in their AIM, which is to form a holy character, and to illustrate the perfection of an infinitely holy God. All the holiness that exists on earth may be referred directly or indirectly to the influence of the scriptures; and all the holiness in the universe results from obedience to the great laws which the scriptures enjoin. Of these "scriptures" Timothy had a knowledge. There are probably few, in any christian community, who do not claim SOME knowledge of the scriptures; for even though they may be professed infidels, they would have it understood, that their infidelity is not another name for heathenism; that they do not reject the Bible without SOME knowledge of what they reject. But I venture to say, if we knew the whole, we should see, that, in a vast majority of these cases they had never read the Bible; and that you could put them to silence, if not by asking them who was the first man, at least, by asking them the most simple question concerning the "second man," the Lord from Heaven. But even where there is not such gross ignorance of the scriptures, as this—where the individuals are accustomed sometimes to read the Bible, and to sit under the preaching of the gospel, and have something of a character for their knowledge of divine truth you will too often find that their knowledge is extremely superficial—that they know little of the doctrines, still less of the evidences of that religion which they profess to regard as supremely important, and to which they render a decent external homage. I wonder not, at the ignorance of the heathen, whether they are such, by the righteous providence of God, or by their own voluntary choice; but that men who have the Bible in their hands, who hear its truths expounded from the pulpit every week, who live in the very atmosphere of evangelical knowledge—that SUCH men, sagacious, inquisitive, and wise on other subjects—should betray an ignorance of the very elementary principles of christianity—would be utterly unaccountable on any other principle, than that "he that doeth evil, hateth the light, neither cometh to the light, lest his deeds be reproved."

But Timothy's knowledge of the scriptures was not only the opposite of absolute ignorance, but far from a superficial acquaintance with them. Of course, the Jewish scriptures are here referred to, as no other were in existence, at the period of his birth and education; and of these he seems to have made himself a thorough master. He was well acquainted with the various histories and doctrines which they contain, and also familiar with the grounds of their divine authority; he could give reasons to justify the diligence with which he studied them, and the reverence with which he regarded them. When he rejoiced in the exercise of his faith, he knew what he believed; when he commended the scriptures to the attention of others, he knew what he affirmed.

But note the DATE of Timothy's knowledge of the scriptures—it was from his early childhood. There is a period at the commencement of our lives, when it is impossible, owing to the infantile state of the faculties, that any impression of divine truth should be communicated; but when Timothy's mind was so far developed as to render it possible that he could be instructed, he began to understand the first principles of divine revelation; and his knowledge increased, as his faculties expanded. No doubt while a child he could successfully hold an argument in favor of his religion with those who were much older and more learned than himself. The child Jesus, a few years before, by HIS wisdom, confounded the doctors in the temple. We are accustomed to venerate hoary hairs; but hoary hairs are never venerable when accompanied by ignorance and vice; but knowledge, virtue and piety, ARE venerable, though as in the case of Timothy they are associated with the simplicity and tenderness of childhood.

How unlike the lot of this youth, to that of multitudes who are left to grow up to maturity in comparative ignorance, of the holy scriptures! I have seen the man who has passed from childhood to manhood, knowing nothing of the Bible, and slumbering in carnal security; and have said to myself, "would that thou hadst been like Timothy, acquainted with the scriptures from thy youth; then there would be some reason to hope that the truths which are treasured up in thy mind, might be rendered instrumental in sactifying thy heart." I have seen the man who has grown up in ignorance of God's word, struggling under the burden of guilt and inquiring with agony, what he should do ; and here again, I have said, " would that the truths of the Bible had early gained a lodgment in thy mind, as they did in the mind of Timothy, and then thou mightest have been prepared at once, to accept of an offered Savior." I have seen the young christian who had known little or nothing of the gospel, till he found the salvation of his soul pressing upon him with urgency, doubting in respect to his own evidences from his inability to try his character by the scriptural standard ; and I have heard him lament bitterly his ignorance of the Bible, and the consequent inadequacy of his armour for the Christian conflict; and I have said yet again, " would that thou too, hadst been a Timothy in knowledge, even though thou hadst not been in piety ; and I should have seen thee with brighter evidences and fewer conflicts; a more happy and useful christian." Where is the advanced christian, where especially is the minister of the gospel, who will not respond to this statement as accordant with his own observation ? Timothy from a child, had a knowledge of the Holy scriptures. How did he gain it ?

The providence of God is to be acknowledged in nothing more than in the circumstances of our birth ; for the least observation must satisfy us that these have a powerful influence in deciding the character and the destiny. It was graciously ordered in respect to Timothy, that while his father was a Greek—a heathen, his mother and grandmother were eminently pious ; for the apostle speaks of his " unfeigned faith" as having " dwelt first in his grandmother Lois, and his mother Eunice." It was no doubt then, through the influence of these excellent persons, that his mind was first imbued with a knowledge of God's word ; and under their faithful instructions that he acquired a taste for the study of the Bible. Suppose that Timothy instead of having had a pious grandmother, had belonged to a family that were exclusively heathen ; and that in his childhood he had been left to the ordinary influences which such relationship would involve; what a different history of his childhood and his subsequent life would have been written from that which has actually come down to us! Should we have heard any thing of his knowledge of the scriptures, or of his unfeigned faith, or of his exemplary services as a minister of the gospel? We know not, what God, in the sovereignty of his gracious and miraculous agency might have done for him; the same bright light that shone around Paul might, for aught we can say, have shone around Timothy; and the heart of the young heathen might have been touched by sanctifying grace, and his life consecrated to the holiest of purposes. But independantly of such an interposition, which would have involved a departure from the common order of Providence, we must believe that Timothy in the circumstances supposed, would never have been heard of as a minister, never as a christian. Thanks to that gracious providence who gave to Timothy a mother who loved her Bible and taught HIM to read it. Thanks to that providence who has given us OUR birth in the midst of christian influences, and who has given to some of us, as he gave Timothy, pious mothers, who have directed our youthful steps in the paths of piety, and have bid us follow them in the way to Heaven!

To be concluded.

THE NATIONAL DEBT OF ENGLAND—

Amounts to nearly $388,000,000,000 a sum not so easily comprehended as expressed in words; but if we look forward to the year A. D. 2000, and back to the year one, and further back 2300 years, to the flood, and further back 1700 years to the creation of man, the whole date will be six thousand years, and the debt is equal to a dollar a minute, for the whole time. What will it be one thousand years from this date?

Selected.

Original.

TO A DOUBTING CHRISTIAN.

BY CHARLES WASHINGTON BAIRD.*

Say poor soul, what is't thou fearest,
  Why, oh why all this distrust?
'Tis the Savior's call thou hearest,
  His who rais'd thee from the dust.
Why wilt thou still unbelieving
  Welcome not the voice of love?
Rise in faith and grace receiving
  Soar oppressive doubts above.

Yes, it is the Lamb invites thee,
  Saying from his glorious throne
'Come, a shining crown awaits thee,
  Come to joys thou once hast known.'
Seize the promise kindly tendered
  Of His strength through whom you win—
Praise to Him be constant rendered
  That He breaks the power of sin.

'Tis of grace the heavenly portals
  Now are open'd unto thee—
Love, the Savior's love to mortals
  Bought your pardon full and free.
Cast your cares on Him who loves you,
  Him who died that you might live—
He by cloud by darkness proves you;
  Faithful then in trust abide.

THE SUNDAY SCHOOL.

Group after group are gathering. Such as pressed
  Once to their Savior's arms, and gently laid
Their cherub heads upon his shielding breast,
  Though sterner souls the fond approach forbade,—
Group after group glide on with noiseless tread,
  And round Jehovah's sacred altar meet,
Where holy thoughts in infant hearts are bred,
  And holy words their ruby lips repeat,
Oft with a chastened glance, in modulation sweet.

Selected.

* A lad 14 years of age, a son of Rev. Robert Baird, D. D.

Original.

THE BROTHER AND SISTER.

BY MRS. EMMA C. EMBURY.

Among the papers of an aged relative, which fell into my hands after her decease, I found two letters, so full of earnest and affectionate expostulation, that I became specially interested, to learn their history. They had apparently been written nearly forty years, and the faded ink—the time-stained paper—no less than the quaint and old fashioned phraseology in which they were expressed bore witness of their authenticity. My curiosity was strongly excited and knowing that every family has its chronicler, in the person of some old lady or gentleman, who has outlived all interest in the present, and finds pleasure only, in recollections of the past—I had recourse to such a friend for information. The story was one of little incident, yet, as conveying a moral lesson of no small import, it may be worth preserving.

Eleanor Hubert, was one of a large family of brothers and sisters—and being neither the eldest nor the youngest—neither the pride nor the pet—she occupied merely, the responsible station, of "one of the children." Possessed of strong affections and a warm heart, she had early distinguished her brother Henry, as the object of her special interest. While she was kind, and gentle to all, she was most devoted in her love to him. He was the junior, and the tenderness which had sprung in her childish heart for "the baby," grew with his growth and strengthened with his strength, until it became the ruling principle of her life. Yet nothing could be more dissimilar than the character of the brother and sister. While Eleanor was all truth and goodness with a quiet temper—gentle manner—cheerful face and a fearless sense of duty; Henry was one of those reckless, thoughtless, yet generous beings, who are usually designated in after life, as "real good fellows,"—"nobody's enemy but their own" etc. His facility of temper rendered him unable to resist temptation, and with every disposition to do right, he was constantly doing something wrong. Like all impulsive persons, he was naturally kind, affectionate, and magnanimous—no one could be more attentive to the claims of tenderness—no one ever acknowledged an error with more readiness and grace—or bore more meekly the punishment of a fault. But that peculiar characteristic of mind which often exercised in the cause of duty might have been honored with the name of docility, became a culpable weakness when it rendered him equally submissive to the influence of evil advisers—of course a youth of such character excited great anxiety in those who best loved him. His frank and handsome countenance, his affectionate manners, his sweetness of temper made him a universal favorite, and many a fault was overlooked—many an error excused for the merry-hearted, and thoughtless boy.

But Eleanor was grave and reflective beyond her years. The disgraces into which her beloved brother so often fell, led her to the discovery of the defects in his character, and in striving to screen him from the consequences of his follies, she learned to trace those follies to their source. Affection taught her to watch the first leaning towards error in his mind, and while yet a child in years she seemed to have become a guardian to the wayward but daring brother who looked up to her with almost reverential tenderness. Her own integrity and sweetness of character rendered her most deservedly dear to her parents, and she was thus enabled to save Henry very frequently from well-merited punishment which might possibly have modified his habits. It was the natural mistake of a young and tender heart and bitterly did she reproach herself in after-days for her ill-judged kindness. Still this very influence formed a strong bond of union between them, and Henry learned to value doubly, that goodness which he could not imitate.

If parents would remember how entirely, " the child is father to the man," they would certainly watch more closely over the first ebullitions of evil passion in the hearts of their offspring. How surely may we trace the bitter streams of "envy, hatred, malice and all uncharitableness" to the tiny fountain of anger or jealousy which first bubbled amid the flowers and verdure of childhood—and how vainly may we hope to leave a heritage of love to those whose expanding hearts have been watered with such envenomed dews.

It is not my intention to trace the course of Eleanor's affection through all the season of childhood. Years passed on and she became a gentle and lovely woman, while Henry grew up to man's estate, gifted with all that could make him a favourite in gay society. Singularly handsome, possessed of various showy accomplishments, together with natural talents of a high order, and especially distinguished for his graphic skill in story-telling, and his fine taste as a singer of convivial songs, he was exposed to many temptations which could scarcely assail a less favored person. The consequences may be readily imagined. His facile temper rendered him an easy prey to evil, when it came in the shape of pleasure, and all the restraints of duty and affection were forgotten. There is an old legend of a christian hermit, who was tempted by the spirit of evil, and was finally brought to believe that he must choose which of three evils he would commit. His choice lay between theft, murder and intemperance—and the good man finding himself in such a strait, selected what he conceived to be the lightest sin. He chose drunkenness, as the least heinous crime, and the consequence was, that while in a state of inebriety, he committed both the other crimes. The story, though but a fable, may serve to illustrate the destructive nature of that deadly vice, which benumbs every noble faculty of human nature, and reduces a man below the level of the beasts that perish.

It was long before Eleanor could believe that her beloved brother had fallen into intemperate habits. She tried to blind herself to the indubitable evidences of his weakness which were seen in his bloodshot eye, his trembling hand and his unsteady step. She hoped that each recurrence of the mischief might be traced to some unusual temptation, and all the influence of her earnest affection was exerted to counteract the evil. Henry would listen to her remonstrances with deep remorse, he would answer her with tears and promises, and ere the dew of penitence was dried upon his cheek, or the echo of his words had died upon the listening ear, he was again the boon companion of those who 'drank to die.' It was this dreadful habit in her brother which called forth the letters of which I have spoken, and if in my story I have somewhat veiled the facts I shall give the letters entire—assuring my readers that they are the genuine remonstrances of an affectionate sister to an erring brother, and bear date forty years back.

Wednesday night, 12 o'clock, 1801.

My dear Brother,

Surely you do not despise your own soul—therefore listen to reproof. Remember the words of the wisest of men "Rejoice O young man in thy youth, and let thy heart cheer thee in the days of thy youth, and walk in the ways of thine heart and in the sight of thine eyes, but know thou that for all these things, God will bring thee into judgment." What say you to this? I know you do not disbelieve it—you cannot—why then trifle away those precious moments which are so rapidly flying and leaving no trace behind—no trace did I say? alas! the recollection of your present folly will embitter your last moments and plant your dying pillow with thorns. I have often heard you say that you meant to take your pleasure in youth, and in old age you would seriously think of religion, but what if you should never see gray hairs? what if death should summon you away in the midst of your pleasures? What if now, even THIS NIGHT THY SOUL SHOULD BE REQUIRED OF THEE? The thought is appalling—oh, let it sink deep—deep in your young heart.

Or suppose you should arrive at a green old age, are you sure that the passions by which you are now actuated will not then predominate? Evil propensities grow with our growth,

'Ill habits gather by unseen degrees,
As brooks to rivers run—rivers to seas.'

Do you not think also that you would dishonor God by giving Him the very dregs of your life? He has said "Remember thy Creator in the days of thy youth"—and think you, He will be mocked by the offering of a heart already worn out in the service of the world? You have been blest above many others, in being born of Christian parents, in having received a religious education, and in being now within sound of gospel teachings. Your own heart will bear testimony against you, for surely you must remember a time when you would have shrunk from the enormities you now commit. Listen to the faithful monitor which God has implanted in your breast, and my words will not have been uttered in vain.

Dear, dear Henry, you have not yet gone far in the crooked path of vice, your foot has but just passed over its flowery bounds and you have not yet been pierced by the hidden thorns which lie beneath the poisoned blossoms. Oh, let me say to you as did the angel to Lot, "fly, for your life." Remember the last words of our sainted mother, when the sweat of mortal agony was upon her brow—"my children, serve the Lord as I have done"—think of all her tender solicitude for you—remember her dying admonitions to you—the wanderer of her flock—and, oh! forget not that the many prayers which she has offered up for you are now treasured in Heaven. I can write no more—tears blind my weary eyes—may you listen with a contrite spirit to the tender pleadings of

Your most devoted Sister.

Henry found this letter on his table when he arose. It was the morning of New Year's day, and he had long been engaged to join a party of roisterers who intended to celebrate the flight of time by dissipation. Touched by his sister's appeal, he remained at home, and Eleanor was made happy by the belief that he was not hardened against all convictions. For nearly two months he resisted all temptation and nothing could exceed his affectionate regard for his sister's wishes. But alas! for human weakness, his reformation was but transitory. I find a second letter dated,

New Years' Eve., 1802.

"My Brother, I fondly hoped there would be no more occasion for my addressing you in this manner, and on this subject. Alas!—even the knotted oak yields beneath repeated strokes, and the flinty rock gives way, but you remain impenetrable. Why is it that your heart which is as wax in the hands of affection should in this matter receive no impression? Remember that "he who being often reproved hardeneth his neck shall suddenly be destroyed and that without remedy."

How can you thus silence the voice of your faithful conscience? ere long she will speak to you in a voice louder than ten thousand thunders. The partition between this world and the next, is very slight—the breath in your nostrils is your only safeguard from the horrors of an eternity, and you are never seized with the slightest illness, that I am not agonized with fears lest death should come upon you like a thief in the night. Oh! that your imagination would paint the terrors of an unprepared death-bed even as they appear to me! every faculty of your soul would then be aroused to guard against temptation. Even a heathen philosopher could say "I am too noble and of too high a birth to be a slave to my body, which I look upon only as a fetter to the liberty of my soul." Cannot you, living under the light of Christian truth respond to his lofty sentiments?

My brother, I will not reiterate my persuasions, for my heart sinks within me, when I remember how utterly futile they have hitherto been. Oh, if you would but let the past time suffice, and henceforth live like a rational being, capable of enjoying the purest and most refined pleasures here, and meet to be a partaker of the inheritance of the Saints hereafter! My beloved brother this is the LAST time I shall ever thus address you—something tells me that my days are numbered, and some other hand must lay an offering of affection before you when next the opening year returns—God bless you, my dear, my erring brother---Oh, that my death might be your life!"

Henry had made fearful progress in vice during the past

year, but the second appeal was not quite disregarded. He strove for a few days against the demon of strong drink, but his faculties were fast becoming besotted and torpid. Affection had lost its power over him, his naturally fine temper became irritable and violent, his once generous heart under the influence of sensual gratifications had become selfish, and the day of reform seemed past forever. But the earnest prayer of a sorrowing spirit is often answered, and Eleanor had not wrestled with her agony in vain.

Ere the THIRD New Years' day Henry seemed irrecoverably ruined—his days were spent in sullen inactivity, his nights in riotous dissipation, and sometimes for weeks he would absent himself from his home. It was after such a season of reckless madness that he returned, worn and seared and sick with his excesses. He did not remember until he was on the thresh-old that it was the first day of the Year, but as he entered the house the words of his sister recurred to him so vividly that they seemed literally written on the wall before him. There was a strange air of desolation and silence around him, as he passed through the wide hall—his steps seemed to echo with an unnatural loudness, and that peculiar odour, which belongs to nothing but the newly framed casket of death, struck upon his senses. A horrid fear took possession of the prodigal's heart—he staggered forward and flung open the door of the nearest apartment. His perceptions had not deceived him, a coffin stood on its blackened trestles in the centre of the apartment—it held the wasted form of his beloved sister!

A long fit of illness followed this fearful shock. Reason was utterly prostrated, and in his ravings the ghostly image of Eleanor seemed ever before him. For many days his life was in imminent danger and for months he was a helpless invalid, but Eleanor's prayer had been heard. HER DEATH HAD BEEN HIS LIFE—Henry from that hour was a sincere penitent, and when a few years later, he followed his sister to the grave he yielded his last breath in the hope of a blessed reunion with her in the world of spirits.

Original.

NATIONAL RELICS.*

BY HENRY M. PARSONS.

A freeman to our nation gives
   Two relics of her earliest age—
The first, the staff of him who lives
   In memory as the patriot sage—
The last, the sword which stainless wrought
That freedom which our Fathers sought.

Among our country's treasures, lay
   These rich memorials of those
Who, in the council and the fray
   Were mightier than their strongest foes.
The cane, the blade, together bear
Fit offerings for a nation's care.

Long let these precious symbols teach
   The watchmen on Columbia's towers,
That they can never hope to reach
   The goal for which they task their powers,
While selfish aims or party views
Prompt the unslumbering care they use.

And did our Fathers leave us not
   A relic richer far than these,
One that should never be forgot,
   But which the statesman seldom sees
With eye that loves its words of truth—
Blest Book! the guardian of our youth.

Up, sons of those illustrious sires
   Who to the forests of the west
Fled from the persecutor's fires,
   And sought within its shade a rest,
And liberty to worship God,
Denied them on their native sod.

Up, and the Bible they have left,
   Bind to your altars and your hearts—
Watch, for of this when once bereft,
   The sun of freedom aye departs.
Guard well the gift your fathers gave,
Gift first, of Him who came to SAVE.

---

* The Sword of Washington and the Staff of Franklin were presented to the nation March 8, 1843, in behalf of Samuel T. Washington of Virginia, a descendant of "The Father of his Country."

THE HIPPOPOTAMUS.

That the Behemoth of the book of Job is the hippopotamus, or river horse, is now fully conceded by all commentators of any note.

The appearance of the hippopotamus when on the land is altogether uncouth, the body being extremely large, flat, and round, the head enormously large in proportion, and the legs as disproportionately short. Authors vary in describing the size of this animal. The length of a male has been known to be seventeen feet, the height seven feet, and the circumference fifteen; the head three feet and a half, and the girt nine feet; the mouth in width about two feet. The general color of the animal is brownish; the ears small and pointed, and lined very thickly with fine short hairs; the eyes small in proportion to the creature, and black; the lips very thick, broad, and beset with a few scattered tufts of short bristles; the nostrils small. The armament of teeth in its mouth is truly formidable; more particularly the tusks of the lower jaw, which are of a curved form, somewhat cylindrical; these are so strong and hard that they will strike fire with steel—they are sometimes more than two feet in length, and weigh upwards of six pounds each. The other teeth are much smaller; those in the lower jaw are conical, pointed, and projecting forward almost horizontally. The feet are large, and each of the four lobes, or toes, is furnished with a hoof.

Original.

WHAT CONSTITUTES TRUE HAPPINESS IN THE CONJUGAL RELATION.

PRIZE ESSAY.*

BY REV. A. A. LIPSCOMB, ALABAMA.

When we contemplate the character of the Divine Being, the highest point that our minds reach, is his perfect blessedness. Imagination cannot ascend beyond it. Thought reposes here. Our conceptions of his natural greatness and our ideas of his moral goodness lead us to Jehovah's blessedness. If the universe teem with the manifestations of his power, wisdom, and love; if one portion of that universe be signally marked by the demonstration of his mercy; it is all intended to conduct our reflections, by a direct path, to this condition of his nature. A most important truth is inferentially established by this fact. It is the truth, that happiness is the ultimate consequence of intellectual existence. If holiness be the law of angels, and heaven their home, it is that they may be happy in glorifying God. The same law applies to man. If he have intellect, passion and sense, it is that he may enjoy his being. Nothing can be more evident, than that happiness must be of a mixed character. Man is neither a disembodied spirit, nor a mere animal. The essentials of both these meet and mingle in him; and consequently, his happiness must accord with the complex elements, that constitute him. Mind is not necessarily degraded by this union. Its supremacy may still be maintained; its dignity supported. Its noblest exercises result from this alliance. If it often suffer from its relation to matter, this circumstance affords it an opportunity of acquiring new fortitude and of revealing its native superiority. Sense is exalted by the connection. No where else does it display such beauty and excellency. No where else does it perform such elevated offices. No where else does it experience such happiness.

---

* To the writer of this Essay, has been adjudged the prize of a silver medal, or twenty dollars.

The domestic constitution is the result of our peculiar conformation. It embraces every faculty of our nature. It presents a sphere for all the endowments, that we possess. It is the only field, in which, all our powers are fully and constantly available. The world of thought is open only for the intellect; the world of matter for the senses; the world of business leaves most of our sentiments dormant; but the home-world—that world within a world—that sacred centre of a wide-spread circumference—furnishes active and ceaseless employment to each part of the two constituents of our being. Worthy was it of being introduced in the garden of Eden. Worthy was it of the consecrating presence of purity and peace. Worthy was it of the songs of the morning-stars. Jehovah lavished his benevolence upon it. The last of his works, it crowned and consummated the whole.

The institution of marriage is the foundation of domestic life. On it society depends. The harmony and happiness of the race rest absolutely upon it. The two great authorities of the world—religion and law—the one holy, heavenly, and divine; the other, imperfect and earthly—have therefore guarded it. Its relation to the purity of morals is witnessed by the historical truth, that whenever depravity has sought to execute its most shameful purposes and bend everything to its vile gratification, it has commenced by detracting from the sanctity and utility of this ordinance. Its relation to law is seen in the fact, that it has been recognised under every form of civilization, and that, in proportion as man has receded from the savage state, he has invested it, with more and more importance and interest. Its relation to Christianity is evinced in the well-known circumstance, that when Infidelity has arrayed itself against her, it has promised the passions of the populace, an entire independence of its wholesome restraints. Fanaticism may fly to the desert and waste its energies in solitude to escape it; morbid sentimentalism may throw the air of platonic friendship around it; Mohammedism may degrade female character and cast its stigmas upon its virtues, and on the other hand, chivalry, and romance may color it too highly and demand too much from it; but law, morals, philosophy, and religion, combine to honor and defend it. If any thing on earth could deserve a miracle at the hands of the benevolent Redeemer, it was this institution. No wonder then, that he opened his glorious career by displaying his miraculous power at the Galileean wedding, and no wonder, that he made such a beautiful exhibition of social sympathies in his dying-hour, by providing for the maintenance of his endeared mother. The interests of a world pressed upon him, at that moment—the hidings of the Father's countenance were then felt; the glory of the universe was connected with the awful mysteries of the scene—but yet, Jesus Christ could think of Mary! Hallowed be the filial relation—hallowed the domestic character of woman—forever! The cross sanctifies them. The death of the cross seals them! The triumph of the cross ensures their prosperity!

No one can contemplate the relation of husband and wife, and not be forcibly impressed with the idea of oneness. Whenever this delightful state is entered, different and distinct interests are instantly united. If selfishness has hitherto reigned in the heart, it must now be expelled. Indeed, the previous existence of that love, which is the requisite of marriage, supposes selfishness to be subdued, for every advance of true affection is at the expense of this principle. Revelation has confirmed this natural view of marriage. "And they twain shall be one flesh." Of no other relation, can this unity be predicated. It is therefore more intimate and endearing, than any social connection known to man. The most varied duties spring from this union. For these duties, each sex is wisely provided. The constitution of man prepares him to act his part, in this economy, and the nature of woman fits her to sustain her position. The qualities, in which one sex is deficient, are found correspondingly developed in the other, and so, their exercise and exhibition form the entire circle of human character. The education of man, can be best accomplished in the society of woman, for she developes those virtues and graces, which, if left to himself, he would be most likely to overlook. The same sentiment applies to woman. The balance of strength and weakness—activity and quietude—sternness and gentleness, is admirably maintained in conjugal intercourse; each attribute is most advantageously brought into action; each acts upon its opposite sentiment. The line of duty is consequently marked out by the constitution of husband and wife. Instinct reveals the path to be trodden, reason sanctions it; and revelation pours light upon it. If the husband be disposed to employ his superior wisdom and authority to the injury of the wife, he is to remember that she is the "WEAKER VESSEL." If the wife be inclined to abuse her position, she is to recollect, that every departure from her social obligations deranges the domestic economy, and deprives her husband, of his rightful due. The authority of the one is to have respect to love; the love of the other is to have regard to authority. Providence has lodged the supreme power of the family in the husband; submission is therefore the first duty of the wife, whenever that submission will not conflict with a higher claim. The law of nature is that the less should be subordinate to the greater; if the obedience of the wife come in contact with the prescribed will of God and involve the sacrifice of conscience, she is bound to reverence that relation which is above all human relations, and anterior to all human obligations. The will of the wife is to conform to the will of her husband in all proper things; such is the law of nature, providence, and grace. The marriage-service binds this, as a holy vow, upon her. If she once violate this primary principle, the fountain of domestic peace is sealed forever. The utmost forbearance is to be used in domestic intercourse. A disposition to press our rights too far is often ruinous to happiness. The dominion of law may frequently be injured as much by excessive rigidness, as by careless relaxation. The spirit of our actions is almost as important as the actions themselves. The parties exhibit character, as perfectly, in the way, in which a thing is done, as in the thing itself. Here there is constant occasion for prudence and discretion. A husband may be correct in the pursuance of a certain course of conduct, and yet seriously err, in the temper of his mind. So it may be in a wife. Let this never be forgotten, for domestic bliss is suspended upon it.

A perfect understanding of each other's disposition, and a settled determination to please each other so far as practicable, is essential to the happiness of both parties. The first few months of wedded-life often form the great crisis in its history. Circumstances daily occur to bring out the actual character; sacrifices are constantly demanded; opposite opinion, tastes, and feelings are ever coming into collision. If the wisest sagacity, and the most affectionate kindness be not employed, at this tender period, the issue will probably be adverse. Individuals are often strenuous about trifles. Such a spirit will never suit matrimonial life. Where no vital principle is concerned, the policy of concession is always judicious and praise-worthy. Did persons exercise becoming caution in selecting those only as partners, with whom they were intimately acquainted, the necessity of this course would not be so great, but unfortunately, it frequently happens that a knowledge of character is to be acquired after marriage. A sad and severe experience is undergone, in this manner; and of all the knowledge, that we obtain, it may be safely said, that this is purchased at the dearest price. When marriage is associated with wild and visionary sentiments, or the imagination has gained an ascendency over sober judgment and the heart yielded to its assumed control, the danger is still more alarming. It is the law of all imaginative excitements, that they should soon die. Like the convulsions in the natural world, they are violent, but quickly ended. Nature has thus clearly and unequivocally intimated, that this part of our constitution—this half-intellectual and half-sensual quality—should hold a secondary place within us. If the wedded-state be entered under its sway, true and abiding affection is often wanting, for imagination loves to counterfeit the heart. The consequence is, that when passion decays, no foundation is left. Jealousies arise, and contentions follow. If persons would take soberer views of marriage, and prepare themselves for its responsibilities, these difficulties would be measurably avoided. Alas, the novel is made the standard authority, and from its false pages, the light-hearted draw their views of wedded-life! If fiction be the teacher, what but fiction can be the result? The affections of our bosoms—those pledges of immortality—those earnests of Heaven—are surely too sacred to be put under such instruction.

To be concluded.

Original.

THE MANIAC AND THE DUELLIST.

PRESENT AND FUTURE MISERY.

BY REV. SAMUEL IRENÆUS PRIME.

A few years ago I visited an Asylum for the Insane. It was a gloomy place—for where is a wilderness of deeper gloom than the howling waste of ruined mind? We passed from one cell to another, and with shuddering surveyed the varied forms of madness which had seized the images of God. As we opened the door of a long hall, the cries of agony that broke on the ear, brought us instantly to the cell from which they came. We looked through the grated door, and in the corner, lay a human form, in the midst of a heap of broken straw. They told us it was a WOMAN. Every breath was a shriek; yet not such a shriek as comes from the sufferer when the knife cuts keenly through the joints and the marrow; but such a shriek as you might think a spirit gives when suffering amid the torments of the lost! Nor was this a transient paroxysm of agony. From hour to hour, day after day, night following night, she cried "Oh Lord, have mercy, Oh Lord have mercy—mercy—mercy"—until her strength was spent! Thus weeks and months rolled by, and still the miserable sufferer knew "no rest, day nor night!"

It was terrible. Many days after I was there, those dreadful screams would ring in the ear, as if were heard the distant wailings of the lost. Even now, though years have passed, when sleep for a brief season is a stranger, those cries of anguish—that woman's wails, will break upon the stillness of the night, and pierce the soul with pain. That was misery. It was an image of perdition; it gave the spectator, a more vivid conception of its horrors than perhaps he had ever before obtained, but it lacked the susceptibility of agony which belongs only to the disembodied soul! But we have another tale of wretchedness to present.

A FEW years ago a duel was fought near the city of Washington, under circumstances of peculiar atrocity. A distinguished individual challenged his relative, once his friend. The challenged party having the choice of weapons, named muskets, to be loaded with buck shot and slugs, and the distance ten paces; avowing at the same time his intention and desire that both parties should be destroyed. They fought. The challenger was killed on the spot, the murderer escaped unhurt! Years afterwards, an acquaintance of mine was spending the winter in Charleston S. C. and lodged at the same house with this unhappy man. He was requested by the duellist one evening, to sleep in the same room with him, but he declined as he was very well accommodated in his own. On his persisting in declining, the duellist confessed to him, that HE WAS AFRAID TO SLEEP ALONE, and as a friend who usually occupied the room was absent, he would esteem it a great favor if the gentleman would pass the night with him. His kindness being thus demanded, he consented, and retired to rest in the room with this man of fashion and honor, who some years before had stained his hands with the blood of a kinsman. After long tossing on his unquiet pillow, and repeated deep, half-stifled groans that revealed the inward pangs of the murderer, he sank into slumber, and as he rolled from side to side the name of his victim was often uttered, with broken words that discovered the keen remorse that preyed like fire on his conscience. Suddenly he would start up in his bed with the terrible impression that the avenger of blood was pursuing him; or hide himself under the covering as if he would escape the burning eye of an angry God, that gleamed in the darkness over him, like lightning from the thunder cloud! For him there was "no rest, day nor night." Conscience, armed with terrors, lashed him unceasingly, and who could sleep? And this was not the restlessness of disease; the raving of a disordered intellect, nor the anguish of a maniac struggling in his chains! It was a man of intelligence, education, health and affluence, given up to himself—not delivered over to the avenger of blood to be tormented before his time—but left to the power of his own CONSCIENCE—suffering only, what every one may suffer who is abandoned of God!

I have this narrative from the lips of the man who saw and heard what is here related, and therefore I repeat it with entire confidence in its truth. These details of mental and moral suffering are recited, not to enlist the sympathy and harrow the tender sensibilities of the human heart, but to illustrate this simple thought; if here, in this imperfect state of being, with limited capacities for misery, with half-developed sensibilities, poor human nature may thus suffer, what may not the immortal mind endure when the clay casement shall fall off, and the naked spirit lies under the wrath of Omnipotence; every faculty of that spirit a living nerve, and every breath a flame of fire!

Let the philosopher who loves to speculate and cavil, or he who fears and trembles lest there be a second death, or he who laughs at the Bible as a cunningly devised fable, let these unite in rejecting the doctrine of future punishments, because the spirit cannot FEEL material fire; let them deny that there is any such locality as that so minutely and fearfully described, where the smoke of their torment will ascend forever. I will not quarrel with them about names. Let it be granted that there is no "bottomless pit;" that there lives no undying worm; that no everlasting fire awaits the wicked, into which they will be turned with all the nations that forget God. If these expressions are not to be understood LITERALLY, they are figurative—the language of strong emotion seizing on the most vivid images to express that which no words can adequately convey—and therefore the misery may be fairly presumed to be worse than if the language were to be received in its literal sense. But if the expressions are figurative, they are not employed loosely or idly by the Holy Spirit who indited them. If they are not intended to teach us, that after death has destroyed this body the soul SHALL live, and if in sin then in misery, as exquisite as language can express or thought conceive, "tell us, O, thou our compassionate God, tell us what they do mean. Let us not be left in ignorance of the meaning of these fearful words, and above all things, O leave us not to be deceived with the thought that they mean nothing, till we wake in woe to mourn our sad mistake." It should be enough for rational men to know that, THAT punishment is certain, that it is involved in the nature of the soul and must be prolonged while the soul lives. And with this knowledge founded on the positive and clearest declarations of the Bible, and graven in the conscience of every nation that ever existed, what rational man will suffer the priceless interests of that immortal soul to be in jeopardy a single hour!

Who, for all the wealth of ten thousand worlds, to be enjoyed for four score years, would consent to become at death, THAT MANIAC coiled in a heap of straw and gnawing her tongue in the anguish of her disordered mind? Who for all the honor that ever wreathed the brows of men, to be enjoyed through life, would consent to be racked at death and for ever with the torments of that man's conscience who could not bear to sleep alone?

And what are these to the miseries that are before every one that lives and dies without a saving interest in Jesus Christ!

> "The wildest ills that darken life
> Are rapture to the bosom's strife;
> The tempest, in its blackest form,
> Is beauty to the bosom's storm;
> The ocean, lashed to fury loud,
> Its high wave mingling with the cloud,
> Is peaceful, sweet serenity
> To passion's dark and boundless sea."

Original.

A TRIP FROM NEW YORK TO BOSTON.

BY REV. A. D. EDDY.

Having embarked on a commodious steamer for Boston, and swept around the Battery, while all on board was gayety and gladness, we passed up the East River where the eye never tires, so rich, so varied so ever new and improving is the scenery of this river. The country seats, schools, hospitals, asylums and retreats which adorn its borders are alike proof of the taste, enterprise and benevolence of the city we have just left.

The Sound soon opens before us and a bright harvest moon is beautifully reflected from its crystal waters. Recounting the changes, pleasures and trials of life while all around are promenading in the buoyancy of youth and the high enjoyment of summer recreation, a sudden and melancholy emotion comes over the mind. "It was here" in subdued tones, the sound falls upon our ear, "the Lexington went down." Like a whisper of death, it caused a general silence, while an offering of tender and affectionate sympathy seemed paid to surviving mourners, and a tribute of regret to the memory of the many intelligent, virtuous and pious entombed in these waters. Oh, the dreams of lover, husband and wife, of fathers, mothers, children and home that came in wildness with the wintry wind and cold waves of that sad hour. This spot will not soon be passed without calling afresh to many minds the sundered ties and buried hopes which that catastrophe occasioned.

At an early hour in the morning we arrived at the beautiful city, Providence, rich in commerce manufactories and public edifices, noted for refinement and hospitality and worthy of admiration for its literary and religious refinement.

Leaving Providence our eye soon rested on the imposing dome of the Boston State-House and the towering monument on Bunker Hill. Boston is not only the birth-place of American liberty, around which cluster recollections dear to the friends of human rights and of mankind; but it is the seat of a deeper, stronger, holier principle. There is felt here a love of religious liberty, which is strong and deathless, at least in the breast of those who know the value of pure religion. It is not merely that our Pilgrim Fathers fled indignant from civil thraldom, and here brake all the ties that bound them to foreign rule, but it is that they loved religious liberty and would sooner sacrifice their all, than not possess and transmit it to their children and the world; that makes them the pride of this nation and the admiration of mankind. It is the moral grandeur of their memory, the intelligence, holiness, bold and sacrificing spirit that adorned them—the broad foundations which they here laid for education, virtue and piety; their far reaching views and policy—these make them live and move among us still, giving sacredness and life to the monuments that survive them.

These make the city and country of the early Pilgrims so replete with interest as you approach the halls of their legislators and the temples where they worshiped. There is no part of the land where the influence of their wisdom, enterprise and religion has not been felt; and it will not cease when the shores of the Pacific shall be crowded with cities, that their sons have built and adorned with sanctuaries where their offspring worship.

Boston has numerous attractions for the stranger. The Common comprising forty acres beautifully laid out and the Old State House, rank among the first of these. We entered and crossed the one thronged with youth and beauty. We soon commenced our tedious ascent to the other. The first object you notice as you enter this venerable pile is the beautiful statue of Washington. You are invited to register your name and without question or fee you are directed to every apartment you may wish to visit and almost every where you meet with choice relics of revolutionary days. The brazen helmet of the hired Hessian is there; and the sword wrested from the strong arm of the Britain, hangs on the wall ! We next ascend by a flight of more than two hundred steps to the dome of this memorable edifice. A most extended panoramic view opens before you. Bustling thousands are at your feet, while tens of thousands slumber unconsciously in the dust beneath. Thus the living multitudes are treading upon each other to the grave ! And yet the dead live ! We felt more strongly than ever before how powerful is the mind to achieve and how mighty the arm to rear enduring monuments of intellectual greatness. We remember the time when there were comparatively few of these institutions of learning and religion.

Boston has many other places of interest to the traveller. The Mission House of the American Board. C. F. M. is one. Here is found the representation of almost every heathen nation on the globe, both in the gross idols of their worship and rude implements of their husbandry and arts; and from this house goes forth a mighty influence.

Fannuel Hall ought never to be overlooked in the objects of revolutionary interest that crowd the New England metropolis. Its location is very forbidding and its appearance, as you approach it, is far from imposing—but when once within its walls, you cannot for a moment resist the inspiration of the spot where you stand. You are in the cradle of liberty—of liberty, not from chains of human bondage, but liberty of thought, feeling, soul, even of that liberty wherewith Christ makes free. It is this, pre-eminently, that hallows these walls, and fills the soul with admiration and awe ; and here is renewed and strengthened a sense of moral and religious obligation, to guard and transmit the principles of religious freedom.

I love and venerate the New England spirit, that still binds and blends learning and religion ; that clings to the Bible as its basis of common law ; making now and forever the charter of its liberty and security, the statutes of the kingdom of God. It is said to be an early decision of some of the New England emigrants, that they would abide by the laws of God, till they could make better. Whether this is true or not, and if true deserving the sneers which skepticism and worldly ignorance have cast upon it, we are ready to ask at this late day; after all the advances of legislation and the cumbersome tomes of statute law, what improvements have men made upon the laws of God and the plain precepts of Christ? Where is there one equitable statute of human legislation that is not based upon the law by Moses?

Our next visit was to Bunker Hill, sacred to the memory of the brave, who yet live in the remembrance of millions. The proud and lofty monument before you, is eloquent in their praise, while standing where their blood was shed and their ashes repose, you seem in silent reverence to hold communion with their spirits.

I am no friend to war and have many doubts as to its necessity in any form. Nor am I confident as to the propriety of those standing memorials of the valor and deeds of blood that crowd the annals of our revolution. And yet we know what human nature is and what it has been. To do justice to our ancestors and learn the worth of that inheritance they have left us, we must review the history of their times; go over the ground of their sufferings and their wrongs; and there find the full justification of their remonstrances, their sacrifices, their conflicts and resistance unto blood. There may be a point where endurance ceases to be a virtue, and there resistance is no crime. The waste of fortunes and of lives must rest on others, not on our venerable sires. God, as on Israel, smiled on them; gave to them victory and to us the purchase of their valor and their blood. But the monument before us was perhaps needless. A boundless continent, with its teeming millions, its rich plains, lofty mountains, its commerce with the world, with its nurseries of science and its temples of religion, are more than marble statues and granite columns to honor and perpetuate the names and the worth of our fathers. When these shall be insufficient, and our degeneracy shall show us unworthy of the names and inheritance we enjoy, then let the monument before us be demolished; for it would stand like some crumbling column or falling pillar amid the ruins of corrupted and wasted Pompei, and reflect not so much the wisdom and worth of our ancestors as the folly of their offspring! And I have sometimes thought, that when men begin to build the tombs of the prophets they justify the deeds of their fathers who slew them.

Looking abroad from the summit of the battle hill, is there no departure from the manly integrity, the sterling worth, christian simplicity and faith in God, which shone so bright in days that are gone. Are there not some, yea many, who know not Joseph, not even Christ, among the thousands, on whom this lofty monument now casts its shade! And yet they are the descendants of the Pilgrims and of the Puritans! We have no sympathy with the over-bearing pride of that modern wisdom and refinement, which looks back with scorn and derision to the narrow views and sickly sentiments of the puritan settlers of New England—"Narrow views!" "Sickly sentiments!" Read Hume. Read all English history. Look at the "sifting of three kingdoms, to plant this continent with the choicest wheat." Look at the monuments, that surround you, shadowing forth the richest intelligence, virtue and religion that God, even in the exuberance of his love and mercy, ever promised to mankind on earth. We mourn, we blush for the men of these times, who can sneer at the Mathers, the Mayhews and their numerous cotemporaries in intellectual excellence and moral worth, or who can refuse respect and veneration for their character, because some transient shadow of the times in which they lived may rest upon them, showing that the clearer sun of the present century had not yet risen. Rather, let us prize their worth and walk by the light which their example still pours upon our path, nor presume on safer guides till we can say at least, "a greater than Solomon is here." Ah, in rejecting these men, we fear, that their religion and their Savior too have been cast aside; and the false philosophy, false religion, transcendental mysticism, now rising as the fogs of a deadly miasma, may spread paleness and death over many, who otherwise might have adorned society and honored the memory of their fathers.

To be concluded.

THE CHILD AND THE CHRISTIAN HERMIT.
No. II.

The child slept long and soundly, for when he awoke, the moon was risen, and was shedding a mild lustre on all the trees. Silence reigned around, but not her "solemn sister" darkness, for many a twinkling star was to be seen above, while the pale lamps of the innumerable glow-worms below, made the earth seem, to the child's eyes, like another heaven. He was roused from his infant meditations by a rustling sound, and turning to the grove behind him, he beheld a beautiful large dog, that came bounding towards him. The noble animal ran fondly up to the child, caressed his hands and feet, pulled his garment gently with his teeth, and evinced, by various actions, that he wished to lead him somewhere.

These MUTE expressions of love were not quite understood, at first, by the child, for he had CONVERSED with the flowers and birds, and insects, and with every green tree and limpid stream—and THEY had talked with HIM; but this dog spoke not. Yet had the child no thought of resisting these kind and repeated signs of friendship. His grateful feelings were all awakened, and he rose and followed the dog, who would sometimes run sportively before him, then return to renew his caresses; now, licking his hands, and then again, gently taking the border of his little tunic in his mouth, as though he would hasten him on.

Brilliantly, indeed, did the full-orbed moon shine in the spangled firmament above.

> "No mist obscured,
> No little cloud disturbed
> The whole serene of heaven."

The child felt his heart glow with unutterable happiness, and he longed to know who made all the glorious worlds that he beheld, that he might praise Him.

The stillness of the scene was now interrupted by a sweet and plaintive note. It was the nightingale; and the child stopped—and held his breath—and listened, in an ecstacy of delight, to the pensive tones of the "night-warbling bird."

The faithful dog stood sentinel by his side; his full dark eyes steadfastly fixed on those of the child, as though he were waiting his commands. And the gentle child felt pleased that the dog seemed to love him so much,—and he passed his little arm round his neck, and continued listening to the song of the nightingale, charmed and riveted to the spot by the sweet melody.

But he had not forgotten the dragon-fly, nor did he wish to do so, for she had been his earliest play-fellow, and he called to mind the joyous hours they had spent together. He thought of the days when she would come and sip the clear dew-drops, and partake of the golden honey with him, telling him all the while sweet stories of the merry life she led among the flowers and mosses of the green wood. He stood musing, till the dog invited him to pursue his way; so, on and on they went.

At length a pale, glimmering light appeared at a short distance, and the child thought of the will-o'-the-wisps he had once seen: and though their melancholy discourse had been so unintelligible to him, as to send him to sleep, yet he remembered and understood sufficient of their gloomy converse, to be aware that it was not pleasing to his tender mind. He hoped then that the light was not a will-o'-the-wisp. He did not feel afraid, for he knew not what fear was. He only knew love and wonder.

But now the dog began to bark, and to run on faster than before, often turning round as if to see if his infant friend were still near him. As the majestic animal approached the light, his barking became louder and louder, when, to the surprise of the child, a venerable figure appeared coming towards him. He was clothed in a full dark robe, that descended to his feet, and was fastened round the waist by a leathern girdle. His form was tall and erect, though his white locks, on which the moonbeams rested, showed that his pilgrimage on earth had been long. Deep and clear, and full of tenderness, were the tones of the aged man's voice, as he drew near, and addressed the child. Then taking him up in his arms, he bore his infant guest to the spot whence the light had proceeded. The child saw that what had puzzled him so much, was a small lamp, that lighted up a hut which he now entered with his new-found friend.

But he thought not long of the light—for he had met with kindness and affection, which had sunk deep into his little heart—and all other feelings, just then, gave place to ONE,— of grateful love.

The aged man had placed the child upon his knee, and gently wiped the dews from off his pale cheek, encouraging him with a benevolent smile, and many endearing words: and the child threw his arms around his neck, and burst into a flood of tears—they were tears of joy, and thankfulness, and love.

Then the hermit arose, and went to the door of the hut, and clapped his hands—and a goat came fleetly across the green sward, and seemed glad to give her milk to the aged man.

And as the child partook of the milk, and some sweet brown

bread, the lips of the recluse slowly moved, and his eyes were raised to heaven. He was thanking God for having preserved the child.

Then the child's tender eyelids became heavy, and the hermit laid him down on his own leafy couch;—and the child slept with the hand of his new-found friend locked in his.

And there was an eye watching over the hut, and over the child, and over the aged man—it was the eye of the All-seeing God. And now—

> "The meek-eyed morn appeared,
> Mother of dews; at first
> Faint gleaming in the dappled east."

And the hermit took the child by the hand, and bade him kneel with him at the open door of the hut.

So they knelt down together, that holy man and that gentle child;—but the former alone uttered the words of prayer and praise; for the child knew not how to address God. He knelt, because he loved to obey the voice of his kind friend, and he listened with a grateful heart and an humble spirit.

The prayerful tones ascended slowly and clearly through the pure air, and as the morning breeze carried the sounds away, they seemed like heralds of peace sent to a distant land.

And they rose from their knees, and re-entered the hut. The goat again afforded her delicious milk, and fruits and bread now graced the humble board.

The child felt happy with the aged man, but yet he longed to go again into the green wood, in search of his dear dragon-fly, and to talk to his beloved flowers. So, as he listened to the "woodland hymns that thick around him rose," he turned his soft blue eyes to the open door, and though he spoke not, yet the hermit saw that his infant mind was dwelling on some dear and distant object.

Then the kind old man spoke tenderly to the child, and encouraged him to tell his simple story; and when he heard it all,—how the child had formerly gossiped with trees, and streams, and flowers, and birds, and insects,—and how he had been distressed the previous day, at the unwonted silence of them all,—and how the loss of his beloved dragon-fly had grieved his little heart—the venerable recluse smiled affectionately on him, for he perceived that a sweet and glorious DREAM had powerfully impressed his infant mind. So he spoke gently to the child, and by degrees convinced him that he had been cherishing a lovely illusion only; but he cheered him under his disappointment by the sweet assurance, that though flowers, and running brooks, and beautiful insects, and bright birds, and glowing stars, could not hold converse WITH him, yet they would, every one and all, speak of their great Creator; for

"In Reason's ear they all rejoice,
And utter forth a glorious voice."

(To be continued.)

Original.

THE YOUTH'S PORTFOLIO.

BY THEODORE THINKER.

NO. II.

DISAPPOINTED HOPES.

"OH ever thus from childhood's hour,
I've seen my fondest hopes decay—
I never loved a tree or flower
But 'twas the first to fade away."

SEVERAL years ago in a retired village of Connecticut lived Emma Willington. When about fourteen years of age she was an exemplary girl and a devoted christian. At this early age a conversation took place between her and a poor widow in the village, a narrative of which I have thought might be interesting to my young readers and furnish them with much valuable instruction. The account is from the aged lady herself.

Emma walking a short distance from home on a beautiful moonlight evening in May, heard a voice as if from a person in distress. Listening she soon ascertained that it proceeded from the dwelling of Mrs. Willmott, a poor woman whom her mother employed to sew for her family. She entered the house to learn the occasion of the distress and if possible to render the family some assistance. Mrs. Willmott met her at the door and exclaimed wringing her hands in anguish, "O, he will die! he will die! what shall I do without George?"

George was her oldest son, and after the death of her husband was her main dependence. He was evidently near his end when Emma entered, and survived only an hour or two The mother was inconsolable, and employed extravagant language in expressing her grief. Emma tried to comfort her, but in vain.

Some days after the funeral of George Willmott, Emma called upon the disconsolate widow, having first sought direction of God in her closet. The tears flowed down her face as she pressed the hand of the afflicted one.

"I have come," she said "to weep with you, and to talk of Him who can dry the tears of the mourner."

"My dear child," replied Mrs. Willmott "I am glad to see you and I thank you for your sympathy; but you know nothing of my sorrow, you are too young to suffer as I have suffered—Oh, I have lost my all!" Tears prevented her from saying more.

"I know that your affliction is severe," said the other in a tone of kindness—you must suffer very much; but Jesus has said "Blessed are they that mourn for they shall be comforted." Dear Mrs. Willmott, here it is in this precious book— she said, opening a pocket testament and pointing to the words.

Mrs. Willmott was a woman who had never thought much

of religion. Like many others, who are obliged to labor hard for a living, she had quieted her conscience by saying that she had no leisure for such matters; and so she intimated to her young visitor, at this interview. "If I was rich, as you are," said she, "and had no more to do, I would be religious. I have many cares which you know nothing about—it is not so easy as you suppose for poor people to be christians.

Emma modestly suggested that religion was for the poor in common with the rich. She quoted another passage—"seek ye first, the kingdom of God and his righteousness and all these things shall be added unto you." Religion she said, "is more important than every thing else. Oh I wish you were a christian. You could bear your affliction so much better were Christ who loves you, precious to you."

If he loves me, "replied Mrs. W." why has he treated me so? I have seldom loved any thing which he has not taken from me. A thousand times has he snatched away my comforts as though he was angry with me. We had a pretty little cottage once and I thought I should be happy with my husband and my children around me. You remember that little house Emma—it used to stand near the pine tree as you rise the hill—but God took it away from me. You remember when that house was burned and almost every thing I had in the world with it. My poor husband lived only a year after that and now that George is gone! God has taken away every thing. I have seen nothing but trouble all my days. Did God love me would he make me miserable?"

"The Bible tells us, Mrs. Willmott," said Emma with earnestness "whom the Lord loveth he chasteneth" God afflicts us for our good. "He does it in kindness to us." But the poor woman did not believe the zealous girl who was trying to comfort her. "I am sure" said she "I cannot see what kindness there is in keeping one in misery all the days of her life.

Emma was silent for awhile. She was grieved to hear one express doubts of the benevolence of God, and hardly knew what reply to make. At length she thought of a comparison by which she hoped to make it clear that God had dealt kindly with her. "My dear Mrs. Willmott" she said, "is not God training us for eternity? He says he is unwilling that any should perish—we are disobedient to him. By nature we do not love him—therefore he corrects us—he chastises us to make us better, just as you correct your children when they disobey you. The reason that he disappoints us and takes away the objects which we love is to lead us not to love this world so much, but heaven more."

The poor disconsolate woman had never thought of this before and she appeared in deep reflection. "Can it be," she inquired half unconsciously, "that God loves me?" Emma was encouraged and improved the advantage she had gained.

"Yes" said she "God does love you, else he would not have sent his Son into the world to die for us. When he afflicts us, it is not because he delights in chastisement, but because affliction is necessary to fit us for heaven. Should we ever desire to go to heaven if we had everything in this world to make us happy?".

"I see it now" said Mrs. Willmott, "how could I shut my eyes to the truth so long. What shall I do to secure such a rich prize? How shall I become a true disciple of Christ?"

"You can obtain this blessing without money and without price" said her juvenile teacher. "Whosoever will, may come and take of the water of life freely." The Savior says, "Take my yoke upon you, and learn of me and ye shall find rest unto your souls." She dwelt upon the love of the Redeemer and pointed this poor woman to his cross.

She then knelt with her, commended her to the Friend of sinners and took her leave. Last summer I visited Mrs. Willmott. Her sands were almost run. Many years had passed since that eventful interview with Emma, but it was almost as fresh in her memory as on the day it transpired. Emma had gone to her rest. She died when about eighteen years of age rejoicing in hope of a blissful immortality.

I had not before heard of her death, and when I learned that her sun had so early gone down, I could not suppress the thought which Wordsworth has clothed in such forcible language—

>The good die first,
>And they whose hearts are dry as summer dust,
>Burn to the socket

The old lady drew from her bosom a little book soiled and time-worn and placing it in my hands she said, "this is the most precious earthly treasure I possess. From this Testament, Emma read to me the words of life. The day before she died, she gave it to me with her blessing and expressed the hope that it would prove as valuable a companion to me as it had been to her."

Having led me to the window she pointed to the churchyard, a few rods distant and said, "Beneath that mound so green, with the willow by its side, repose the ashes of that dear girl. I planted the violet and the forget-me-not on that grave, and often have I bedewed them with my tears. She is now we trust, an angel near the throne of God. How much am I indebted to her instructions, counsels and prayers who taught me the way to Christ and Heaven."

"On that day when she came to me with her little testament I trust I found peace and joy in a crucified Savior. Though I have since been a vile sinner I hope my sins have been washed in his blood. I have since looked upon disappointments in a new light. They now seem the richest of blessings. God has taken from me almost every thing which I loved, but what a precious boon have I in exchange! He has given me a Savior who is "chiefest among ten thousand and the one altogether lovely." Blessed Savior! Soon shall I see him face to face, and that dear child who first led me to his cross."

>"Home of the weary! where in peace reposing
>The spirit lingers in unclouded bliss—
>Though o'er its dust the curtained grave is closing,
>Who would not early choose a lot like this?"

Original

HONEY-SUCKLE AND HUMMING-BIRD.

In the heat of mid-summer, the humming bird hies
Where the odors from delicate woodbines arise,
Not attracted by beauty, but sweetness which wells
Through the day and the night from their innermost cells.

Thus united, a beautiful emblem they prove
Of earth's truest friendship—the soul's purest love,
Refreshing but transient, for autumn comes o'er them;
Yet joy should be ours that the spring will restore them.

Engraved by Daggett, Hinman & Co. from the original Painting by C. Harding.

THE PATROON.

Yours affec'ly
S. Van Rensselaer

For the Christian Family Magazine.

THE
CHRISTIAN FAMILY MAGAZINE,
AND
ANNUAL.

OUR MORTAL AND IMMORTAL DESTINY.

BY THE EDITOR.

EVERY THING on which the eye can rest has its brief day. From the tender herbage and flower of the field, to the sturdy oak and stately cedar of the forest, aye, and the century plant which casts its fruit once only in a hundred years—all things, in rapid succession, have their rise, progress and end.

The whole kingdom of animated nature, bears the same marks of transitoriness. From the anamalcula and countless insects that swarm through all matter, and have their birth, growth and end in one brief day, to the monarch of the sea, air and land, yes, to man the lord of Creation—all things, with rapid stride, hurry on from their birth to their maturity and mortal end, as though time, with his uplifted scythe were eager to cut them down; and the grave were impatient to gather all flesh to its dark and silent empire!

Nothing here is stable—the very slabs and monuments of enduring marble, that were erected to commemorate the name of our grand-sires, are fast crumbling down. We see in the vista of the mighty past, grave built upon grave and ashes heaped upon ashes—and the earth has become one great charnel-house of death! The monarch and beggar—the conqueror and reptile, mingle their dust in harmonious forgetfulness! Who, then can be proud? Reader, wouldst thou feel thy lofty aspirings give way—thine inordinate thirst for any thing save the riches, honors and glories of Heaven? Go—stand, but one half hour, in the midst of that great congregation of the illustrious dead, in Westminster Abbey—where kings and nobles, conquerors and prelates, historians and scholars, poets and philosophers 'have laid their glory by.' Select as your post of observation the upper SHRINE; cast your eye down upon this mighty panorama of death—this wilderness of tombs! 'Behold the chambers and pillars and funeral trophies' of the immortal dead; and you may feel the crimson current of life chill around the heart and run cold through all its channels, while you reflect on the end of man!

How full of silence and gloom—of shadows and fallen glory is this place—and yet amidst the touching stillness that reigns around the dead, the lightest foot-fall and whisper, reverberates through all these spacious vaults and chambers of the tomb! Here you see names that once were the glory and admiration, or the terror and scourge of Europe. Here are encoffined the blade and battle-axe of feudal times. The spear and sceptre that once caused the civilized world to grow pale; and which made whole realms a field of slaughter. Go down to the tombs of kings and conquerors, and in spite of a vigilance that never sleeps and lamps that never go out, you will see how dishonored is the memory of the dead! 'The coffin of Edward the Confessor has been broken open, and his remains despoiled of their funeral ornaments; the sceptre has been stolen from the hand of the imperial Elizabeth, and the effigy of Henry the Fifth lies headless. Not a royal monument but bears some proof how false and fugitive is the homage of mankind! Some are plundered; some mutilated; some covered with ribaldry and insult.' And, in spite of lasting marble, guards of brass and bars of gold and all that human skill can devise to deck the tomb and shield it from the wastes of time, you see every thing here crumbling to ashes; yes, and the Abbey itself, this great Mausoleum of the immortal dead, without renewed skill and constant efforts, will soon become one mighty pile of ruins!

If you give wings to thought and survey the monuments

of decay that cover the globe, you will consider the spot where you stand but a drop to the boundless ocean!

Tell us if you can, where are the 100 000, cities of the Old World? Where is, even the SPOT, where once stood mighty Carthage, Babylon and Troy. Wave after wave, at last has left the pall of oblivion upon their glory. And in the wastes of ages the faithful tongue of history has become dumb forever! Shall we then strive, to make much of earthly glory? Shall we eagerly desire to build our immortality on this side of the Tomb? What are all the dazzling honors and hoards of gold and imperial pomp of the world at the verge of the tomb? The dying man will tell you, these are poor indeed. Could an unearthly voice from the skies proclaim their worthlessness, it would be this—so poor are these, that cast at the feet of the Redeemed, they would not so much as adorn the streets of the new Jerusalem! But why stand we here moralizing upon the empire of decay and death; and lay so much stress upon time, which at best, is but the infancy of our being—but the dim twilight of an immortal day. Lift up your eye and see only a little in the distance a more congenial and glorious clime—where the sun never goes down—where no autumnal blasts or wintry frosts, or wasting sickness or parting scenes, or pangs of remorse, or demoralizing sin, shall ever come—but where, blessed be the name of God, one unbroken, everlasting scene of beauty and vigour and youth shall be enjoyed!

Heaven, immortality, life eternal---O, the rapture these words are intended to inspire, while in the house of our pilgrimage. How should they incite us to hold on our way; in our labours and prayers; in our watchings and fastings; our trials and conflicts.

Fresh courage christian—Is your record on high, through the riches of grace—Heaven awaits you—the crown of unfading glory is at the end of the race. The prize of life eternal is for those ONLY, who are victorious. The glories of the life to come will more—infinitely more than repay thee for all thy care and concern; for all thy labor and pains-taking, for thyself and for the souls of others. Through faith and patience, Christ will never forsake thee—he will calm thy perturbation; hush the tempests of life; still the troubled ocean and cut thy pathway through mountains to the skies!

But perhaps, some who may read this paper are without hope and without God in the world. What then, is your prospect? What your destiny? O, if there be a God, if the Bible be true, no time is to be lost; the great work of life is all left undone. All that is worth a wish, of an enduring nature, is at stake; and may perchance, be staked upon your speedy, well-directed efforts, to secure the crown of glory. Life is short and infinitely uncertain—the grave is at your feet and death may stand ready to strike you down. The solemn realities of dooms-day await you. On your glorious spring-time of grace must hang the golden harvest of eternity!

HON. STEPHEN VAN RENSSELAER.

SEE STEEL ENGRAVING.

The Hon. Stephen Van Rensselaer who by common consent bore to his death the hereditary title, Patroon, anciently attached to his inheritance, was born in the city of New York, on the first day of November, 1764, and died at his residence in Albany at the age of 75. By the death of his father, in early life, and his mother's second marriage with Rev. Dr. Westerlo, he was brought under the influence of that devoted servant of the Lord. But the deepest and most salutary impressions made upon his character in childhood were always gratefully referred by himself to the instructions of his judicious and pious mother.

Mr. Van Rensselaer received his academical education at Kingston N. Y., and commenced his collegiate at Princeton but afterwards removed to Cambridge where he graduated in 1782. He was twice married, first, in 1784 to Margaret, daughter of Gen. Philip Schuyler whose services and worth are identified with our Revolutionary history, and second in 1802 to Cornelia, daughter of Wm. Patterson one of the Judges of the Supreme court of the United States. This lady and nine children, of the marriage, survive the husband and father.

With no ambition for military or political distinction the subject of this notice acquired an enviable and enduring reputation by his services in the field, particularly at the battle of Queenston, and by his counsels in the Assembly and Senate of his native State and as a representative in Congress of the city and county of Albany. He was also as Lieutenant Governor an able coadjutor of John Jay during the six years in which the government of New York was conducted by that able statesman. He was first elected to the Assembly in 1789, and in the course of the next forty years there were but few important measures of our state government, in which his influence and good judgment were not recognized.

When but twenty-two years of age, with every alluring prospect which distinguished parentage and princely wealth could present, he deliberately chose to enter upon a religious course, by a public profession of his faith in Christ. A long life illustrated his sincerity and a happy death attested the value of his trust in the Savior.

In public life he was free from the prejudices of party and by a ready perception of the right of all questions presented for his consideration—and by an integrity and honesty which could not be corrupted, he secured and maintained a commanding moral sway in the numerous deliberative bodies with which he was connected. But he was pre-eminently distinguished in popular estimation by his private charities and his connection with various foreign and domestic benevolent Societies. His munificence flowed in an uninterrupted and never scanty stream. It diffused itself, through associations for the dissemination of learning, for the support and spread of Christianity, and descended to a thousand firesides of the poor and despairing. But his benevolence was unostentatious, the promptings of a warm and affectionate heart in which burned the hallowed flame of the Redeemer's love.

Through life he abounded in prayer, and almost to the hour of his death, he was a diligent reader of the Bible. He was equally devoted to the cultivation of personal holiness, and of consequence ever conscientious and uniform in his attention to the external duties of his christian profession.

During his last protracted sickness, his piety shone with increasing brilliancy in his sole, but confiding reliance for pardon and eternal life on the atonement by Christ and in his meek and chastened resignation to the will of God.

"Let us meditate upon this most instructive example. To what multitudes, and with what emphasis does it speak? Come hither ye rich and gay, ye elevated and aspiring, and attend to the words of truth and soberness. With affluence and standing, such as few can boast, you have seen "what manner of conversation he had" in the world. He made not riches the object of his idolatry, nor allowed them to minister to the lusts of the flesh or the pride of life; he employed them as became a faithful almoner of Providence, in doing good, dispensing benefits to thousands. Amidst the allurements and temptations which surrounded him, he kept himself unspotted from the world. Under circumstances, usually regarded as little favorable to a course of humble and consistent piety, he presented the rich, and varied and resplendant beauties of the Christian character. Learn here the worth of honors, the uses of wealth, and above all the excellence of true religion. In dignity, in real grandeur, in elevation and usefulness, such a man rises to an immeasurable height above what the world can produce. And his reward is infinitely more desirable. "The memory of the just shall be blessed." The honors he laid at the foot of the cross, are succeeded by the "crown of righteousness that fadeth not away;" the riches he scattered with such beneficence, are replaced by "durable riches at God's right hand." Go, child of prosperity, votary of greatness, "'GO THOU AND DO LIKEWISE."

EDITORIAL.

THE MORAL RUBICON OF LIFE.

BY THE EDITOR.

The interchange of prosperity and adversity, which checker the scenes of this life, is not the result of blind chance or of mere fortuitous circumstances. Our days of sunshine and gloom; of joy and sorrow are not visited upon us in regular order, or under the direction of fixed laws, like the return of the seasons—they are the allotments of an all wise Providence and are designed to promote our highest moral welfare; they are signally intended to have a disciplinary or remedial influence on our character, as probationers for eternity.

Were life one prolonged and glorious summer of unfading beauty and unimpaired fruitfulness—were our seasons of languishing and sorrow; of sickness and separation to cease forever, we should be too much inclined to regard our sojourn here as a paradise, rather than a pilgrimage—and we might be induced to look upon the wealth, honor and friendship of this world as enduring treasures and strive to make our Heaven below, rather than struggle to lay up our treasure on high.

But there are seasons of SPECIAL INTEREST; trying ordeals, to which men are sometimes brought in this life—these are tests, which are calculated, not only to try their principles, but they are to have a moulding and directing, if not decisive influence on their character and destiny forever.

Many no doubt, long before they have spent the morning of life, have passed this MORAL RUBICON of their existence; and from the bed of their last sickness, and from the eternal world, will look back upon this ordeal as the point, from which they took their stand for eternity, for bliss or wo!

Thousands can date the beginning or end, of their prosperity or adversity, from a single incident in life. Multitudes, can point to some singnal visitation of Divine Providence; some golden season of prosperity or some trying emergency which resulted in a complete change of their purposes and plans; of their character and conduct through life. "There is a tide in the affairs of men, which taken at its flood leads on to fortune; neglected all is lost"—and lost forever!

This touching sentiment, runs in an unbroken chain, through the history of Nations, as well as of individuals.

The glory of Napoleon sunk in deep and everlasting eclipse, when, like a destroying angel he grasped at the sceptre of Russia and his heart panted for the crown of universal Empire!

Cæsar, must needs cross the Rubicon before a day of cloudless prosperity opened upon his path.

Luther must see his friend and companion struck dead at his feet, by a thunderbolt from the wonder-working hand of Jehovah, before those fires of the glorious Reformation could be kindled, that one day will spread over all the world.

Moses with the riches and glories of Egypt at his feet passed the eventful ordeal of character; a test which will stand as a monument of admiration to the church to the end of time. "He chose rather, to suffer affliction with the people of God, than to enjoy the pleasure of sin for a season."

The young man in the Gospel, reached the crowning era of his existence when he deliberately preferred his riches, to the favor of Jesus Christ.

In the conduct of Eve, the mother of Mankind, we have a most striking example.

"She plucked, she ate—
Earth felt the wound and Nature from her seat
Sighing through all her works gave signs of wo;
That all was lost."

Some of our respected readers, as they cast their eye over this article, may be able to recur to some season of prosperity or sorrow that has ever since had a powerful bearing on their character and conduct—and which, it may be, has resulted in their elevation or disgrace; and which will be remembered, with deep and unfeigned thanksgiving, or sincere and unavailing regret through life—yes, which may have a tremendous influence upon their posterity from age to age!

With what interest did angels hang around the scene, when

the chaste, the holy-minded Joseph, was tempted to depart from his steadfastness and purity. Oh, what, in God's esteem was suspended on his decision, in this unexampled instance ! What a firm and appropriate answer he gave. He did not reply— " How can I do this great wickedness and sin against my own soul; or against Potipher?"—No, but—" How can I do this GREAT WICKEDNESS and sin against GOD ?" Had he yielded, what a fall it would have been? What a dire stroke to the people of God, at that most critical epoch? Rivers of tears and oceans of blood, could not have atoned for his wrong !

Our great, practical object is, to induce the reader, to PREPARE for those sealing seasons; those momentous ordeals; when men are made to pause in the career of their probation—when from the stand they take ; from the course they adopt, they may date their rise or ruin forever !

Pharaoh, Ephraim, and Felix are striking instances in illustration. " When Paul reasoned, of righteousness, temperance and a judgment to come, Felix TREMBLED." Conscience, though bound with the cords of Sampson, broke from its slumbers— But, did Felix yield to the majesty of truth ? to the power of the Spirit of God, at this moment of matchless interest ? No, he said, " Go thy way for this time, when I have a convenient season I will call for thee." And from the awful silence of the scriptures, on the subject of his character and doom, we have no possible reason to suppose that he ever had another call of divine mercy.

Seasons of prosperity, like those of adversity, are among the most important means which God employs in bringing men to the test of their principles ; to the seal of their destiny.

Afflictions are God's ministers. When he speaks by the rod, it is perilous not to heed his voice. After seasons of unimproved affliction, how many have found, when tears were too late, that a cloud of darkness had settled upon their minds ; that those golden seasons of tenderness and concern for their salvation had fled forever ; that they were compelled to take up the lamentation—" The harvest is past, the summer is ended and we are not saved."

Others have come forth, from the furnace of affliction, with their moral nature refined and purified. How often has the failure of health; the loss of property; the destruction of fond and long-cherished hopes or the separation, by death, of loved friends, arrested the attention of the careless and been instrumental in bringing them to view their perilous situation by nature; and of embracing the Savior to the salvation of their souls.

Behold that young mother bending over the cradle of her first born; as it reciprocates her smiles and entwines itself around her heart-strings; her bosom beats high with emotion, in the prospect that opens before her; when that child shall bud and blossom and ripen into manhood and become the solace of her later years and the staff of her age—But alas, suddenly the rose fades from its cheek; the greedy canker-worm commences its prey at its heart; the frost of death nips the flower in the bud and the portals of the tomb close upon it forever. How the soul is moved; the fountain of tears is broken up and the heart melts like wax, by the stroke of Heaven. The sun-light fades away from her path and the world to her, becomes a prison. Stricken and childless, she is led to see the unspeakable vanity of earthly treasures—In her solitude, she sighs after joys of an enduring nature, at the foot of the cross; and, blessed be God, she finds in the consolation of our holy religion 'a balm for every wound'—and to the remotest period of her existence will she have occasion to thank God for this affliction.

Not less decisive is the influence of prosperity on the character, for good or for evil, especially on the young. If prosperity has not a tendency to soften the feelings, and render the heart more susceptible to the influences of the Spirit of God; it will make it more callous—and when a few such seasons shall have passed away, UNIMPROVED; the soul may become wedded to the vain and delusive enjoyments of this world; and feel no concern as to its preparation for the life to come. How often, have the lovers of pleasure, on their dying beds, been impressed with the conviction, that they have wasted life in the pursuit of trifles? Behold that young man who has been nurtured in the lap of ease and prosperity. Life is full of glee; his heart leaps for joy while his wealth and honors are increased; he anticipates no reverse of fortune, no season of gloom and sadness, that shall check the tide of his worldly prosperity. But suddenly the scene is changed. His estate, by an unforeseen incident, is swept away and his summer friends forsake him.

While his heart is made sad, he feels how fleeting and unsatisfying are the treasures of this world. Does he improve this season of sadness to the salvation of his soul? Does he seek the favor of God, by repentance and reconciliation to the Savior? These intervals are often fraught with consequences of the deepest moment—improved or unimproved, their results will reach onward eternally. Numerous passages, in the word of God, forcibly indicate that there are bounderies, beyond which mercy cannot pass—indicate that men sometimes outlive their day of grace! "My Spirit shall not ALWAYS strive with man." "Let him alone, he is joined to his idols." "Seek ye the Lord, while he may be found; call ye upon him while he is near." And what are we if left to ourselves?—if abandoned by the Spirit of God? Better for us, that we had perished at the shrine of Molock—or groped our way, to the eternal world, under the dim light of nature.

FEMALE INFLUENCE.

BY HON. DANIEL WEBSTER.

It is by the promulgation of sound morals in the community, and more especially by the training and instruction of the young, that woman performs her part towards the preservation of a free government. It is now generally admitted, that public liberty, the perpetuity of a free constitution, rests on the virtue and intelligence of the community which enjoys it.

How is that virtue to be inspired, and how is that intelligence to be communicated? Bonaparte once asked Madame De Stael in what manner he could most promote the happiness of France. Her reply is full of practical wisdom. She said—"Instruct the mothers of the French people." Because the mothers are the affectionate and effective teachers of the human race. The mother begins this process of training with the infant in her arms. It is she who directs, so to speak, its first mental and spiritual pulsations. She conducts it along the impressible years of childhood and youth; and hopes to deliver it to the rough contests and tumultuous scenes of life, armed by those good principles which her child has first received from maternal care and love.

If we draw within the circle of our contemplation the mothers of a civilized nation what do we see? We behold so many artificers working, not on frail and perishable matter, but on the immortal mind, moulding and fashioning beings who are to exist forever. We applaud the artist whose skill and genius present the mimic man upon the canvass—we admire and celebrate the sculptor who works out that same image in enduring marble—but how insignificant are these achievements, though the highest and the fairest in all the departments of art, in comparison with the great vocation of mothers! They work not upon the canvass that shall fail, or the marble that shall crumble into dust—but upon mind, upon spirit, which is to last forever, and which is to bear, throughout its duration, the impress of a mother's plastic hand.

I have already expressed the opinion which all allow to be correct, that our security for the duration of the free institutions which bless our country, depends upon the habits of virtue and the prevalence of knowledge and of education. Knowledge does not comprise all which is contained in the broader term of education. The feelings are to be disciplined—the passions are to be restrained—true and worthy motives are to be inspired—a profound religious feeling is to be instilled, and pure morality inculcated under all circumstances. All this is comprised in Education.

EXT.

Original.

VISIT TO THE CALDEIRA,

THE LARGEST CRATER IN THE WORLD.

BY HENRY M. PARSONS.

CALDEIRA signifies a boiler, in the language of the Portuguese, and is generally applied by the inhabitants of the Azores, to the hot springs which abound in many of those islands. With the prefix of the definite article it is used at Fayal, to designate the great extinct volcano in its centre by which that island was undoubtedly produced, at no very remote period. The voyager thither, seldom visits its most romantic and sublime scenery as the summit of the Caldeira is sixteen miles from the city of Orta, and the ascent exceedingly difficult and laborious. Our attention was directed to this spot by the American Consul, and we determined to gratify our curiosity by a visit, although forewarned of the expense to our physical energy, at which it would be purchased

The general appearance of Fayal when viewed from the sea is that of conical hills rising higher as they recede from the shore and overlooked in the back ground by a lofty mountain. On a nearer approach, deep and extensive ravines are disclosed, while through chasms hollowed by torrents or volcanic action, cultivated hills invite by their dress of unusual luxuriance. In some places a solitary cabin stands on a beetling cliff—in others, a low, white cottage is planted in a vineyard and shaded by orange and myrtle.

The island contains between twenty and thirty thousand inhabitants. The city of Orta its capital, is situated on the eastern side at the bottom of a beautiful semi-circular bay, about two miles broad, with a grand amphitheatre of mountains above, crested with the evergreen faya from which the island derives its name. We had ascended a hill a mile from this city on our way to the crater as the sun arose. The elevated peak was before us, glowing in its beams, apparently very near, but in reality at the distance of fifteen miles. The varying rays of light produced by reflection upon the ferns or party-colored rocks afforded one of the most splendid exhibitions in optics we had ever beheld. The rude but neat dwellings of the peasantry are scattered along the road for three or four miles, beyond which the path is unre-lieved by any vestige of civilization. At the base of the Caldeira we forded a muddy stream and began an almost perpendicular ascent of several hours continuance, halting occasionally to recruit our strength from the basket of the guide, or gather fresh incitement to pursue our toil in the mingled admiration and astonishment which a glance at the scenery beneath us awakened. When our cicerone who kept a little in advance, planted his foot on the edge of the mighty crater and shouted his triumph in his richest dialect, a view midway down the yawning abyss, paralized our remaining energies and we sank upon the shelving side of the mountain with a pervading sense of awful and unlimited grandeur. While our first impressions derived from a partial view were intense and overpowering, a momentary sight of the immense basin as a cloud settled into it, was not calculated to dispel or weaken them. From the narrow edge of the crater which is nearly level, circular and six miles in circumference, our eye fell more than three thousand feet upon a lake five miles in circuit from whose centre arises an indented cone of seven or eight hundred feet in elevation. When the cloud was lifted from the aperture, we stood for many moments in silent admiration of one of the grandest exhibitions of natural scenery which the earth affords, sensible of the weakness and insignificance of man and the limitless power of Him at whose voice the earth trembleth.

Most of the sides of the caldron shelve regularly, but in some places they are broken in, while ferns and clumps of myrtle or box hang in profusion from fissures in the precipice. At the base on the north side, huge fragments are strewed about; the large masses standing erect or piled irregularly upon each other, as we discovered by the aid of a glass, without which the most prominent objects were but indistinctly visible. The whole scene has a wild and sombre aspect from the water-worn lava, pumice, and every variety of rock met with at the island, which compose these enormous escarpments. The more elevated extremities of the strata towards the south, overhang each other, black and craggy, in the form of insulated columns. While we noticed one pyramidal mass of tuff near the summit, apparently six hundred feet in height, the stratification as beautifully preserved as in a work of art, a report like the crack of a rifle echoed and re-echoed from the sides of the crater and aroused our fears for the stability of our giddy platform. The assurance of the guide that a Portuguese at the bottom was employed in felling trees, did not dissipate them instantly. That one could descend, appeared so utterly impossible that we should have thought him sporting with our danger had we not discovered through a glass a moving speck that corroborated his assertion. It should be remarked that while the climate of the Azores happily precludes the necessity of wood for other purposes than those of preparing food, it is difficult to procure a sufficiency for this, and the reward of the woodman, reconciles him to his labor, though he passes days in the Caldeira and is obliged to lash to his back a few sticks at a time when he begins his incredibly toilsome ascent. Our guide pointed to a spot where we could test the practicability of a descent. We went down several hundred feet by a zig-zag, artificial path and abandoned our purpose of continuing to the bottom only because invited by the unsurpassed beauty of the scenery which a circuit of the summit promised. As we again attained the edge, a large sea-bird came sweeping in graceful circles from its visit to the lake below. As it passed above us, it seemed a beautiful similitude of the soul rising on the wings of faith from the caverns of despondence into the clear sunlight of unwavering trust.

The waters of the Caldeira though on a level with the sea are fresh, clear and less than a dozen feet in depth, abounding in beautiful but tiny fish. Those who have visited Vesuvius and Ætna have seen a lake of fire raging continually beneath them, but if silence heightens sublimity they may behold at Fayal a grander reality than even those boiling lakes present. The mouth of the famous volcano of Italy, is less than two miles in circumference and that of Sicily does not exceed three and a half, while the Caldeira is more than six, with a depth exceeding either a thousand feet—such a depth that the wind never curled the sleeping waters—such a depth that the sunlight never played, nor a moon-beam rested on their bosom.

The circuit of the summit afforded us a rich prospect of twenty three villages surrounded with gardens and vineyards, scattered around the bases of numberless truncated hills. Across the channel arose the lofty Pico, its peak enwreathed with clouds or gilded with the sun. In the distance, St. George and St. Michael lay like specks upon the bosom of the quiet deep. The path we traversed was seldom more than ten feet wide, and in some places for several hundred yards, it was not three, with a precipice on one side many hundred feet, on the other as many thousand. We were singularly fortunate in the day we selected for the excursion as it is seldom that the mountain is free from clouds for a single hour. Once or twice while we made the circuit of the summit they curtained the view beneath us for a time, but when the sun poured its flood through their opening, deep and solemn emotions corresponded with the solemnity of the scene. But that which completed the magnificent picture was the beautiful and gorgeously sublime effect of sunset among the peaks below. To gaze upon the soft rich light as it tinged the lofty summits and glanced afar upon the mirror wave—to see the deep and spreading shade cast by the mountains on the sea in bold, fantastic forms—to behold a scene like this, was a climax filling the mind with a healthful relish of the majestic works of the Creator and lofty aspirations for that moral fitness which prepares the soul for contemplation of the unspeakably glorious scenes of Heaven.

Original.

TIMOTHY.

INFLUENCE OF EARLY MORAL INSTRUCTION.*

NO. II.

BY REV. WM. B. SPRAGUE, D. D.

Who can calculate the blessings involved in this most hallowed of all earthly gifts—a pious mother? The mother sustains a relation to the child, in some respects MORE interesting and endearing than the father. The child is cast more immediately upon her care; it makes its first home upon her bosom—it is first attracted by her smile; her plastic hand is the first to mould the elements of its character. And where the spirit of piety has been enkindled in her breast and breathes in her conversation and deportment, the earliest influence to which the opening mind is subjected is a religious influence; and even before its faculties have begun to unfold, she has consecrated it to God in faith and prayer. Behold that christian mother, watching the first dawn of intellect, as the period for commencing a course of moral culture adapted in its beginning to the feebleness of an infant's mind! Behold her kneeling by the cradle in the silence of her chamber, and asking the Father of all mercies to take the little immortal into his keeping; the Spirit of all grace to become its sanctifier! Behold her as it begins to exhibit signs of intelligence, endeavoring to lift its infant thoughts upward; and as its capacity expands, to impress it with a sense of the presence of God, and its own dependance and accountableness. As it advances through the different stages of childhood and youth, mark the fidelity with which she inculcates upon her offspring the great principles and duties of religion; mark the care, the assiduity, the unceasing vigilance which she manifests in keeping him from the power of temptation; mark the pathetic earnestness, the persevering zeal with which she sets before him the danger of a life of sin,

*Continued from Page 219

the importance of escaping from the wrath to come, and of securing an interest in the great Redeemer; and finally, mark the tender and never-failing interest with which she follows him into the world, with her anxieties and prayers whithersoever he may go; and if she is permitted to witness the answer to her prayers and the reward of her efforts in the conversion of her child, see how the tear of gratitude and joy glistens in her eye, as the thankful exclamation flows from her lips, " This my son, was dead and is alive again; he was lost and is found." Oh, if there be a spectacle which attracts angels from heaven to earth, it must be that of a pious mother, such as young Timothy had, laboring by her instructions, counsels and prayers, to render a beloved child wise and holy unto eternal life.

But Timothy was blessed in having pious ancestors, on one side, for at least two generations; not only his mother Eunice but his grandmother Lois, was eminent for her piety, and it is quite likely, that he may have owed much to the grandparent as well as to the parent. Possibly she might have instructed him in his childhood; she had no doubt been instrumental in forming the character of his mother to virtue and piety; and thus the same faith which dwelt in her, descended to him. Who is there that does not look with veneration upon an aged mother in Israel, imparting from the stores of her knowledge and experience to a circle of grandchildren around her, and lifting her feeble hands to bless them in the name of her covenant keeping God? And where this privilege is not enjoyed, how delightful the thought to any christian mother, that not only her children, but children's children, to the latest posterity, may enjoy the benefit of her faith and of her prayers; that she may meet in heaven multitudes of her descendants, who had come into existence ages after she had entered into her rest! Can any thought be more hallowed, more transporting to a christian mother than this?

I have noticed particularly the influence of a pious mother and a pious grandmother, in imbuing the youthful mind with the knowledge of God's word; because there is special reference to this in the case we are contemplating. But there are other influences of great importance which are adapted to secure the same happy result. A pious father as well as a pious mother may be instrumental of accomplishing this object; but most, is always effected by a united parental influence. And as there are a multitude of children neither of whose parents have the disposition to communicate to them any religious instruction, we have reason to bless God that by means of sabbath school instruction multitudes of children are constantly being trained up in the knowledge of God's word, who would otherwise scarcely rise above the ignorance of heathen. And though I would by no means admit this as a substitute for a faithful parental training, where the parents are themselves living in the fear of God, yet I would hail it as a most important auxiliary to parental influence under ANY circumstances; and I cannot doubt that it is the duty of all parents to avail themselves of it so far as may be in their power. Let parents do what they can to give a right direction to the minds of their children, and in connection with this, let them have the benefit of sabbath school instruction; and certain it is that their advantages for becoming wise unto eternal life will be greater than those of the generations who have gone before them. But if parents expect to find in the advantages of the sabbath school a substitute for their own faithful efforts to mould the character of their children—an apology for neglecting the duties which God both by his providence and his word has enjoined upon them, then rely on it, the sabbath school becomes to such children, anything else than a blessing; better both for the children and their parents that it never had an existence.

Timothy derived from his early knowledge of the scriptures many important benefits. What TEMPORAL blessings it might have secured to him directly or indirectly we have no knowledge; but as godliness is profitable to the life that now is, it is quite probable that Timothy both in his youth and manhood, enjoyed the blessings of THIS world in many respects, far more than he would have done, if he had not had the advantage of a pious education. But the great benefit that resulted from his having been thus early acquainted with divine truth, was the formation of religious character. Truth is the foundation of all vital and practical religion; and if the mind of Timothy had not been brought in contact with God's truth, through the influence of a pious mother or by some other means, it is impossible that he should ever have had the principles of religion implanted in his heart. If you would estimate the amount of blessing which his early religious knowledge secured to him, take into view all the blessings which were connected with his religious life, in respect to the present and the future. Think of the probable evils from which he was saved in THIS world, and the bright and cheering hopes which sustained him in the prospect of a world to come. Above all, think of the power which his religion gave him to meet death without dismay, and of the glorious reward which awaited him in heaven, and which he is receiving now, while we meditate upon his fidelity. I do not say—that a knowledge of the scriptures in youth, will be followed by the same blessed consequences to you my young reader, that it was to Timothy; for I cannot tell whether you will possess the same docile and humble spirit that he possessed; whether you will be disposed as he was, to reduce to practice the great truths which you are taught; but I may say with perfect confidence that so long as you remain ignorant of God's word, there is little hope of your spiritual renovation, whereas if its truths are treasured up in your mind, you carry about with you, if I may be allowed the expression, the materials for your sanctification. And hence we find that a large proportion of those, who are ever converted are those who have been taught God's truth by their parents, or in the sabbath school, or by some other instrumentality, in the morning of life. Is it then, too much, to hope that if like Timothy, you know the scriptures from your childhood, like him also, you will early become the subject of renewing grace, and will be a sharer in the consolations of religion here, and in its glorious rewards hereafter.

But Timothy was honored in some respects, above what most young persons can expect; he not only became a true disciple, but a devoted minister of the Lord Jesus, and enjoyed in a peculiar degree the friendship of the great apostle, being an active coadjutor with him in his labors, and being honored with two important letters from him, which constitute part of the inspired record. How delightful must it have been to this young minister to be the intimate friend and associate, of such a man as Paul; to be directed by his counsels and sustained and encouraged by his prayers; and how incomparably more delightful must it be now to enjoy the privilege of a hallowed intercourse with him in that better world of which both have long been inhabitants. Suppose now, my young friends, that you become early acquainted with the scriptures, that you not only know the truth but feel its sanctifying power; that you stand forth in the character of a decided and consistent young christian—it is not certain indeed, that the voice of providence may call you to the same office to which Timothy was called, but it certainly DOES call you into some field of usefulness, where you have the privilege of devoting yourselves to the best interests of your fellow men. You certainly cannot hope for the privilege which Timothy had, of having Paul for a companion of your labors; but other good men stand ready to be your associates and coadjutors; and the day will come, when even Paul himself will become your companion not indeed in the labors and conflicts of earth, but in the joys and praises of Heaven. Is not this encouragement enough to enter on a life of piety—encouragement enough to imitate Timothy's example in becoming diligent students of the Bible?

REPENTANCE—

A GERMAN PARABLE.

A CERTAIN farmer reared with his own hands a row of noble fruit trees. To his great joy they produced their first fruit, and he was anxious to know what kind it was.

And the son of his neighbor, a bad boy, came into the garden, and enticed the young son of the farmer, and they went and robbed all the trees of their fruit before it was fully ripe.

When the owner of the garden came and saw the bare trees he was very much grieved, and cried, Alas! why, has this been done? Some wicked boys have destroyed my fruit!

This language touched the heart of the farmer's son, and he went to his companion, and said, Ah! my father is grieved at the deed we have committed. I have no longer any peace in my mind. My father will love me no more, but chastise me in his anger.

But the other answered, that is foolishness, your father knows nothing about it, and will never hear of it. You must carefully conceal it from him, and be on your guard.

And when Henry, for this was the name of the boy, came home, and saw the smiling countenance of his father, he could not return his smile; for he thought, how can I appear cheerful in the presence of him whom I have deceived? I cannot look at myself. It seems as if there were a dark shade in my heart.

Now the father approached his children, and handed every one some of the fruit of autumn, Henry as well as the others. And the children jumped about delighted, and ate. But Henry concealed his face, and wept bitterly.

Then the father began, saying, my son, why do you weep?

And Henry answered, Oh! I am not worthy to be called your son. I can no longer bear to appear to you otherwise than what I am, and know myself to be. Dear father, manifest no more kindness to me in future, but chastise me, that I may dare approach you again, and cease to be my own tormentor. Let me severely atone for my offence, for behold, I robbed the young trees!

Then the father extended his hand, pressed him to his heart, and said, I forgive you my child! God grant that this may be the last, as well as the first time, that you will have any action to conceal. Then I will not be sorry for the trees.

Original.

A SABBATH SCENE.

BY MRS. M. L. GARDINER.

The day was one of loveliness, the sun in splendor shone—
On castle, tower, and mountain top, its brightest beams were thrown.
The bells chimed forth in sweetness, upon the gusty air
And hearts of humble gratitude met in the house of prayer.

'Twas a day of thrilling interest, hundreds and hundreds came-
The crowded aisle was filled with those who owned the Saviour's name.
The man of God raised high his voice, his heart with fervor glowed;
The old, the young, the beautiful, around the altar bowed.

Peace sat serenely on the brow, which oft was knit with care,
Grace threw her spotless robe around the fairest of the fair;
The mother with the daughter came, the sire the son embraced,
And e'en the orphan, all alone, look'd heavenly as she passed.

Angels above delighted bent, the rapturous scene to view;
Bright seraphs spread their golden wings, and near the temple drew;
The echoing heavens with praises rang, to God's Eternal Son,
And saints in humble reverence bow'd, before the great Three One.

O, 'twas a day through coming time, will tune the Christian's lyre,
A day which through eternity, will nobler thoughts inspire;
Within the groves of Paradise, delighted there, they'll tell
What strong emotions swayed their souls, what burning tears here fell.

O, may the scene, the blessed scene, on earth be oft renewed,
More precious souls be gathered in, more stubborn wills subdued;
The gospel chariot, light convey, o'er a benighted world,
The King of Glory guide its way, with banners bright unfurled.

Original.

MEMOIR OF MRS. ANN S. L. GILBERT.

BY MRS. L. H. SIGOURNEY.

Mrs. Gilbert, was the daughter of Reuben Langdon, Esq. and Mrs. Patience Langdon, and born at New London, Connecticut, on the 8th of May, 1809. A part of her childhood was spent in her native city, after which by the removal of her parents, she became a resident of Hartford. Her ancestors, on both sides, were highly respectable. Her maternal grandfather, the Hon. Sylvester Gilbert, of Hebron, is still living, at the age of 87, with unimpaired intellect, respected for the fidelity with which he discharged the offices of Judge and Member of Congress, as well as for his venerable years and sincere piety.

The first unfoldings of the character of Ann S. Langdon, were pleasant and promising, and entire obedience to parental authority was easily enforced. She early manifested and continued through life to evince the most tender filial attachment, and one of the comforting assurances from her beloved father, at her dying pillow, was, that she "HAD ALWAYS BEEN A GOOD CHILD." Soothing must such a testimony from revered lips be, to the soul, about to take its solemn passage from all earthly things.

The subject of this memoir, when old enough to attend school, won the regard of her teachers, by loveliness of deportment, and attention to their commands. Her conscientiousness in observing even the slightest regulation was remarked by her associates. On one occasion, where a rule had been made, to enter the school-room with a courtesy, she happened to come before the teacher, and when only two or three of the pupils had assembled. Still she complied with the prescribed form of good manners, at which they laughed and said, "Well, Ann Langdon, you always must do just right, whether there is anybody to see you or not."

She was for several years, a member of the "Hartford Female Seminary," while it was conducted by Miss Catharine Beecher, and graduated there, at the age of 21, with its highest honors. While connected with that Institution, she became a member of the North Congregational Church, then under the care of Rev. Mr. Spring. She had long been religiously impressed, and for a year and a half previous to her public profession, had indulged a hope that her peace was made with God, through the reconciliation of a Savior. But judging her heart and life, with severe scrutiny, she hesitated in taking the solemn step of union with the visible Church, until the persuasion of friends, induced her to consider it as a duty. Though she tremulously assumed these hallowed vows, she was upheld and cheered by a sweet sense of the divine approbation.

"I can truly say, she writes, that I never before enjoyed so much of religion. I see more and more, the difference between my past and present character, particularly in the circumstance of attachment to the things of time and sense. I feel my affections greatly weaned from these objects, and it is my daily prayer that they may be set more supremely on God."

She became much engaged as an instructor in the Sabbath school, not only in her own church, but in a somewhat neglected district, at the distance of two miles from her home, where the classes were superintended by an older sister, and often records in her journal, earnest aspirations for the improvement of those under her charge, and that their intercourse might result not only in a "mutual feeling of deeper interest, but in bringing the blessing of the Almighty upon both teachers and pupils."

In the autumn of 1830, she sustained the loss of a very lovely little sister, of a remarkably religious character, to whom she was most tenderly attached—

"I was called, at one o'clock in the morning, she writes, to part with my dear little sister Ellen. So sudden was the stroke, that I could not realize it. Yet I was led to say, that it was infinitely less than I deserved. The first night after her death, was the longest that I ever past. I did not close my eyes to sleep, until the morning began to dawn. But I think I never before felt such entire confidence in God. I cannot admit the thought, that this dispensation should pass away without producing its proper effect. It is my earnest prayer, that God will sanctify this affliction to all of us. May it lead us to more watchfulness, wean us from this vain world and help us to set our affections on heavenly things."

So anxious was this young disciple, not to lose the intended fruits of this lesson of sorrow, that she expressed a fear lest even her intellectual pursuits at the Seminary, might divide her thoughts from the serious contemplations that it had awakened, and hopes, "that as long as her soul shall inhabit this clay tabernacle, it may remember and improve this loud call of God's providence."

Among the many excellent precepts which Miss Beecher faithfully endeavored to instil into the minds of those entrusted to her care, was the one that they should strive to lead lives of usefulness, and render the knowledge which they acquired instrumental to the good of others. Moved by the opinions of one, whom she so much respected and loved, she became for a short time an assistant teacher in the Seminary where she received her education, and then consented to act as Principal in the Female department of an academy in a neighboring state.

In the anticipation of this employment, she writes, "there are some things pleasing, as well as painful. Yet I feel more than ever, willing to be placed, wherever I can be made the instrument of good."

The self-denial requisite for a young lady to leave the comforts of a delightful paternal mansion, and without the incitement of pecuniary necessity, to undertake the laborious office of a teacher, among strangers, is neither slight, nor transient. To any inquiry what had induced her to assume such a situation, she would reply, "the admonitions of Miss Beecher, that young ladies should make themselves useful."

An interesting fragment of a Journal, preserved by her

friends, narrates with great simplicity, her manner of life, during this period of absence from her pleasant home. At one time, it represents her, as remaining long after the usual hour of dismission, to arrange questions in history, or prepare the writing books for her pupils, at another, to prevail on a thoughtless one, to learn a neglected lesson, at another, to converse with one who had failed in duty, until a promise was gained to retrace the retrograde course, and persevere in paths of goodness. Then a few lines record her high satisfaction that one young lady is "doing so finely in Algebra," and again utter the lamentation in which so many faithful teachers have sympathized, "Oh! that I could learn for all my scholars." Sometimes, a rural walk or ride, restores the spirits that had for a moment drooped, or her heart always ready to receive, impressions of happiness, rejoices in the gift of a boquet of flowers, principally because it reminded her of similar attentions on the part of her "own dear father."

Here, notwithstanding her constant avocations during the week, she bestowed a portion of her only day of rest, upon an Infant Sabbath School Class, and calls herself seriously to account, for not devoting more time to studies peculiarly for their instruction. It would seem that her labors in the great field of education, though arduous brought their own reward; for in reviewing the period thus employed, she says, with her characteristic humility—

"My stay in Monson, was protracted beyond my expectations, and on the whole, has been pleasantly, and some of it, I trust, profitably spent. I have made some feeble efforts for the good of those placed under my care, and may God pardon my unfaithfulness, and help me in future to be more devoted to his service."

After her return to her parents, she evinced her accustomed zeal in promoting the happiness of the family, lightening the cares of her mother, and seeking her own spiritual improvement. She listened with deep attention to discourses from the pulpit, and often wrote an analysis of them from recollection, in the following manner.

"Oct. 21, 1832 . This evening, Dr. Hawes preached at the Centre Church, before a large audience, in behalf of the "Ladies Benevolent Society," a most interesting sermon, from the text, "To do good, and to communicate forget not."

In the beginning, he showed some of the ways, in which preventive Charity might profitably operate.

1. By furnishing the poor with employment.

2. By training up indigent children and youth, in habits of industry and economy.

3. By furnishing the poor, with the means of intellectual improvement.

4. By supplying them with moral and religious instruction.

He then enlarged on some of the advantages of preventive, over remedial charity.

1. It calls into exercise, far better feelings, both in the giver, and receiver.

2. It is far cheaper.

3. Far more effective.

4. Far more comprehensive.

Charity, whether preventive or remedial, is the fruit of the Gospel. Until lately, it has been a prevalent error, to act rather on the principles of remedial, than of preventive charity. The exigences of our country, demand a vast increase of preventive charity; and the great benevolent societies of the day being conducted on that principle, are deserving of support and approbation."

On the 7th of May, 1833, the subject of this Memoir, was married to Rev. Edwin R. Gilbert, of Wallingford, Ct. and entered on the duties of a new, and important relation. Her affectionate and amiable disposition, her native grace of manner, and the cheerful patience of a heart whose highest consolations flowed from an Eternal source, conspired to make her new home, the abode of happiness. Mutual affection and confidence lightened every care, and the request recorded in her private papers, at the time of their engagement, seemed mercifully granted, that they might " walk together, in christian love, and fellowship, pursuing with alacrity the path that conducts to Heaven."

The love of intellectual pursuits and desire of extended usefulness, which her education had fostered, did not interfere with the close observance and diligent performance of whatever concerned the order and welfare of her family. Her knowledge of those minuter points on which household comfort depends, and the virtues of her heart, as exemplified in the duties of every day, were fully appreciated by her husband, and it is a privilege to be permitted to quote his own expressive words.

"My dear wife was a most excellent housekeeper. She loved domestic duties, and looked well to the ways of her household. It was her aim to have a place for every thing, and every thing in its place. She understood the art of preparing in the best manner, every thing for the table. I have never seen any one who I thought might excel her in the science of housekeeping. And for all this, she was much indebted to her dear mother, who wisely felt, that in the accomplishments of her daughter, a knowledge of good housekeeping ought not to be wanting.

Her countenance exhibited brightness, sweetness, and great kindness. Those who were not particularly acquainted with her, did not fail to remark the gentleness and cheerfulness that distinguished her. She was not wanting in spirit and energy and indeed, possessed a large share of those traits, but great amiableness was predominant in her character. Grace heightened all her good natural traits, and she wished to cultivate them, to make her character more what she thought a christian's should be.

She was a most excellent wife to me, as a minister of the Gospel. All my people who knew her, loved her, and those who knew her best, valued her most. Indeed, I had no idea, how much they loved her, till since her death, which is felt by them, as a public affliction.

Chiefly through her instrumentality, a Maternal Association was formed, in which she exerted a most happy influence

She gave it very much of its life, and I could see that the mothers who were interested in that Institution, loved her more and more."

Mrs. Gilbert seemed to omit nothing which could be desired in the example of a christian, and the wife of a minister. She was faithful in her correspondence with her numerous friends and were it not for the narrow limits, to which this memoir is necessarily confined, it would be pleasant by extracts from her familiar letters, to show how sweetly and frankly her feelings unfolded in the epistolary style.

The reader will not be disappointed, to hear that she excelled as a mother. One who in the instruction of the children of others, had been emphatically in the language of Scripture " apt to teach" would not naturally fail in duty towards her own. On this point also, " her husband riseth up, and praiseth her."

" She had, he says, a peculiar faculty of managing her children, discerning their dispositions, understanding their wants, cultivating in them, sweet and happy tempers, and training them with morals, and good manners. She thought much, she felt much, she prayed much for our dear children. Oh! how much have I loved, and valued her, as a mother."

She was the mother of four children, and called to part with two sons in their infancy; her first born, at the age of a year and a half, and the third son at four months. After her first bereavement in a letter to her beloved parents, she says tenderly,

" That we feel lonely, I need not tell you. But our prayer is, that we may be filled with all the fulness of God, and that we may find our comfort and consolation in Him. We have no reason to fear, if we put our trust there.

Once in a while, the feeling comes over me, Oh, that my dear little boy could enjoy with us, the fruits and the flowers of the summer. But we have every reason to believe that his sources of enjoyment, as well as his power to enjoy, are far higher, far nobler than ours. May we all be prepared to participate in them."

A daughter who was but a few weeks old, at the time of her mother's death, was baptized at her funeral, receiving her own name. But the little one was soon called to follow her blessed mother, and the second son is now the only survivor of those fair olive-plants that once bloomed around her table.

Her health became feeble for several months previous to her decease, though not so decidedly, as to preclude the hope of recovery, until a short time before that event took place. Her mind continued in a submissive and peaceful state, and she often expressed the sweet hope that "Jesus Christ was her friend." She repeatedly alluded to her own unworthiness, and seemed with the meekness of a little child, to cling to the promises of her Heavenly Father. During the greater part of her sickness she was able to converse with comparative ease, and cheerfulness sat on her countenance, as she spoke of her increasing confidence in her Saviour.

On the last Sunday of her life, apprehending that her dissolution drew near, she spoke much to those who were around her bed, sent messages to absent friends, and was frequently engaged in fervent prayer. This scene was again repeated, on the afternoon of the following Thursday, when recovering from deep and deadly faintness, and supposing that the King of Terrors was at hand, she poured out her soul in supplication to God, and then took leave with great affection of her husband hoping that they should meet in heaven, and ever be dear to each other. She conversed most tenderly with her beloved mother, saying "God will take care of me. I believe he will take care of you. Does Christ comfort you?" She sent love to all her dear kindred, and other friends and committed her soul to its Redeemer.

Then she relapsed into a quiet slumber, from which she scarcely awoke, until she slept in Jesus, on the afternoon of Saturday, Feb. 13, 1841, in the thirty-second year of her age. Her obsequies were attended on the following Tuesday, and her remains brought into the church where for eight years she had been a worshipper, earnestly desiring the spiritual good of the people, who now assembled to lay her in the grave, and to sympathize with her bereaved husband.

I cannot close this imperfect sketch of a beautifully consistent character better than by borrowing a passage from the funeral sermon, preached on that day, by the Rev. Mr. Griggs, of North Haven.

"Though she had scarcely completed thirty-two years, she had done the great work of life. As a daughter, a sister, a wife, a mother, she had performed her part well. She believed on the Lord Jesus Christ, lived the life of the righteous, died the death of the righteous, and is now entered into rest. May the bereaved husband and children, all these mourning relatives, all this sympathizing people cherish her spirit, and attain her end."

Original

WHAT CONSTITUTES TRUE HAPPINESS IN THE CONJUGAL RELATION.

PRIZE ESSAY.*

BY REV. A. A. LIPSCOMB, ALABAMA.

One of the most serious errors, that can occupy the mind is that, which regards marriage, as an end in itself. Such is not a correct view of this important relation. If it be so contemplated, each party will inevitably feel, that nothing more remains to be effected. The object was possession. That secured, all vigilance of thought ceases—the disposition to please vanishes—affection relapses into indifference, and kind-hearted attentions become unknown. The true idea of marriage is, that it is a means, and not an end—Providence designed it to sustain this character. If it have most responsible duties—if it bring the most solemn of all engagements, it is with reference to our happiness, and consequently, wedded bliss is

*Continued from p. 235.

only to be sought in the faithful discharge of wedded obligations. The husband and wife virtually separate themselves, in a measure, from the outer world, and covenant before God to promote each other's pleasure. The first and last sentiment of their minds should be, that they are to be a mutual blessing. To look to the external world for their happiness—to seek it in the crowded saloon—to repair to the next neighbor's house to find it, is a sacrifice of the great principle, on which, such a union is based. Let the parties be thrown upon themselves for pleasure, and marriage will be constantly viewed as a means to secure it. Every thing will be avoided, that would tend to mar domestic tranquility. The business of each day will be, to remove all grounds of irritation—to soothe asperities of temper—to cultivate increasing nearness of relation, and to form their natures in the same mould. Married persons should ever remember, that their happiness hangs on the perpetuation of those sentiments and feelings which originally drew them together. The interesting days, that preceded their union, ought to be unceasingly lived over, and over until their spirit becomes the spirit of life. Who can recur to those moments, when love had been but recently enshrined in the heart, when fancy had but one image before her vision—when memory was lost in hope, and hope merged in the certainties of reality, and not realize that the past has a wondrous power over human emotions? Blissful was that prelude season, bright and beautiful like the days that steal upon us, in the wintry time, as sweet harbingers of the soft spring! Anxiety quickened the play of feeling; and affection, tender and ardent, made every heart-string give forth the richest melody. The intensity of romance, was equalled, without its follies; and the valor of chivalry was realized, without its vices. Was there a moment then, when an unkind word would have been uttered? Was there an hour then, when the society of the chosen one, would not have been preferable to any other fellowship? Let the married preserve those fervent feelings, generous sentiments, and noble principles—let them be corrected by experience, and matured by wisdom—let them reign supreme in the bosom without changing into reserve and indifference, and it will be found, that though flowers wither and foliage fades, the joys of the spirit have the element of immortality within them.

The respective spheres of husband and wife ought to be kept sacred by each other. Any attempt to destroy the line of separation between them will be succeeded by the same results, that always follow an infringement of natural law. Each one has a prescribed part to perform. To vary from it, is to produce disorder. A meddlesome disposition is the bane of domestic comfort. It is invariably associated with narrow views, and captious feelings. As a feeble member of the physical frame is ever drawing disease to itself, so this temper is continually attracting circumstances of peevish excitement. It has as many eyes as Argus, and they are all CROSS-EYES, in a double sense. A strict watch should be exercised over the mind, in respect of this besetment. It grows so rapidly, that it must be checked in its incipiency. The strength of conscience must be made to bear upon it. The minds of numerous individuals are so constituted that INFIRMITIES are not felt to be evils. Moral principle, is therefore not called in to aid in their extermination. Strange fallacy of judgment! Nothing is beyond the jurisdiction of conscience—nothing is unworthy of close attention, that involves correct sentiment, and elevated feeling. A pin may destroy life as well as a dagger. A small substance in the eye may affect the sight. We call these things insignificant; they are LITTLE matters. Are they indeed? So much the greater blame is to be attached to us, if they be suffered to distract domestic life. Are they LITTLE? Try to overcome them, and you will see, that Omnipotence will have to aid you in the effort. The serenity of the fireside circle is seldom endangered by vice. Fortunately for the world, the most vicious of human creatures are not generally found in the bonds of marriage. Petty trifles form the trial and the exposure. The very things, that public opinion cannot reach are the things that wreck the hopes of wedded blessedness. To have the entire control over them is an important feature in domestic culture.

If it be desirable, to cherish an affectionate spirit, it is equally desirable to cultivate such manners, as will accord with it. One has lived in the world to little purpose, who has not observed the effect of agreeable behavior. Persons, who have no other pretensions to recommend them, often win their way through society, by this means alone. However erroneous the criterion may be, there are but few, who do not regard manners, as expressive of character. A good temper, and disagreeable manners are sometimes strangely found together. The rough bark of a tree may cover a smooth skin. Domestic life should present a happy union of a kind spirit and kind manners. Nothing should be overlooked, that can promote elevated sentiments. If perfect politeness should be any where exhibited, it should be in the relation existing between husband and wife. There are constant opportunities occurring, for the display of an affectionate and fervent attachment. There are innumerable little attentions, that may be shown by each other, with no inconsiderable advantage. A tender look—a soothing word—a trifling act expressive of esteem, are not without influence. They strengthen love. They impress the memory. They render intercourse pleasant. Manners have a reflex action upon the spirit of their subject, as well as a direct action upon the mind of their object. If there were no other reason, this should lead to their diligent cultivation. The truth of these observations applies especially to the sterner sex. Good husbands are not always fortunate in their manners. The feelings of their wives are frequently hurt by their hasty words and inconsiderate acts. A source of unpleasantness is thus kept constantly open. Discord not seldom arises from these apparently insignificant causes. When we remember, that the ills of life fall the heavier upon delicate woman—when we remember that the trials of marriage oppress her, the more severely, can any carefulness of manner be too great, in our conduct towards her? No rules can be laid down on the subject of manners; but this may be said, that if the mind of each party subordinate its gratification to the will of the other, and manifest an appropriate and corresponding style of action, the end will be obtained. The duties of marriage are both negative and positive. We are to abstain from every thing, that would lessen the power of affection, and also, exert all our agency, to add to the pleasure of the wedded state. The united pair should feel that they are to live for one another, in humble subjection to the law of God, and with ceaseless reference to the glory of God. Inferior only to that highest and holiest sentiment, the sentiment of religion, this conviction should be enthroned within them. If adversities should overtake them—if fortune should, in the language of the world, frown upon them, and if the firmament above, and the landscape below, should be dark and dismal, such a principle, associated with all that is tender and endearing in human feeling, will only bind them the nearer to each other, as the storm that strips the foliage from the tree, seems but to make its roots strike the deeper into the firm earth. Impulse is short-lived; romance soon decays—but such love expires only in the grave. It partially renews the faded scenes of Eden, and almost images the communion and companionship of Heaven.

The benign influence of christianity should be sought to consecrate the domestic relations—to hallow the love of husband and wife, and to breathe its blessed benediction over their daily intercourse. The office of this benevolent agent is two-fold; it implants a new affection, love to God, and it purifies and ennobles the natural affections of the heart. If its glory is seen in the former, it is also seen in the latter. Oh, how holy is human love, under its operation! The thought of immortality adds joy to every other joy. A common Heaven animates husband and wife by its hopes; a common Savior is their constant guest. Could we look on the objects of our regard in the light of Infidelity, what encouragement should we have to cherish affection? If they are to perish so soon, if they be but little better than the beasts, that descend to the dust, then what is there to call forth our love? The heart cannot bear such mockery. It will not endure it. Never, never never! Better not love at all, if there be no hereafter! Better never form an attachment, if death is to triumph over soul and body! Thus Christianity chimes with our natural instincts and affections. It sanctifies human love, and enshrines it within the same sanctuary, that contains the love of God. The altar within the vail, where the Schekinah rests and the cherubim watch, is dedicated to the glorious Supreme—the altar in the outer court is devoted to the chosen object of earthly affection.

Original.

A TRIP FROM NEW YORK TO BOSTON.*

BY REV. A. D. EDDY.

Mount Auburn is a beautiful spot and is among the leading objects of interest in this part of New England. We approached it however, with no favorable impression as to its moral influence. We had long doubted the propriety of so adorning the tomb and making splendid the charnel house of human corruption. Let death have its gloom and the grave still hold its dreary empire over the mind. Let no one think lightly of dying, from the flowers and the sweet shades where the slumberer reposes from his weariness and pains, nor court its triumphs from the splendid marble and the wreathed myrtle that honor the memory of the dead.

But all these philosophizings were dispelled the moment we entered the silent windings of this vast burying place. And if Abraham religiously provided for the resting of his bones in Machpelah, and there deposited the ashes of his beloved Sarah—if Joseph of Aramathea laid in his own new tomb the body of the Redeemer, let us honor our dead by a suitable depository from the noise and gaze of the crowded throng, and leave there a memorial of their character.

*Concluded from p. 243.

Amid all the monuments we saw, and all the impressive solemnity they imparted, one exceeded all the rest. Embosomed in the natural shrubbery of the place, remote from observation we saw a single grave a little elevated and undistinguished by a monumental stone as if this simple mound, was all that could perpetuate the memory of one so dear, so much beloved. Perhaps the mother laid here her last support and retired from the lowly grave doubly widowed; or the orphans in sorrow laid in this shady spot their last parent and had nothing to leave behind, but this mound eloquent of their loneliness and grief. It impressively contrasted with the stately piles and spacious vaults that crowded around us at every step.

We here found the monument of the young friend who was the companion of our early studies—the grave of many whom when living we admired and now dead, we venerate. And though we saw occasionally, an inscription that greatly shocked our sensibilities we returned with the full conviction that the moral influence of the place is good.

New England is the home of Churches and the nursery of the ministry. In this immediate neighborhood are no less than three Theological Seminaries. Andover stands pre-eminent as the oldest, and best endowed of all our American schools of theology. We visited this Institution, whose associations we wish might ever be preserved. Not less than three hundred thousand dollars have been expended in the endowment of this Seminary, and it is now rich in all the resources essential to the best education which the church can demand in her ministry. It is a prevailing opinion in New England that a learned and pious ministry is essential to the best interests of that enlightened people—that the ministry should be respected—that it has divine claims on the confidence of men, and that no one can be a good citizen, or a safe member of society, not to say a christian who despises or undervalues this ordinance of heaven.

To no one cause, can we more safely trace the general intelligence and morality of New England, than to the learning and piety of its ministry. This Institution shares largely in the honor of preserving and increasing these essential qualifications for the sacred office. May it long be preserved from those influences, which in other countries and in other times, have essentially changed the character of Theological Institutions and made them more the nurseries of error and irreligion than of truth and piety.

There is a respect manifested towards the christian ministry in New England which we admire. A class of ministers, elevated by their literary and religious resources, cannot but be valued and sustained by the wise and virtuous; and no people can afford to loose the benefits of such ministrations. How much does New England owe to her evangelical ministry, and how much does that community forfeit which is destitute of its services. The respect due to it, and the support it demands, are to be measured by the divine authority that ordained it and the invariable blessings that have attended the faithful discharge of its duties; and when this whole land shall have what New England now enjoys, or seeks to enjoy, a learned and pious minister for every congregation of a thousand souls, then may we dismiss all fears for the rupture of our civil ties and the loss of our civil immunities. Domestic evils would fast die away; public calamities be less grievous or more easily borne; political asperities would be softened and instead of sectional jealousies and mutual recriminations, our entire nation would resume the confidence, of one common brotherhood. We have more confidence in the evangelical power of the gospel ministrations and the diffusive spirit of christianity than in the wisdom of any legislation where this spirit and these ministrations are unknown or undervalued. When will the time come, when members of Congress will rise in the halls of our national legislature during its excitement and divisions and propose in the spirit of Franklin, an invocation of the divine blessing and a day of fasting and prayer. The descendants of the Pilgrims will no more sacrifice their industry and frugality, than their intelligence and religion. These united, New England will remain what we would have all America become, the admiration of the world.

THE CHILD AND THE CHRISTIAN HERMIT.

No. III.

It was a cheering sight to behold the meek and trusting child, seated at the feet of his pious friend, listening to all he said with affection and delight.

And when the hermit spoke of that great Being, whose throne is in the highest heaven, and YET who deigns to dwell in the hearts of the contrite and lowly—who is present in all parts of the universe at the same moment,—who is the Creator and Preserver of every thing,—governing all events by his wisdom and goodness,—looking into the heart of every human being,—knowing their secret thoughts as well as their actions, —when the hermit dilated on these things, the child was lost in feelings of awe and admiration, and he longed to hear more and more of so great a God, and to learn to please him.

Then the aged man took the child into the green wood, and there he pointed out the beauties of the variegated foliage. Here, was a venerable oak, spreading its leafy arms far and wide, offering a cool shade to the wanderer during the heat of the day. There, a stately elm, which ever greets the merry spring with its light and cheerful green, waved its ample branches gaily in the breeze. There, again, the poplar, straight and tall, reared its spiral head to the skies. The mountain-ash, with its scarlet berries, entwined its branches with those of the elegant white birch; and, not far off, the holly, glittering with its armed and varnished leaves, tipped with coral, embellished the forest glade. And now the child stopped to admire the beautiful larch, gracefully tapering from the base to the summit. The hermit told him of the elastic nature of this tree; how it bends before the most violent gale, and regains its erect position as soon as the rough blast has passed over it. "And we, my child," he added, "must bow submissively to the storms of life, should the Almighty, in his wisdom, suffer them to burst over our heads; and He will, in his own good time, raise us up again, nor will he permit us to be destroyed."

The child did not quite comprehend the hermit's discourse, but he hearkened to it with meek attention, wishing to be instructed. Often did he pause to examine the studded and fluted trunk of the white beech, overspread with a variety of mosses and lichens. The lime, the majestic pine, and the overshadowing branches of the horse-chestnut, next claimed his wonder and delight. Nor were the sycamore and maple overlooked; their bark smooth and polished as satin, and their verdant boughs forming an impenetrable shade.

As they slowly left the embowered spot, the aged man again reverted to the great Creator of all.

"The noble oak," he said, "and the minute weed which springs up at its foot, are nourished by the same earth, and watered by the same gentle dews of heaven; and so it is with man,—the high and the low are alike His care; neither can subsist without his blessing."

The child felt glad when he heard all this, and he looked fondly into the old man's face as he spoke, and a tear of gratitude glistened in his dark blue eye, while a happy smile played around his pretty mouth.

They returned to their rustic dwelling, where all that contributes to health and peace was ever to be found.

As the shades of evening drew near, and the child felt the influence of sleep stealing over him, the benevolent recluse gently placed him on a leafy bed which he had prepared for him; first, however, teaching him to invoke a blessing from Him who condescends to hear the weakest infant's prayer.

And soon the child's fair eyelids closed, and he slept the sleep of innocence.

The pious man now trimmed his little lamp, and taking from a nook the volume which is dear to every Christian heart, he sat him down to feast upon its sacred truths. Ever and anon he turned to gaze upon that gentle child, who lay in sweet repose, his little hands gracefully folded on his bosom. Light and joyful seemed his slumbers; his forehead, white as the purest snow, was scarcely shaded by his glossy auburn hair,—his cherub-cheek glowed like a blushing rose,—a placid smile was on his coral lips,—while his soft low breathings seemed to whisper all was peace within.

The aged man lifted his soul in prayer to God, that He would bless this little one, and cause the seed of holiness and love to take deep root within his heart. Pleasing to the Almighty is the prayer of age for helpless infancy; and as it rises to the throne of grace, it seems to bring a blessing on the suppliant. At his side the angel of innocence holds her vigil; every evil spirit stands abashed, and dares not tempt; and all unholy thoughts are put to flight.

It was noon when the child was led by his aged friend to the summit of a steep cliff, whence they beheld the "multitudinous ocean."

Many a white sail was to be seen gracefully moving over the blue waters. The mid-day sun was shining in all his splendor, and the sea-birds skimmed lightly over the surface of the mighty deep. All seemed happy, and the child felt happy also. He pressed the hand of his venerable guide closer within his own, and waited for him to speak.

The hermit noticed his inquiring eye, and, pointing to the

vast expanse before them, he said, "My child, again thou beholdest the wonderful works of God. 'The sea is his, and he made it, and his hands prepared the dry land.' Those ships contain many human beings, and are all bound to some port. Some are near the haven of their hopes; some have yet many days and nights to plough the waves, ere they arrive at their destinations. But the same providence watches over all. The God who is with us, is with them also. He is the faithful Pilot, who can guide the vessel in safety through the rudest storm. See now, yon brave seaman climbs the giddy mast: he has reached the top, and his life appears to depend on that frail rope. But an invisible hand holds him up, and keeps him safe, while suspended o'er the foaming waves. That hand is God's."

The child grew more and more amazed at such great, such universal love. His little heart was overflowing with affection and delight. He did not speak, but suffered the good hermit to lead him back to his moss-covered hut in silent joy.

On the threshold stood the dog, displaying by various gestures his satisfaction at their return. The child rushed forward to caress him, and when the noble animal licked his hands, and fondly leaped upon him, or, in sportive glee, rolled himself on the soft enamelled grass, he laughed aloud, from pure and unalloyed gladness. Again the aged man clapped his hands, and the pretty goat came bounding over the plain; and they sat them down to enjoy their frugal meal. The dog shared their repast, and many a feathered songster perched fearlessly around. The timid hare and rabbit, too, entered unscared into the lowly dwelling:—and the child remarked where these uninvited but welcome guests could easiest get at the crumbs that fell, and THERE he took delight in dropping them.

Sweet charity seemed to rule his infant thoughts: charity, which is loving "and is kind,"—which seeks the ease of others, not her own, and never looks for praise.

To be continued.

WEDDING HYMN.

WORDS BY WILLIAM CUTTER.

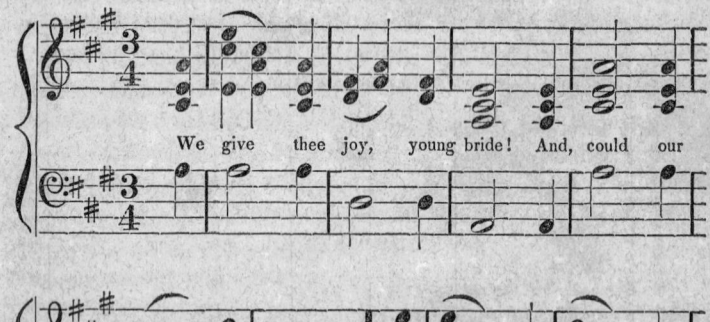

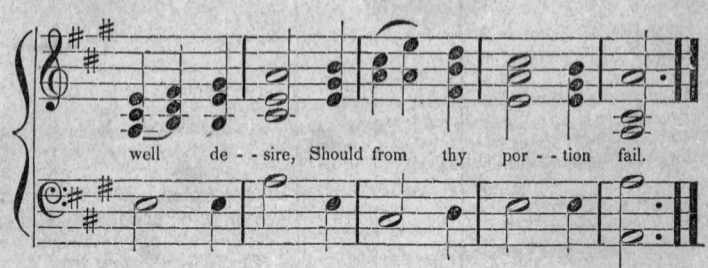

We give thee joy, young bride! And, could our prayers a- -vail, No gift the heart may well de- -sire, Should from thy por- -tion fail.

2.
We give thee joy, young bride!
  Not that ideal light
Which lingers round the dreams of youth,
  But aye eludes the sight.

3.
We give thee joy, young bride!
  Substantial, changeless, pure —
Such as can satisfy the heart,
  And through all time endure.

4.
We give thee joy, young bride!
  May all the scenes of life
Find thee rejoicing in thy lot,
  A faithful, happy wife.

5.
We give thee joy, young bride!
  And, when life's scenes are o'er,
May thou and thine in bliss remain
  United evermore!

Original.

THE GERANIUM, AND THE CHAF-FINCH.

While the bird nestles close to this delicate flower
Whose fragrance gives zest to its favorite bower,
How mellow its notes and how shrill as they rise
Perfumed with sweet incense, and float to the skies.

So the Christian who clings to the merits of Him
Whose love like his glory will never grow dim,
Wakes a song of rejoicing, the sweetest he sings
Till death to his spirit lends heavenly wings.

THE PROFFERED KISS.

For the Christian Family Magazine.

THE
CHRISTIAN FAMILY ANNUAL.

DURATION AND VALUE OF THE SOUL.

BY THE EDITOR.

The spark that falls from the steel, bears some proportion to the effulgence of the sun; the mote that floats in the sunbeam, bears some proportion to the dimensions of the globe; a moment, some proportion to a million of years; a farthing to the wealth of the world.

But what imagery can give an adequate conception of the duration and value of the immortal soul.

Its Duration. When a thousand times ten thousand ages shall have run their ample round, and are forgotten; these multiplied by the sands on the sea shore; by the leaves of autumn and by the stars of heaven ten thousand times ten thousand, the soul will only have entered the morning of eternity—all beyond will be eternal life.

If a bird could convey to some remote field of space only a single grain of sand, and return once in a thousand years, what a vast period would elapse, ere a molehill, not to say, the Alps or the Andes would be removed? And yet, when each Mountain and Continent and Island, and the Globe itself should thus be deposited in the distant fields of space, Eternity, vast eternity would only be commenced!

The value of the soul. Of its value, we can say nothing adequate—no pencil can delineate, no tongue can tell, no imagination conceive. the worth of an immortal soul.

The mind of the loftiest archangel in glory, would labor in vain in the attempt. We can form some estimate of the wealth of Cresus; of the costly gems that deck the brow of nobles; of the millions upon millions that cluster around the thrones and palaces of Eastern monarchs—and yet, when all this immense wealth and treasure is weighed in the scale against the value of a single soul, how empty it appears.

Estimate the value of that glorious luminary and of those lesser lamps that spangle the spacious vault of Heaven, and cheer the path of myriads through all the vigils of the night—and compute if you can, the loss that the world would sustain, were these lights, by some stroke of heaven, quenched in everlasting darkness. By no arithmetic could this loss be estimated—and yet, in comparison with the loss of one soul, all these dwindle into absolute and everlasting insignificance.

We can form some idea of the cost of those inglorious laurels, those blood-stained honors, which clothed the brow of military conquerors, who, to secure the crown of universal empire, like Alexander and Napoleon, made whole nations a field of slaughter, at the expense of myriads of lives and countless treasure. Place in the scale against the value of ONE SOUL, the immense price, which those imperial honors cost, and all the glory which the princes of the world have awarded to their names—and to the dying man, how small, how worthless, how contemptible they appear? The soul of the poorest beggar at the gate, with the love of Christ in his heart, and an interest in Heaven in prospect, is infinitely more valuable, in God's esteem, than all these. Could we possess all the wealth, friendship, honor and power that heart can wish, and that this and every other world can bestow; and yet, in the trying scene of our last sickness, be compelled to feel that for these we have lost the soul—how trifling, would these treasures and glories appear?

If this is the estimate which we, in the possession of health and reason, place on the treasures of earth and on the priceless soul; how great will appear its value when death has done his work and the soul shall take its exit to the bar of the

Judge to receive its final sentence of reward or doom?

In attempting to represent the value of the soul, how we feel the poverty of our conceptions, as well as of our language? What will be our view of the capacity, dignity, destiny and value of the soul when the effulgence of a thousand suns shall break upon our ravished vision and we shall see as we are seen and know as we are known?

O, could we summon to our circle one of the prophets, or apostles, martyrs or angels, who have long glowed and burned in the presence of the Eternal, and ask him to describe the worth of the soul—His tongue would falter in the attempt. He could convey to us no adequate conception of its value but in the mighty language of the skies. He would tell us. As well might an infant of a day, drink in and enjoy the conceptions of a Kepler or of a Newton, while measuring the heavens, or tracing the laws of matter and motion.

That great moral problem, which stands on the page of the Bible—"What shall it profit a man if he shall gain the whole world and lose his own soul; or what shall a man give in exchange for his soul," would have lost half its grandeur, had the Savior attempted to solve it by any measure within the range of finite arithmetic? He simply states this grand proposition, and, as though this were all that could be done, he leaves the question to be pondered in time, and answered alone in eternity.

How often in our moments of leisure or amidst the darkness and solitude of night, when all nature was sunk in repose; or perhaps, in the unclouded scenes of prosperity, or in the hour of distress and sorrow, has the soul been impressed with a sense of its exalted nature, of its inexpressible value. Then, how the riches and glories of the world faded away? Gold became dross, honor a name, power a bubble, crowns and kingdoms a breath of empty air. All these, in comparison with a deathless soul appeared trifling as the mere daisies of the day.

We have attempted to form some idea of the worth of the soul, by comparing it with things of the greatest value in our world; and we have seen in the comparison, that things sublunary—Gold, gems, crowns, empire—ALL THINGS, placed upon the scale against the soul, are light as the dust of the balance.

Before we can form any true estimate of our immortal nature, we must lift the curtain that covers the great Future, and contemplate its capacity, its susceptibility of enjoyment in the lapse of eternity.

If it be admitted that the capacity of the soul, for enjoyment, will be enlarged forever ; the conclusion is irresistible, that in some remote period of eternity, one soul will have possessed more bliss than all that has ever yet been enjoyed by all the hosts of Heaven—and yet, when this measure of fruition shall have been attained, the soul will only have entered the dawn of vast eternity!

After all that can be said of the soul, no figures or comparisons can give us any adequate estimate of its infinite worth, unless we can measure its value by the PRICE that has been paid for its redemption. And what price is this? Not the cattle on a thousand hills; nor ten thousand rivers of oil; nor the sacrifice of myriads of lives, or of all the glorified intelligences around the throne of God and the Lamb—No—not these—But a price has been paid for its redemption far, yes, infinitely greater than all these—It is a price of blood; it is the sacrifice of the adorable son of God!

Who, then, we seriously inquire, can treat lightly, so valuable a treasure, so priceless a gift, as the IMMORTAL SOUL?

> "What matter whether pain or pleasures fill
> The swelling heart one little moment here?
> From both alike how vain is every thrill,
> While an untried eternity is near!
> Think not of rest, fond man, in life's career;
> The joys and grief that meet thee, dash aside
> Like bubbles, and thy bark right onward steer
> Through calm and tempest, till it cross the tide,
> Shoot into port in triumph, or serenely glide."

Original.

THE PROFFERED KISS.*

BY H. M. PARSONS.

There is language, oft unspoken,
   Whose deep truth the heart may prove—
Do not then reject the token
   Of a fresh and guileless love.
It may be that, youth departed,
None will sue as gentle hearted.

How like strains of music falling
   Sweet and plaintive on the ear,
Are those moments when recalling
   Childhood's smile and passing tear,
Gentler, purer thoughts we nourish,
Which unsought, can never flourish.

Group of beauty! care and sorrow
   Do not check your bounding hearts—
Not a dream of dark to-morrow
   To your joy its shade imparts.
We could wish the dreams you cherish,
Might not from your bosoms perish.

But the rose your cheeks impressing
   Will by slow degrees decay,
And the toils of life depressing,
   Snow-flakes on your spirits lay.
These are lessons meant in kindness
To remind of moral blindness.

Yet through life there's hope above us
   If our faith can pierce the sky,
Yes, there is One Friend to love us
   And repress the rising sigh—
He, our gloomiest doubts can scatter—
He, temptation's weapons shatter.

Does the summer of our being
   Warm—expand the flowers of youth,
Whose rich hues another seeing
   Will unshrinking seek the truth?
Let the winter gather o'er us,
Love and peace are still before us.

      *See Frontispiece.

Original.

LIGHT LITERATURE.

BY A. V. WYCKOFF.

The degeneracy of our national morality must be evident to the observing patriot and christian. The influence of powerful evils have been long secretly at work, depriving it of its primitive sternness and purity. The eager desire with which multitudes embrace the selfish doctrines of scepticism, and the general laxity of moral sentiment are sure indications of the growing corruption of the public mind. The numerous causes of this, cannot all perhaps, be distinctly pointed out; but there are some prominent ones which we can easily distinguish, and which may well excite distrust.

Among these more palpable causes of the decline of our national morality, is one, which deserves our serious attention. We allude to the INFLUENCE OF A LIGHT, AND OFTEN IMMORAL LITERATURE. However much, this is cried down by caterers, for the public taste, and sneered at by others interested in the matter, it should not on that account, be the object of less consideration, but rather should merit the more careful examination.

The cheapness with which fictitious works are furnished at the present day, throws them far and wide upon the country. The very press has been turned into an engine of destruction. Night after night the clanking of its machinery may be heard in this work of ruin; day after day it issues forth its polluting sheets to gratify the morbid appetite of the public. The natural consequence of the wide diffusion of these works is, that the minds of thousands become enfeebled. Their appetite, once corrupted is never appeased—like the insatiate grave, it never cries 'enough.' Their tastes become vitiated, and they no longer have a relish for sound productions. Their ideas assume a romantic tinge, and if the characters exhibited and illustrated in the fictions they have perused, do not conform to human nature they waste their time in useless regrets, and in futile endeavors to come up to the standard marked out. Nor is this strange, when we consider the circumstances of the case. The reader has been dwelling a while in the ideal world of the novelist. He has been absorbed in contemplating its magnificence. He has been dazzled by its splendor and gorgeousness. He has been bound by some mysterious chain to its beings. Their vices have cost them no pain or remorse; they are painted as heroic and sublime. In that ideal world there are enchanted castles and fairy bowers. Music is heard there, more sweet than has ever ravished mortal ear. Beauty is more blooming than has ever met mortal eye. Virtue is more pure than ever man has known. Happiness is there, with scarce a regret, love with scarce a sigh. The bewildered reader turns from this revel of imagination, to the stern realities of the world, feverish and excited. Perhaps his mind has not been moulded and strengthened by education, or fortified by strong religious principles. It then becomes controlled by habits of association which unfit it for deep thought, and reflection. The imagination of the reader has been pleased but his intellectual powers have not been stimulated and nourished. Worst of all the heart is left cold and neglected; there is nothing to satisfy its yearnings for something higher and better, nothing to soothe its anguished feelings—nothing upon which it can muse with delight, and embrace with confiding hope.

We know that these productions of fiction may be brilliant efforts of genius, and moral sentiments may be interwoven in the thread of the narrative, clothed in all the beauty of language; but genius prostituted, can never claim our admiration, nor will the pleasure derived from the beautiful thoughts of a writer be a sufficient inducement to incur the enervating influence of his productions. He must be little aware of his danger indeed, who would have recourse to fiction, to refresh his mind with sparkling thoughts. Who would endure the deadly blasts of Arabia, for the sake of breathing its spicy incense for an hour, or chain himself in the dark mine to gather around him, and fondle for a while the masses of gold. Genius exerted only for the sake of injury we should shun, for its splendor like the fitful light that flickers over the mouldering remains in the grave, is engendered and nourished by corruption, and dazzles but to lead astray

But the great mischief is, that much of the wide spread fiction of the present day is highly immoral. In a strain of apparent moral discourse the most pernicious sentiments are insinuated, and under the garb of friendship and truth, the maxims of Satan are taught. In an unguarded moment the poison is infused into the bosom of the unconscious reader; there it rankles long and deep, till the well springs of happiness are polluted, and the soul is covered with moral leprosy. As these works are scattered through our land they reach the innocent and pure—rouse their slumbering passions, and light the fires of corruption in the human heart. O! who can tell how many a hope they have wrecked, how many a loved one they have robbed of their purity. We might mark them in their course, as we mark the burning lava, carrying moral desolation and death wherever they reach. We shudder, as we see the bloated victim of immorality wending his way to the dark abodes of corruption, or hurrying to join his scoffing associates, to mingle in the revellings of infidelity; thus shipwrecking his soul and cursing his God. But may we not, with greater reason shudder at the wide diffusion of those writings which conveyed the first principles of vice into his heart, and may we not severely reprobate those who spend their lives in the dissemination of these principles under the imposing garb of fiction. In their hands virtue loses all its attractions, and is covered with ridicule and contempt. Religion, is but fanaticism, a gross system of imposition, or at best, behind the spirit of the age; and the mild principles of benevolence are unworthy of the dignity of men. On the contrary, vice is brought forward in bold relief, and decked in her most gorgeous colors she proffers honor and prosperity. Her votaries, are made to appear as angels of light, and her service brings ease and renown. When literature like this, is widely diffused through our country, who could expect that morality should remain untainted? Can man inhale the pestilential atmosphere without experiencing its dire effects or drain the poisoned bowl with impunity?

Fiction, of certain kinds when employed for the sake of conveying moral and intellectual instruction, is productive of good consequences, but when it is employed merely as a means of tickling the fancy and gratifying a morbid taste, inculcating vice, and casting contempt upon religion and our social institutions, it is time that the American and the philanthropist should lift their voice against its evils, and arouse their energies to counteract its effects. Duty to their country and God demands this, and the dictates of duty they should follow, notwithstanding the bitter opposition of men. Let them not be deterred by the hue and cry that the spirit of the age demands the circulation of fiction, for the SPIRIT OF PHILANTHROPY is interwoven with the spirit of the age, and that spirit delights neither in 'moral corruption nor in intellectual weakness'

Original.

THE WOODLAND WALK.

BY THE AUTHOR OF "BLIND ALICE."

Louisa Vivian at seventeen, was a girl of pleasing appearance, of agreeable manners and cultivated intellect. Her father, a gentleman in easy circumstances, lived all the year at the country seat which had been his father's. A neighboring town had grown up to his domain, but no temptation which the desire of wealth could proffer, had power to win from Mr. Vivian any part of that beautiful woodland which surrounded his mansion and through which, beautiful walks tastefully arranged, led to the town or city, as it had of late become, on one side, and to the river on which it was built, on the other. When we said that a walk through the woodland led to the city, we did not mean to represent it as the only mode of communication. A wide avenue along which two carriages could with ease drive abreast, extended in front of Mr. Vivian's house for half a mile, where it met the public road. A wide arched gate terminated the avenue and was joined at each side by a substantial picket fence, which secured the grounds from the intrusion of animals. A smaller gate served the purpose of foot passengers, who approached or departed from the grounds through the woodland walk, already mentioned. The mansion had no architectural beauty, but there was something in its vine-covered porch and old fashioned roof harmonizing with the scene around it, in which nature had been left untrammelled, though not unaided, by art. Within, the modern improvements which minister to comfort and refinement were not wanting, and above all, there was ever a kindly welcome for their friends, a cheerful reception for their acquaintance, hospitality for the wayfarer, and sympathy and charity for the suffering poor, from the excellent Mr. and Mrs. Vivian.

In this pleasant home had Louisa Vivian passed her life, except two years which had been spent at a boarding school of celebrity in New York. From this, she had only returned a few months when we introduce her to the reader. Louisa had known but one misfortune in her life. She was an only child. No brother or sister, claimed with her the tenderness of her parents, the attention of visitors or the service of her father's domestics. Louisa was affectionate and not ungenerous by nature, but the object of undivided care and interest to all around her, we can scarcely be surprised that the Upas tree of selfishness should have sprung up in her heart and threatened to shed its poison over her life. This evil was the more dangerous because it did not manifest itself in a glaring or vulgar form. Louisa had always been ready to share her cakes or her toys with her playmates, her books or trinkets with her companions at school, and now, the beggar found ready access to her purse, and the waiting maid, as she trimmed her bonnet with the scarce faded ribbon, or tied around her neck the gay handkerchief, her young lady had given, lauded her generosity. But Louisa, had never relinquished a taste, suppressed a desire, or controlled an emotion, for an other's sake. She knew not what it was to subdue repining and regretful thoughts, to bring back by mental effort the sunshine to her heart and the smile to her face, lest her clouds should throw their shadow on another's peace. Do you think we demand of her an impossible achievement? By the blessing of God on humble prayer and persevering effort, this may be, and has been often done, and the result is that perfect, unbroken peace, which the world can never give.

One morning in the flowery month of June, Louisa declining her father's invitation to walk or ride with him, sauntered into a small shaded sitting room, and taking a book from the centre table, threw herself into a rocking chair and was soon apparently absorbed in the sorrows of Ethelinda, or Elfrida or some other of those "perfect monsters which the world ne'er saw," whose impossible adventures too often make the staple of Circulating Libraries. Around the window near her clustered the rose, and honey-suckle, whose mingled odor filled the room in which she sat. The morning breeze made soft music among the branches of the old trees, and as it lifted their verdant screen and gave entrance to the dancing sunbeams, a thousand dew drops, like mimic suns, flashed back their radiance. But what knew Louisa, in the artificial world which a forced and sickly imagination had conjured around her, of all this wealth of beauty and natural, healthy enjoyment? Nothing, absolutely nothing. So absorbed was her attention by the book she was reading, that she heard not the opening of the door behind her, and started with surprise, as a pleasant voice beside her asked, "In Dream land Louisa?" "Miss Milton!" exclaimed Louisa, as with a half sigh and half smile, she closed her book and rose to welcome a lady apparently ten years her senior, whose countenance was far more expressive of the enjoyment which we are accustomed to regard as the companion of youth, than that of her younger friend. The contrast thus exhibited, seemed to be observed by Mrs. Vivian, who had entered with Miss Milton, for, with a smile which had in it something of sadness, she said, "Miss Milton, I wish you could teach Louisa the secret of being always happy as you seem to be."

"I should think it a secret easily learned, by one so pleasantly situated as Louisa. My directions to her would be, only to keep her senses awake and her heart open to the thousand sources of enjoyment, with which God has surrounded her."

To be concluded.

Original.

BURIAL SCENE AT SEA.

BY H. M. PARSONS.

For several weeks after we had left our native shore, favoring airs had wafted us on our course. But the wind began to freshen and through the night our vessel plunged and rolled under double-reefed top-sails. At sunrise there was a sudden calm, but the appearance of the clouds scudding across the heavens and a dark mantle of vapor along the western horizon, portended an approaching gale. The ship rocked on the heavy cross-seas and the sails flapped to and fro against the masts while the peterel whistled his shrill call as he flitted around us.

The hardy seamen had scarcely close-reefed the top-sails before the storm came on. The sea-water lifted from the surface by the gale, swept across the ship, while the waves jerked her with fearful violence. A heavy sea striking forward carried away the bulwarks, deluging the deck. At this moment the mate rushed from below, exclaiming—"We have sprung a leak," an annunciation which sent a dismal foreboding to the boldest heart. An hour later, the scene was appalling. The ship lay to under bare poles, every sea making a breach over her and every clank of the pumps increasing the terror of the crew.

As hope departed, an invalid youth who had hitherto remained below summoned all his strength and reached the deck. Turning to the Captain he inquired in a calm and subdued tone—" Is there no prospect but a watery grave ?"

"None that I can see" he replied. "We have done all that man can do and if this tempest continues long, we must inevitably perish. God only can deliver us."

"They who put their trust in Him are safe," replied the youth, "even amid the roar of the angry elements. I hoped when I entered upon this voyage that it would please the Almighty to return me to my home and my loved ones, in the enjoyment of invigorated health. But before I embarked I gave myself and my friends unreservedly to Him who sought me, when a wanderer, and led me to his fold, and in this solemn hour I would not if I could, recall that surrender. I have no fears for myself," but turning to the collected ship's company, he added "I have many fears that few of you are prepared to meet the awful fate before us, as the Christian only can. Let us bow to that Great Being who alone can still the tempest—who alone can enable us to look beyond— above this scene and find a Savior waiting to be gracious."

Amid the fury of the blast, the youth poured forth his heart to God, and there were none to treat his prayer with trifling or indifference. At such a time with what vividness does the future press upon the soul. How does the great man feel his littleness—the strong his frailty—the wise his ignorance—the rich his poverty—the bold contemner of religion his need of pardon through the Lamb of God. But Oh ! what folly can equal that of postponing until an hour like this, or of deferring to the last sickness, a prepartion to meet our final Judge. Surely, it is not a favorable opportunity to seek neglected mercy, when the mind is agitated with conflicting thoughts, and harrowing fears.

The effort of the youth was to much for his feeble frame, and the Captain conveyed him to his berth.

Two hours longer, did the tempest continue with unabated force, and when it broke, the ship was a melancholy and crippled thing. But for days after the leak was stopped, there was not a heart on board, from which the memory of the hours of danger was obliterated. The voice of blasphemy was hushed, and many a vow of reformation made when escape seemed hopeless, was still unforgotten, though unredeemed.

The ocean was gently fanned by a mild south-west breeze, on the fourteenth evening that succeeded the subsiding of the gale, as the invalid was brought again on deck, that he might inhale the invigorating air It had been evident since his embarkation that every hour at sea, was diminishing his strength. His eye had now assumed an almost unearthly brightness, and his countenance betokened the progress of disease.

"I would speak yet again with your ship's company" said he, "while reclining in the Captain's arms." When they had gathered around him amid-ships at the call of the commander, the youth proceeded—"I thought to die while the elements above and around me, were warring for the mastery over us all—but I take my last look upon the expanse of ocean when the winds are hushed and when the sun beams with uncommon mildness, and would not have it otherwise. O, it is sweet in the last moments of life, to feel the grace of a merciful and Almighty Savior extended to the spirit as it enters the dark valley of the shadow of death. Listen to the voice of a dying Believer, and remember his last admonition—Delay not, to make your peace with God." His voice faltered, and he slept, nay,

"It was not sleep, it was not rest
But glory opening to the blest."

While the bell tolled at twilight on the following day, there was a paleness on the faces of those who had assembled to commit the departed to the sea. At the sudden splash in the waters many a heart followed the disappearing form not to its resting in the caverns of the deep, but to that world where the ransomed by a Savior's blood, shall never sin nor suffer more.

SOLILOQUY OF THE SOUL.

BY REV. HERMAN HOOKER.

" The Lord is my portion, saith my soul." I have tried all creatures, and would rest in them no longer. They cannot return me the good I would confer, much less the good I need. The love with which I have loved them, they have turned into sorrow, and made that wither and recoil within me, which would assimilate to them and convert them to something like, yea better than myself. I would try them no more, and like a leaf torn from its elevation, and borne by the violence of the storm, till it meets with a sure obstruction and falls the image of quiet, I would rather remain in such a lodgment as I have, and though detached from the place in which I had sought to bloom, yet feeling changes and storms no more.

I have not found the water or the bread of life in the springs or the productions of earth. I have exhausted every thing. I have the "lively prints" and "fair ideas" of a good I have never attained. I have had friendships and alliances, and they contain not, and but poorly resemble what I seek. I must have something lovelier, purer, and safer; and I cannot despair of what I am made to require. I am not myself a delusion, though I may be deluded. I can find nothing on which to rest out of God. He who can confer on me lasting happiness must be superior to myself. I must feel that I am a learner, and yet not unlearned in his excellence. He must have something for me to love; like the vine, I shall wither and die, if I have nothing to embrace. I must be able for ever to ascend and descend, and find him above and below me still. I must have something for curiosity and discovery as well as for adoration and praise, and in God I find all I need.

Such is the soliloquy of the soul declaring its nature in the expression of its wants, and exulting in the discovery and participation of a suitable good. Its course must be onward, and upward, and without end. It must have something to love supremely; and it will love and embrace nothing as a sufficient good so long as it can see any thing above or beyond it that is better. Admitted to the open presence of the Majesty on high, it sees nothing beyond; it is comprehended in an incomprehensible blessedness; it is lost in a boundless radiance, a visible glory, a fulness of every good; it neither slumbers any more, nor is weary any more, but runs its endless courses with excitements ever fresh, and with a recompense full of glory.

Selected.

TRUE COURAGE.

Dare to be honest, just, magnanimous, true to your God, to your country, to yourselves and the world. Dare to do to others as you would have them do to you. There is a moral courage, which enables a man to triumph over foes more formidable than were ever marshalled by any Cæsar. A courage which impels him to do his duty—to hold fast his integrity—to maintain a conscience void of offence towards God and towards men—at every hazard and sacrifice—in defiance of the world, and of the prince of the world. Such was the courage of Moses, of Joseph, of Daniel, of Aristides, of Phocion, of Regulus, of Paul, of Luther, of Washington. Such is the courage which sustains every good man, amidst the temptations, honors, conflicts, opposition, which threaten him at every stage of his progress through life. It is not a noisy, boastful courage which pushes itself into notice when there is no real danger, but which shrinks away when the enemy is at the door. It is calm, self-possessed, meek, unostentatious, retiring; but when the fearful hour arrives, then you shall behold the majesty of genuine christian courage, in all her native energy and grandeur, breathing the spirit of angelic purity, and grasping victory from the furnace or the lion's den, when none of the millions of this world's heroes would have ventured to share her fortune. "I fear God, and I have no other fear," is one of the sublimest sentiments ever felt or uttered by man.

Selected.

Original.

THE STORM.

Adown the mountain's rugged side,
　Across the spreading plain,
Above the ocean's swelling tide,
　The tempest holds its reign.
The forest's pride, the golden grain,
　Are laid along its path,
And far upon the heaving main,
　The waves resound its wrath.

Yet fiercer is the storm to those,
　Whose dreams of life have proved
But thorns beneath the blushing rose
　Which they have nursed and loved.
When friends, wealth, fame and pleasure die,
　What clouds o'ercast their mind.
No ray illumes their darken'd sky,
　No refuge can they find.

But if with conscious guilt, the soul
　Should pass death's dreaded night,
Justice, her thunder tones will roll
　Forever, on its flight.
Remember ye, who never gave
　One penitential sigh,
A storm will come you cannot brave,
　The frown of Him on high.

Faint not O Christian, though a train
　Of trials, doubts and fears,
Fierce conflict in your heart maintain,
　Through all life's passing years.
The clouds will break—the storm will cease,
　The winds be hush'd in rest ;
And light, the light of endless peace
　Irradiate your breast.

Original.

THE CHEVALIER OF THE LEGION OF HONOR AND THE BIBLE.

BY REV. ROBERT BAIRD, D. D.

On a Sabbath in the summer of 1835, while attending the French Protestant Chapel in the city of Paris, which with my family I was in the habit of frequenting when not occupied in preaching, a gentleman and his wife came in and took a seat immediately before me. My attention was soon called to the appearance and conduct of these persons. They acted at first, like those who had not been in the habit of attending a place of public worship. Every thing seemed strange to them. But when the service commenced, I remarked that they listened with deep attention. During the sermon, as well as the singing of the sweet hymns which were used on this occasion, tears in abundance rolled down their cheeks. The text was "I have set the Lord always before me." The minister was the excellent Pastor, Audebez, one of the best French preachers in Paris. Sabbath after sabbath they came to the chapel, until they could no longer forbear to speak to Mr. A. and ask him to visit them. He went, and they told him the following history of their lives.

Having a little property, they had lived with great simplicity in a retired part of the city, devoting much of their time to reading and seeking such amusements as that great Capital so abundantly furnishes to prevent men from thinking of their immortal interests. Year after year thus passed away. They frequented no church for their minds were imbued with the infidelity which prevails among so many of their countrymen.

One day, the Chevalier as he passed through a street, saw a Colporteur selling Bibles. Inquiring the price, he was struck with its being so inconsiderable. He resolved to purchase one. Carrying it home, he told his wife what he had done. "Why did you buy it," said she. "Are you not aware that no one in France believes the Bible, especially in respectable circles?" "That is true" said he, "but as it was so cheap, I thought I would buy it as a piece of antiquity," COMME PIECE DE ANTIQUITE as he expressed it. With this explanation his wife was satisfied, and they sat down to its perusal. On their progress through the first part of it they were greatly amused with the old stories which they found. But while reading the book of Psalms, they became awakened to a deep sense of their sins; and then they began to read with earnestness. They read it through and through—they prayed to God to have mercy upon them. Month after month rolled away. At length they found peace in believing, and immediately commenced the worship of God in their family; even before they had any knowledge that such a thing was practised in any other family, for they were wholly ignorant of the religious world.

As soon as they had found Christ they regarded it as their duty to inquire whether there were any in Paris who knew any thing of this wonderful religion which they had found in their Bible. For this purpose they went to a Roman Catholic Church in their neighborhood. It was High Mass. They tarried till the service was about half concluded, when the wife said to her husband, "let us go home; these people do not know the Great God of our Bible." They went home, and for months seemed to have given up all expectation of finding any one who was acquainted with this religion.

At length the woman having occasion to enter a shop to buy some article, endeavored to persuade the person who kept it to purchase a Bible. "Oh," said she, "the Bible is a beautiful thing," LA BIBLE EST UNE BELLE CHOSE. As she said this, a pious lady came in and added, "Yes, the Bible is a beautiful thing; but the preaching of the Gospel is another beautiful thing." "I can readily believe it" said the wife of the Chevalier "but where can one find it in Paris?" "Oh," said the other, "if you will go to such a street," giving the name "and to such a number and ascend to the third story, you will there find a chapel and may hear the preaching of the Gospel." They went the following Sabbath, and there I met them under the circumstances just related.

How strikingly does this narrative illustrate the utility and importance of distributing the Scriptures! Here we find a family made acquainted with the Great Salvation by the perusal of the Bible. I have known an instance, in which one New Testament was the means under the divine blessing of the conversion of five individuals in a village in the eastern part of France. Who then, that loves God's word, would not do all in his power, to place it in the possession of the millions who are destitute of it, in France and other Roman Catholic Countries.

And what a convincing proof of the sufficiency of the Sacred Scriptures to enlighten, convert and sanctify the hearts of men, when attentively and prayerfully read! Here we have an instance in which the reading of God's word without the aid of notes, comments or "traditions of men" brought two souls to a clear knowledge of eternal life and instructed them in the duties of a christian family. What an illustration of the truth of the Psalmist—"The entrance of thy word giveth light, it giveth understanding to the simple.

THE FIRST LIE REBUKED.

Our mother had taken infinite pains to assure us of one great truth—the Omnipresence of an Omniscient God—and this I never could for a moment shake off. It influenced us both, in a powerful manner, so that if either committed a fault, we never rested until through mutual exhortation on the ground that God certainly knew it, and would be angry if we added deceit to another error, we had encouraged each other to confession. We then went hand in hand to our mother, and the

THE FIRST LIE REBUKED. 29

one who stood clear of the offence acknowledged in the name of the transgressor, while both asked pardon.

Never did children more abhor a lie; we spurned at its meanness, while trembling at its guilt; and nothing bound us more closely and exclusively together than the discoveries we were always making of a laxity among other children in this respect. On such occasions we would shrink into a corner by ourselves and whisper, "do you think God does not hear that?"

Self-righteousness, no doubt, existed in a high degree; we were young Pharisees, rejoicing in the external cleanliness of cup and platter; but I look back with great thankfulness on the mercy that so far instructed us; an habitual regard to truth has carried me safely through many a trial, and as a means, guarded me from many a snare. It cannot be too early or too strongly inculcated; nor should any effort be considered too great, any difficulty as too discouraging, and reprobation as too strong, or I will add, any punishment too severe, when the object in view is to overcome this vice in a child.

Once I remember having been led into a lie, at the instigation, and through the contrivance of a servant girl, for whose benefit it was told. Suspicion instantly arose, from my dreadful embarrassment of manner; a strict investigation commenced; the girl told me to face it out, for that nobody else knew of it, and she would not flinch. But my terrors of conscience were insupportable; I could ill bear my father's steady eye fixed on mine, still less the anxious, wondering, incredulous expression of my brother's innocent face, who would not for a moment fancy me guilty. I confessed at once; and with a heavy sigh my father sent to borrow from a neighbor an instrument of chastisement never before needed in his own house.

He took me to another room, and said, "Child, it will pain me more to punish you thus, than any blows I can inflict will pain you; but I must do it; you have told a lie; a dreadful sin, a base, mean, cowardly action. If I let you grow up a liar you will reproach me for it one day ; if I now spared the rod I should hate the child." I took the punishment in a most extraordinary spirit ; I wished every stroke had been a stab ; I wept because the pain was not great enough ; and I loved my father better at that moment, better than even I, who almost idolized him, had ever loved him before. I thanked him, and I thank him still ; for I never transgressed that way again.

The servant was called, received her wages, and a most awful lecture, and was discharged the same hour. Yet of all things that sank deepest in my very soul, were the cries of my little brother, and the lamentable tone of his soft voice, pleading through the closed door, "Oh papa, don't whip poor Charlotte ! Oh, forgive poor Charlotte !"

It is sweet to know we have a brother indeed who always pleads, and never pleads in vain for the offending child ; a Father whose chastisements are not withheld, but administered in tender love ; judgment being his strong work, and mercy that wherein he delights, and the peaceable fruits of righteousness the end of his corrections.

Selected.

THE DIAMOND, THE PEARL OF GREAT PRICE.

A ROUGH diamond lay in the sand, among many other ordinary stones. A boy picked up some of them to play with, and carried them home, together with the diamond, but he knew not what it was. The father of the boy, watching his play, observed the diamond, and said to his son ; Give me that stone ! The boy did so, and smiled, for he thought to himself—what will my father do with that stone ?

But he took and skilfully cut the stone into regular facets, and polished the diamond, which then sparkled gloriously.

Behold, said the father, here is the stone which thou gavest to me. Then was the boy amazed at the brilliancy of the stone and cried—Father, how hast thou wrought this change?

I knew, said the father, the value and hidden properties of the crude stone, and I removed the crust in which it was enveloped, and now it shines with its natural splendor.

In process of time, when the boy had grown up to manhood, his father gave him the precious stone, as an emblem of the heart that is freed from base passions and purified by virtue.

REMARK. The Boy was made very rich by the gift of his Father. The child that possesses the Pearl of GREAT PRICE, a new heart, is rich indeed; and with all the treasures of the World, without an interest in the Savior's love, he is poor indeed! Ed.

Original.

THE LONE WIDOW.

ON a cold unpleasant day in May, which might well have been taken for a November day, but for the fresh green of the grass and trees, I looked from the window upon the cheerless prospect. Beside me stood a lady, in deep mourning. Sadness rested on her countenance, yet occasionally a smile passed over it betraying the natural cheerfulness of her disposition.

On the lawn in front of us stood a small lilac tree, bearing a single blossom—it had opened amid sunshine, the song of birds, and the pleasant breeze. Dark clouds were above it, cold winds shook it rudely, and it seemed striving but vainly, to catch one gleam of the sunshine that had welcomed its birth.

"Look" said my companion, "at that solitary lilac." "Yes, said she, it is a lone one." Half smiling, she sighed deeply, while her eyes as they met mine were filled with tears. She resumed her seat, and seemed lost in deep and painful thought—perhaps she called to mind the happy days when that lilac was first planted; perhaps, she thought of the hand that watered it, now cold, and mouldering—of the eye which watched and welcomed its opening buds, now lustreless and dead, or like me, was struck with the resemblance between her situation, and that of the lone lilac, as I had thoughtlessly called it. She was born under the sunshine, nursed in the lap of plenty and beloved by all around her. Eighteen months before, she was blessed with all on earth that could make her happy—the fondest of husbands, the kindest of mothers, the loveliest of babes, were hers. Such was her situation, when the blight came. Disease and Death fell upon the happy family—her fondest hopes were crushed—he whom she loved better than life was stretched upon a bed of suffering; the strong man was brought low, his powerful mind grew feeble, memory failed, and naught was left but the wreck of that noble spirit. Yet even here, our Heavenly Father showed his mercy. Though on every other subject the sufferer's mind was impaired, still on the one, all-important, the hope of life beyond the grave, it was clear—every other string was broken, but, touch that and the harp sent forth sweet music. While thus he lay hovering between life and death, the destroying angel smote the bud of promise, clasping in his cold arms, the youngest and loveliest of all. Anxiety for the suffering one sustained the almost broken-hearted mother, but Death had not yet finished his strange work and while she was watching over her husband's sick bed, he suddenly snatched away her mother. Three months passed, and her husband was no more. She was indeed, a LONE WIDOW—two little children were all the ties that bound her to life.

Years past—silently I had marked the course of the widow. She had found a few friends, her children had been blessings to her, and promised soon to become useful members of society. Dark clouds had rolled over her, the storm had lasted long; now the rainbow of promise was seen; a brighter day dawned, she forgot the severe lesson she had learned. Again, she trusted to earth, as if the joys of life could never fail. With pride she gazed upon her son, the image of his sire, and fondly hoped that he would be the comfort of her life, the solace and support of her age. Mistaken woman! Night came on, the rainbow's brilliant hues vanished. Consumption seized her son. Slowly and steadily he wasted away, gently descending to the tomb; but a ray of light marked his path, for the bright hopes of the Gospel were his. Now the widow's idol was again torn from her. She was left with a delicate daughter to struggle on, as best she might, in a cold and heartless world. At first, she was left to murmur against her God, and against HIS love, who had so often chastised her, but soon a change came over her and she was happy—happier far than when she was the pride of affectionate parents, happier than when a blooming bride, in the sunshine of prosperity; happier than when she imprinted the first warm kiss, on the brow of her first born. Strange! that she should be so happy; her husband, her mother, her babe, her manly son, all gone to the grave, while she was left in the midst of adversity; a lone widow! Why was she happy? God had breathed peace into her soul—had shed the calm light of resignation over her path—had shown her that his dealings with her, had been through tender love, and that as he saw her heart cling to Earth, he had taken her earthly treasures to Heaven.

INSCRIPTION ON THE TOMB STONE OF MRS. HEMANS.

"CALM on the bosom of thy God,
  Fair spirit rest thee now;
E'en while with us thy footsteps trod,
  His seal was on thy brow.
Dust, to its narrow house beneath;
  Soul, to its place on high:
They that have seen thy look in death,
  No more may fear to die."

Selected.

Original

FAMILIAR ILLUSTRATIONS OF PRAYER,

FOR CHILDREN.

BY WILLIAM CUTTER, ESQ.

ELLEN was a very quiet and thoughtful little girl of about nine years of age. She had always been an attendant on the Sabbath School, since she was old enough to read, and was conscientious in endeavoring to follow the directions of her teacher. On one occasion, she came running into the house, as if in great haste to get something. But it was not her playthings that she wanted. She took a chair, and sat down by the side of her mother, and said, "Mother, my teacher asks me almost every Sabbath, when I go to school, if I have learned to pray." I told him, that I always say, "Our Father" every night when I go to bed, and every morning when I get up, and still he continues to ask me if I have prayed this week, or if I have learned to pray. What does my teacher mean, mother? How can I learn to pray, but by saying, 'our Father who art in Heaven,' as you always taught me?"

"I will tell you, my dear," said her mother; "but first tell me why do you say your prayers every night and morning?"

"Because you always told me to, mother, and said I should be naughty, and God would not love me if I did not."

"Is that all the reason, my dear?" Don't you pray to God because you love him, and because you know he hears your prayer, and will give you what you ask?"

"I don't know, mother, how CAN such a little girl as I pray so—I can't see God.'

"No, my child but"——

Just at this moment, company came in, and Ellen was obliged to go away, without receiving an answer, or feeling that she knew how to pray better than before. The company staid so late in the evening, she was obliged to retire, and say her prayer as usual, wondering what her teacher could want her to do more. But she thought much of it, and laid awake a long while, trying to imagine what her mother would say to her on the subject.

The next morning, when Ellen awoke, she was quite sick. Her head ached very much, and she did not know what to do. She tried to get up, but when she moved, her head pained her more and more. And she began to cry, and call her mother. "Oh! mother," she said, as soon as her mother opened the door, "I am very sick, and my head feels very badly, what shall I do? mother do help me". Her mother told her to lie down, and keep as still as possible, while she went to prepare some medicine for her, that would make her feel better. Ellen did as she was told, for she knew her mother loved her, and would do all she could for her. Very soon her mother came and took her away into her own room, where she had caused a good fire to be made, and where also she had prepared the medicine, which she thought her little girl needed. Here she watched over her all day and night; and when Ellen wanted anything she would call her mother—and this was very often, for she was feverish and thirsty.

The next day, Ellen was better, and in the afternoon was able to sit up a little while, and talk with her mother. "My dear," said her mother, "I will tell you what you wished to know about prayer, the other day. When you awoke yesterday morning, and felt sick, why did you call me?"

"Because, mother, I felt very badly, and did not know what to do for myself."

"But why call me, when I was not in the room, and you could not see me?"

"Because, I thought you could hear me, and would come to me, and I am sure you love me, and will always try to make me well when I am sick."

"And what made you think that I could do any thing to make you feel better?"

"Because you always do, when I am sick."

"Well, my dear Ellen, if you will remember this, it will

help you to know something about praying to God. You could not see me, and yet you called me, and you believed that I should hear you, you must feel just so about God, when you pray to him. You must feel that he is always near you, though you cannot see him—for the Bible says, he is every where. You believed I should hear you, and come to you, when you called me. So you must believe that God will always hear you, when you ask any thing of him, because he has promised to do so, and he loves to have little children pray to him."

"You thought I could help you, because I love you, and you say I always have helped you when you was sick before. God loves all his creatures, but especially he loves those who love him. He is your father, and gives you every good thing that you need. And you ought to love him, and believe if you want any thing that is good, and ask him for it, he will give it to you. When you called me, you felt that you could not do any thing for yourself—you did not know what to do. So you must feel, when you pray to God, that you need his help, and must perish without it. Will you think of this, my dear child, and try when you say your prayers to night, to remember all I have told you?"

"Yes, my dear mother, I will—and now I remember, my teacher has often told me I was a sinner, and that sin was a disease, and no one could make me well but God. I mean to ask God, to night, to cure me of sin. When you say your prayers, will you ask him too, mother?"

WASHINGTON AND HIS MOTHER.

Young George was about to go to sea as a midshipman; every thing was arranged, the vessel lay opposite his father's house, the little boat had come on shore to take him off, and his whole heart was bent on going. After his trunk had been carried down to the boat, he went to bid his mother farewell, and saw the tears bursting from her eyes. However, he said nothing to her; but he saw that his mother would be distressed if he went, and perhaps never be happy again. He just turned round to the servant and said, "Go and tell them to fetch my trunk back. I will not go away to break my mother's heart." His mother was struck with his decision, and she said to him, "George, God has promised to bless the children that honor their parents, and I believe he will bless you."

Original.

RE-UNION AND INFLUENCE OF THE SANCTIFIED FAMILY CIRCLE.

BY DANIEL R. HEATH.

Of all the sources of enjoyment with which earth is filled, few things are more productive of real enjoyment than the re-union of a happy family circle.

The meeting of near and dear friends after the lapse of years, to whom it has pleased Providence to assign different spheres of action, brings to mind many of the scenes of earlier life, and calls from the records of time, the remembrance of parental fondness and love.

How solemn, how interesting the scene. How impressive to the reflecting mind, that through all the vicissitudes of a life in this business world, the influences which had been exerted upon the youthful mind had had their proper effect, and produced in maturer years the result we contemplate. The prattling boy, who once sat upon the knee of an anxious father, receiving from his well stored mind the inestimable truths of Revelation, now presents himself before the parent, the full grown man with vigorous mind, and unclouded intellect, and conscious of his dignity as being the son of such a father. Dignity how illustrious! To be a Christian, a pattern to the world.

And a daughter too, who received from a fond mother, her first lessons in virtue, and the inculcation of those divine truths which lay the foundation for the developement of the amiable qualities which constitute the true dignity of female character, she also appears in all the innocence and loveliness of womanhood. How delighted now is that venerable pair in beholding those whom they had so well equipped for the stormy sea of life, and upon whose billowy surges they have so far rode triumphant. What a trophy this, of the diligent and anxious solicitude of pious parents. A reward more valuable than the favor of Princes, or the wealth of empire. Once more seated around that revered altar, which years before, had been consecrated as the shrine of sincere devotion, the aged father now takes from its place, the 'old family Bible,' which for years, had borne testimony to the fidelity of its owner, and reads from its inspired pages as did the patriarch of old, suitable passages for their edification. And then the venerable man with characteristic humility bows to the throne of Grace, supplicates the divine favor, and returns heartfelt thanks to the Almighty giver of all good, for his watchful care and super-abundant mercy in preserving the lives of his numerous family and permiting them once more to surround the same fire-side, and participate in the same precious enjoyments that had blest their earlier days.

What a pleasing sight, what a blissful reward, conferred upon the declining years of the pious parent. Would that thousands of fathers and mothers in this Christian land would emulate their example—that every fire-side might become an altar to God, and every house a Bethel from which might ascend perpetual praise to his name. Would that every christian father and mother, would properly appreciate the inestimable privilege that God has given them of acting so prominent a part in the cultivation of the mind and heart. Would that they were conscious of the tremendous weight of responsibility that rests upon the parent in the discharge of his incumbent duties. Would that every parent might consider that each of his family circle, will, not many years hence act a part in wielding human society, and that his influence will then correspond with the mould that was given to his character while young. To think that here is a mind that at some future day, is to exert an influence upon the affairs of nations and perhaps constitute the pivot upon which the destinies of nations are to turn, is a thought that should occupy the mind of every parent, and incite him to the full discharge of his duties.

What a thought that fifty years hence, those who now occupy places of influence, honor and trust will be counted among those who were, but are not, and their places be filled by those who are trained to follow them—that men now in infancy, are to rise in due time and hold the reins of civil government, to whose wisdom and genius we are to look for the preservation of the principles of republican government. And who, are to be the champions of truth? Those who now compose that interesting group, the family circle. Yes, from the family circle, they shall go forth, who shall stand in the temple of liberty, and upon the walls of Zion, and control the destinies of this great and growing republic.

INFIDELITY.

It was amid the luxury of Greece and Rome, the bosom of the wealth of Indostan, of the pomp of Persia, of the voluptuousness of China, of the overflowing abundance of European capitals, that men first started up, who dared to deny the existence of a Deity. On the contrary the houseless Tartar, the Savages of America, the negroes without foresight and without a police, the inhabitants of the rude climates of the north, such as the Laplander, the Greenlander, the Esquimaux—see God every where, even in a flint.

Pierre.

ORIGINAL.

PATMOS. 7s double.   HASTINGS.
(ARRANGED.)

1. Je-sus, lov-er of my soul,
While the bil-lows near me roll,
Let me to thy bo-som fly
While the tem-pest still is nigh;
Hide me, O my Sav-iour, hide,
Till the storm of life be past;
Safe into the ha-ven guide,
Oh, re-ceive my soul at last!

2. Other refuge have I none,
  Lo! I helpless hang on thee:
Leave, oh leave me not alone,
  Lest I basely shrink and flee:
Thou art all my trust and aid,
  All my help from thee I bring;
Cover my defenceless head
  With the shadow of thy wing.

3. Thou, O Christ, art all I want;
  Boundless love in thee I find;
Raise the feeble, cheer the faint,
  Heal the sick, and lead the blind.
Just and holy is thy name;
  I am all unrighteousness,
Vile and full of sin I am;
  Thou art full of truth and grace.

THE IRIS, OR RAINBOW.

How oft have I viewed thee, all glorious and bright,
In the pride of thy birth-place, thou vision of light;
Like an angel of gladness, in mercy designed
As a token and herald of love to mankind.
There, too, where the floods of the desert resound,
Thou reignest unmoved by the tumult around;
And the eye may repose on thy soft smiling beams,
And the fancy may hail thee the Nymph of the streams.
Oh! thus, when the moments of sorrow are nigh,
When the stern voice of Nature shall call us to die;
At that thrilling hour, when in anguish and pain,
Our spirits return to life's pleasures in vain;
May Peace with her soft silv'ry pinions be there,
To chase from our bosoms the phantom Despair;
May Hope, gentle Hope, with her sweetness illume
The darkness that shadows the depth of the tomb.

RURAL DEVOTION.

Engraved for the Christian Family Magazine.

THE
CHRISTIAN FAMILY ANNUAL.

LETTERS TO THE YOUNG,
ON THE WAY OF SALVATION.
BY THE EDITOR.

RESPECTED READER, As an affectionate counselor, as a kind, elder brother, I have long desired to present, for your serious consideration, several topics of more than ordinary interest. And the first shall be, The Way of Salvation. My object, in a series of short letters, will be to give a candid, explicit, practical answer to this important inquiry, "What must I do to be saved?"

The greatest question that ever agitated the world is, Who shall at last eternally be saved? The redemption of this fallen province of God's empire has awakened a thrilling interest in Heaven, and has resulted in the most wonderful, magnificent exhibition of Divine condescension and benevolence ever witnessed in the universe. The angels, those lofty intelligences, who once struck their harps in living melody around the throne of God, on their rebellion were cast off without a day of grace, "and are reserved in everlasting chains under darkness, unto the judgment of the great day."

Not so with man. After his apostacy a probation was given him, a Saviour was promised, a ransom was provided, salvation was offered, and this proclamation was sent forth—"He that believeth and is baptized shall be saved, and he that believeth not shall be damned."

I design, hereafter, to explain and enforce the terms of acceptance, the way of life. In this introductory letter, the single object I have in view is, to earnestly bespeak your immediate attention to this great subject, which has not only awakened so much concern in Heaven, but which has resulted in the incarnation, sufferings and sacrifice of the son of God, in the gift of the Holy Spirit and of a Divine revelation, in the establishment of a church and of a preached gospel.

Youthful reader, the safety, the salvation of the immortal soul, next to the glory of God, is the only all-absorbing interest which can reasonably command your undivided attention on this side of the grave. Though short and hurried the term of mortal life, from infancy to maturity, from the cradle to the coffin, it is the measure of your probation, and must fix unchangeably and forever, your destiny in the world to come— As in the natural world, the autumnal harvest succeeds the season of seed-time—the sunshine and showers of summer, so in the moral, the impressions of childhood, the character and conduct of youth and of riper years must constitute the momentous seed-time, of which an immortal life beyond the tomb will be the harvest. For "Whatsoever a man soweth, that shall he also reap. He that soweth to his flesh shall of the flesh reap corruption; but he that soweth to the Spirit shall of the Spirit reap life everlasting."

If the topic of discussion were the loss or gain of a kingdom, it would arouse you to the most vigorous action. But how trifling will all the dazzling glories of royalty appear in a dying hour; in the great day of assize, when God shall make up his jewels, and award to men and angels according as their works have been?

Were the riches and honors of the whole world laid at your feet, and should you turn away from these with cold indifference, what but madness would this act be pronounced? And what shall we denominate the conduct of the deluded sinner who sleeps in moral supineness over the dearest interests of the soul, while he is momentarily liable to be summoned to the bar of the Judge?

The most prolonged life is but the dawn—the dim twilight of an endless existence, and yet, short and uncertain as is your sojourn here, it is your glorious seed-time—eternity is the harvest.

Is he not a FRIEND who sounds the note of alarm when you are in peril, and who flies to your rescue? Did consumption fasten on your vitals, would it not be a mark of friendship should your physician tell you of your danger, and urge you, before it should be too late forever, to apply a safe and sovereign remedy? Did an assassin stand by your bedside, and hold to your breast a fatal dagger or bludgeon—or were your burning roof just ready to fall in upon your defenseless slumbers, would not that man be considered a friend who should sound the note of alarm and snatch you from the jaws of ruin? But what are the dangers which thicken around your mortal footsteps, and which may speedily result in the destruction of your frail body, compared with those that threaten the immortal soul?

Youthful reader, as your friend, let me seriously urge you to secure an interest in the Saviour without delay. All that can awaken hope and excite fear should lead you to give no sleep to your eyes nor slumber to your eye-lids, until you have made your peace with God. The most refreshing encouragements and promises in the Scriptures are made to the young. "They that seek me early shall find me." "Remember now thy Creator in the days of thy youth, while the evil days come not, nor the years draw nigh when thou shalt say, I have no pleasure in them."

No picture upon which the eye of man or angels can rest, is more beautiful than that of youthful piety.

> " A flower, when offered in the bud,
> Is no mean sacrifice."

How sincerely to be pitied, how deeply to be deplored is the condition of that man who has squandered the season of youth, who beholds life, like a distant landscape, disappearing from his view, and old age and the tomb rapidly approaching.

If he has not tasted those refined pleasures, those animating hopes and consolations which are the solace and support of the Christian, what in this life, can give him lasting satisfaction? If he has stored his mind with the richest treasures of learning and philosophy, and can boast of numberless, devoted friends—if he is loaded with the rarest honors which this world can bestow, and all the wealth that heart can desire; what will this avail him in retirement and solitude, in sickness and old age, or in the trying hour when death shall put an end to his day of grace, and hurry the soul to the bar of the Judge?

Think of the situation of the husbandman who suffers the spring to pass away without breaking up his fallow ground, or entrusting the precious seed to the earth; who is compelled not only to look upon his field as waste, but as over-grown with thorns and thistles. How small his prospect of a comfortable subsistence! The natural season of culture and fruitfulness is passed away, and he is left to adopt the lamentation, "The harvest is past, the summer is ended, and I am not saved." Thus it may be with those who waste the moral spring-time of life.

No axiom in mathematics is truer or easier of demonstration than this; A well-spent youth is the only SURE foundation of a peaceful life, of a happy old age. Not one was ever found who regretted commencing the service of God in early life. Oh, if any one thing would be the least possible inducement for a good man to go back to the cradle and live life over again, it would be that he might, from the earliest dawn of reason, through childhood and youth, be devoted soul and body to the service and kingdom of God.

What a change has taken place within a few years? It is a remarkable if not an alarming fact, that comparatively few, within the last twenty years, have been savingly brought to the knowledge of the truth, and added to the churches, who were not in the morning of life. The result of the most careful examination has shown that nine out of ten —in other instances, nineteen out of twenty—were hopefully converted in early life. Once it was entirely the reverse.

If this statement be correct as a general rule, how perilous it must be to put off the work of the soul's salvation beyond the golden season of youth! The light is so bright, the motives and means of grace are so powerful, that it may now be said with an alarming emphasis, "God's spirit will not always strive with man." "Behold now is the accepted time, behold now is the day of salvation."

Oh, it is truly ignoble to put off the all-important and glorious work of your salvation; to crowd the concerns of a life into the moments of an uncertain future. Thousands have done this, and before that "convenient season" came, the winding sheet and cold clods of the valley covered them.

Tell me what 'sacrifice has age to make when he comes bowed down with infirmities, to lay his first offering on the altar? His riches—But can they longer minister to his enjoyments? His palsied hand can no longer tell over his gold. His decayed sight can no more gaze with delight on the accumulated possessions to which his days of strength had been devoted. His honors—Have they not already withered upon his brow? Will he now separate himself from his boon companions? Alas, the populous grave has gathered them into its silent dominion; they have forsaken him. Does he fly from the world? Say rather that the world is slipping from beneath his trembling feet. Ah, who can avoid the supposition that his motive is mercenary, his object selfish. Love does not lead him, with full-hearted devotion, to worship in the temple; but he goes under the power of fear to lay hold on the horns of the altar in God's sanctuary. God forbid that I should mock any, who give up their whole heart to God, even at the latest hour. But he who is driven to the service of God only by the failure of all other sources of enjoyment, will be liable finally to fail of Heaven. Not so with those who 'remember their Creator in the days of their youth.' They make a sacrifice which God has promised to accept, who seek the Lord early. Think of this, dear youthful reader, and be wise in time; and may God give you the rich blessing of His great salvation.'

Original.

THE WOODLAND WALK.*

BY THE AUTHOR OF "BLIND ALICE."

Mrs. Vivian was called from the room as Miss Milton concluded. Louisa did not reply to her, though a deeper shadow fell upon her face. After a few moments of silence, Miss Milton, who had been attentively regarding her young friend, said, "What is the matter, Louisa? Are you not well this morning, or has something occurred to grieve you?"— Still Louisa was silent, but her lip quivered, and tears filled her eyes.

"My dear girl, you distress me," said Miss Milton approaching her, and taking her hand tenderly. "Will you not tell me what causes your sorrow? You may confide in me with safety, Louisa?"

Louisa drew her hand away coldly, and averted her face as she replied, "I have no cause for sorrow, Miss Milton; at least, you think I have none. But we cannot all feel alike, I am sure," she added, with a very audible sigh; "I wish my feelings were not so quick." "Do not wish that, Louisa, for a delicate sensibility will enable you to perceive more quickly, and enjoy more keenly, all the delights of creation. Recollect, one of your favorite poets makes it consist in being 'soonest awake to the FLOWERS,' as well as 'the first to be touched by the THORNS' of existence. To suppose that sensibility consists only in sensitiveness to sorrow, or in the indulgence of that causeless sadness which is the mark of a sickly mind, is an error, from which I think your good sense will preserve you. But put on your bonnet, and come out with me. You will find preachers of cheerfulness abroad."

"I will go with you if you desire it, certainly, Miss Milton, but I can scarcely hope to find any thing very cheering in a walk through woods, where every tree is an old acquaintance. If I could go to new scenes——but it is useless to wish that; my father will not go, and I must live and die here." This

* Continued from page 20.

was said with such sadness that Miss Milton saw at once in this dissatisfaction with home, this desire for novelty—perhaps for the excitement of gay society, the thorn among Louisa Vivian's flowers. Louisa left the room as she ceased speaking to put on her bonnet, and the subject was not resumed till they had commenced their walk. Miss Milton then said, "So you think you are well acquainted with every thing in this wood?"

"Certainly; I have walked in it often enough to be so."

"I have walked in it, at least, as often as you have, and yet, Louisa, I find something new in it at every visit; and I doubt not that every year of my life, I shall continue to find here objects which will gratify my taste, awaken my intellect, and inspire more profound veneration for that Being whose creative power is manifest in the tiny flower and the humble insect, and who, as the 'Ancient Mariner' teaches us, not only made, but 'loveth all.'" Louisa said nothing, and after a while Miss Milton added, "But I have something to do this morning, in which I want your aid. Here," exhibiting as she spoke a small colored engraving, "is a flower, which, I learn from a monthly magazine, blooms in this neighborhood during this month. I have no specimen of it in my herbarium, and I am out this morning in search of it. If you will turn into the wood on that side, I will take this, and we will meet at the gate in half an hour, you have your watch, I see, and report our success. Do not pass any flower without selecting a specimen, for there may be others that I have not." The ladies separated.

Miss Milton, punctual to her appointment, was at the gate in half an hour; though without the desired prize. Not finding Louisa there, she turned back towards the point at which they had parted, pursuing her way through the wood instead of by the path. She had gone more than two-thirds of the way when yet deeper in the wood, she saw Louisa's white dress. She was stooping, and when at Miss Milton's call, she turned to her, her hands were full of flowers, her face flushed with exercise, and her countenance animated in expression.—

How unlike the languid, spiritless Louisa of the morning!— "You have it—you have it!" exclaimed Miss Milton, with all the eagerness of a botanist, as her friend drew near and exhibited her treasures." "And see how beautiful this is, and this." "Yes—yes, but I have those. They are beautiful specimens, however. Bring them along. We will press them, and they will serve for some friend's herbarium, which may not be as well stocked as mine."

"I wish I understood botany; I would have an herbarium, too," said Louisa, as she sat an hour afterwards in Miss Milton's parlor, looking over her beautiful and well-preserved specimens, which were always accompanied by the botanical description of the plant, and frequently by a painting of the flower as it looked before severed from its parent stem.

"Nothing is easier, dear Louisa. An hour's study will teach you the terms used by botanists, and with the aid of some good botanical work, you will then have no difficulty in recognizing and classing your specimens. To make an herbarium is the surest as well as the pleasantest way to learn botany."

Her friend's suggestions were adopted by Louisa, and the gatherings of the morning were consigned to her. No longer were the morning hours of Louisa Vivian wasted in inaction, or worse than wasted in the perusal of books which dwarfed her intellect, and exhausted her sensibilities. Her observation aroused, through every sense streamed into the awakened mind and heart, new delight and beauty from creation. As the flowers withered at the approach of winter, she found other objects of interest in the birds, the small quadrupeds, and even the insects which still inhabited the leafless woods. She never again complained that there was nothing new around her home. From every walk she brought some mental acquisition; and guided by her pious parents, all her acquisitions ministered to a profounder adoration of the Creator.

Mrs. Vivian could never sufficiently evince her gratitude to Miss Milton for having taught Louisa to be as happy as herself.

TRUE GREATNESS.

BY MRS. ELLIS.

"Mother," said Henry Ashton, a thoughtful-looking boy of fourteen, "I wish you would tell me what is meant by true greatness."

"You have asked me a comprehensive and difficult question," replied his mother, "but it is one so worthy of your utmost attention, that I will endeavor to assist you in investigating the subject for yourself, rather than adopt the method your brother likes so much better, of simply telling you what I think, and then leaving your thoughts to wander at will to any other subject."

"One gets quicker over things in that way," observed his younger brother Frederic, a little ashamed of so direct a reference to himself.

"You may well call it getting over things," observed Mrs. Ashton, "for your way of proceeding is very much like that of the farmer, who should walk over his fields of corn, instead of reaping their produce, and storing it up for after use."

"No, mother," said Frederic, "you cannot compare it to anything so bad as that, for the farmer injures his corn by treading it down." "And if you," replied his mother, "do not exactly injure all the subjects you get over so quickly, you injure your own powers of thinking." "How so?" asked Frederic in some astonishment. "Have you never noticed," continued his mother, "that those persons who will not take the trouble to think to any purpose, grow weary of everything, and finally weary every body else by their weariness and discontent."

"But interrupted Frederic, "as soon as they find time to think, or a subject worth thinking about, they can do so at any time." "No, no," replied his mother, "you are greatly mistaken there. We are all the creatures of habit, and a man who has never taken the trouble to think in the season of youth, can no more do so when arrived at middle life, than he who has kept his bed until the age of forty can rise up and make a pleasant excursion on foot to any place he chooses to visit. Besides which, the power of thinking is not merely given us to serve as pastime for the present moment. It is a power, every effort of which has reference to the future ; for by the habit of thinking in youth, we lay up treasures for old age."

" Oh, dear !" said Frederic, heaving a deep sigh, as if the effort were a great deal too hard for him to make, or as if old age were a very long way off, and a sort of thing he did not feel himself at all called upon to contemplate just then.

" I have one more remark to make," observed his mother, " and then we will return, if you please, to the subject with which we began." "And think about it, I suppose, until dinner-time," interrupted Frederic. "That will be as you are disposed," replied his mother, " for, mind me, I cannot compel you to think. I can only advise and entreat you to cultivate this one faculty of your nature, which, above all others, distinguishes you from the brute creation. But I was going to observe that persons who will not take the trouble to think to any purpose are always weary and uninterested, for this simple reason ; that having glanced slightly over many subjects without examining one, nothing is new to them, nothing is fresh, and enlivening, and full of interest to them, as it is to persons who have made use of their own minds."

Frederic now looked up in his mother's face with an expression of inquiry, for this very freshness and interest was what he was perpetually in search of; and he thought, as many foolish and mistaken persons do, that it was only to be found in a rapid succession of subjects, instead of in—what is one of the grand secrets of human life—making the most of a few.

It was well for Henry Ashton, both as a present and a future good, that he was a thoughtful boy ; for he could thus amuse himself with his own reflections while such discussions as the above were going on between his mother and Frederic ; and before they had arrived at any settled conclusion upon the subject at present under consideration, he had taken up the picture of a shepherd boy reclining upon a grassy bank; and if his secret thoughts had been examined, it is more than probable he would have been convicted of a wish to be himself reclining on the banks of that flowing stream, while his peaceful flocks were grazing by his side, or wandering unheeded on the distant hills.

"I am constantly under the necessity of steering between two difficulties," Mrs. Ashton was accustomed to say. "I have one son who thinks too much—or rather who mistakes musing for thinking, and another who will not think at all — Thus, while I do my utmost to engage the attention of the latter, the former is giving up his mind to some day-dream of his own, neither profitable to himself or others; while, if I endeavor to interest him so as to excite him to useful action, the other has probably escaped from me altogether, and is either at the top of the cherry tree over my head, or running races with his dog across a neighboring field. How clever," the good lady used to add, "must those people be who keep schools, and manage all the young gentlemen at once, by the same rule, even to the number of eighty or a hundred. No wonder the march of intellect goes on so rapidly amongst us." "You have not yet told us," said Henry Ashton, "what is true greatness, and I almost think I know." "Let me hear your opinion, then," said his mother, "and that may help me to a clearer explanation of my own."

"I think," said Henry, still gazing at the picture of the shepherd boy, "that true greatness consists in living separate from the vulgar things as well as the vanities of the world, and in thinking only of what is high, and beautiful, and sublime." A loud laugh from Frederic Ashton put an end to his brother's explanation of true greatness.

"You have done it now, Henry," said he; "if you mean that true greatness consists in lying upon a bank all day, with one's eyes cast up to the clouds, and never going home to eat one's dinner or make one's self comfortable, no wonder there are so few people truly great. According to your notions, whatever they might be in mind, they would be little enough in body. Look here, Henry."

And the boy threw himself, as quick as lightning, upon the green lawn, in the attitude of the shepherd, and casting up his eyes, looked as solemn and contemplative as it was possible for him to look under any circumstances. With a movement as rapid, he was again upon his feet, and dashing his hand, with what he considered a masterly stroke, upon that part of the picture where a warrior clad in armor was to be seen, " That's the fellow for me !" he exclaimed, while retreating a few paces, and flourishing his father's walkingstick in the air, he put himself in the attitude of a warrior about to rush upon his foe.

Accustomed to this kind of bravado, Mrs. Ashton and Henry took little notice of a performance which had about as much to do with what to them was true greatness, as the death-blow of the puppet has with the stroke by which a hero dies.

" If, my dear Henry," said his mother, " the occupation of your shepherd is supposed to consist of mere musing, of that dreamy sort of meditation upon the blue sky and sailing clouds which has no reference to any thing upon this earth, or the duties which devolve upon us as its inhabitants, I must say that I think the result upon character and conduct, in such a case, would be far indeed removed from that which is truly great. But if, as in the case of Sir Isaac Newton, you suppose him to be engaged in contemplating with the eye of a philosopher, the great and glorious universe around him, not only with regard to its vastness and its beauty, but to the simple HOW and WHY of every thing it contains, then I agree with you that any one, though a shepherd, may still be a great man."

" Truly great, I suppose you mean," observed Henry.

" You mistake me there," replied his mother. " To be truly great involves principles beyond the laws of matter, and which I should scarcely reckon under the head of philosophy, as that word is most frequently applied."

To be continued.

Original.

TO A CLERGYMAN, A CHRISTMAS PRESENT.*

BY MRS. L. H. SIGOURNEY.

May the simple gift we send,
Tell you of the grateful friend,
Who, with those he lov'd, was fed
Oft by you with living bread,
Heavenly manna, freely strewed,
Rich repast of angel's food.

When your hearth or board around,
Wife, and child, and guest are found,
And to them, with reverence meek,
Of His ceaseless care you speak
Who our favor'd land supplies
With the bounty of the skies,
And with peace and plenty sweet,
Fills it with the finest wheat,
In the winged thought of love,
Soaring high to Him above,
In the prayer that seeks His throne,
With its warm, prevailing tone,
Friend and teacher, fain would we,
Though away, remembered me.

THE BUTTERFLY.

Child of the sun! pursue thy rapturous flight,
Mingling with her thou lov'st in fields of light;
And where the flowers of paradise unfold,
Quaff fragrant nectar from their cups of gold,
There shall thy wings, rich as an evening sky,
Expand and shut in silent ecstacy.

——Yet wert thou once a worm, a thing that crept
On the bare earth, then wrought a tomb, and slept;
And such is man; soon from his cell of clay,
To burst a seraph in the blaze of day.

---

* These lines were written at the request of a respected friend, to accompany the gift of a barrel of flour, which he was in the habit yearly of sending to a former revered pastor. It were to be wished that Christians more frequently allowed themselves the pleasure of following this good example, and of freely imparting their temporal things to those who faithfully minister to them in spiritual things.

Original.

THE CHARM OF THE SOUTHERN SKY.

BY HENRY M. PARSONS.

Distance from country, home, and loved ones is never more forcibly realized by the wanderer from a northern clime, than when crossing the tropic ocean, he watches night after night the familiar stars of his childhood, as they disappear one by one below the horizon. Nor, if his perception of beauty is vivid, can he ever so correctly appreciate the loveliness and magnificence of the starry world as when he sees the southern constellations rising one after another, and completing the most splendid pageantry of the heavens with the symmetrical and resplendent cross, overhung with the starry crown.

This observation is fortified by the concurrent testimony of the illiterate sailor and philosophic traveller, as well as by the extravagant descriptions of the excitable and imaginative voyager. One who has sailed across the Equator must have remarked the grandeur with which the planets were invested to the least observant of the crew, in the clear sky of the tropic sea. They who have read the "Personal Narrative" of Humboldt, cannot have forgotten his impressions of the southern constellations, conveyed in faithful and eloquent description.

Our conceptions of the real beauty of the northern sky are feeble, not alone in consequence of familiarity, but because of the misty atmosphere through which we generally behold it. Unquestionably our impressions of the superior brilliancy of the southern constellations, is derived in a great measure from the transparent medium through which we view them. When the evening clouds have vanished, the light streams in every direction from the blue dome of Heaven, with intense and unequalled lustre. Often there is not the least discoverable mist to interrupt the vision or dim the glory. The magnitude of the planets appears incredibly increased, and their distance as greatly diminished. Even the scattered nebule assume a distinctive splendor in contrast with the blackness of fields of space. When there is an unobstructed range for the eye over the entire horizon, from an elevated position on ship-board, the view is magnificent unaided by the poetry of imagination, for the four large stars which form the cross, and the seven which make an oval and form the crown, are the poetry of truth. The first is a burning memorial of the sufferings on Calvary— the latter a beautiful emblem of the Redeemer's reward.

Gazing upon these natural features of the southern sky, we are reminded that the evidence of God's love to man is not less because he does not perceive that evidence. Thousands live and will die without one view of the southern cross, and yet that cross shines on, and will shine on long after they have slept the sleep of death. Reality of heirship to eternal life through the Saviour is known and will be known, though multitudes reject His proffered grace.

The rapture of which the mind is conscious in surveying the southern cross cannot be communicated by description.— It is realized in actual, unclouded vision, such as it has been our privilege to enjoy. They who would discover the loveliness, the amazing glory of the plan of redemption, must come within the influence of the gospel. They must take an humble attitude at the foot of the tree on which the Son of man was crucified, and with no veil between, must look upon Him " who was wounded for their transgressions, and bruised for their iniquities." Then will they experience a joy before unknown, and the more they contemplate the condescension of the Saviour will their hearts expand with love and hope.

Our own feelings on first beholding the southern cross were so rapturous and intense that we can never forget the scene. If such emotions can be known with the infirmities of the material which confines the spirit on earth, when we gaze upon the handiwork of the Almighty, who can estimate the bliss which the Christian will possess when he shall enter the city of the New Jerusalem, which " has no need of the sun, neither of the moon to shine in it, for the glory of the Lord shall lighten it, and the Lamb is the light thereof." Who can fathom the happiness of the redeemed when the music of the spheres shall have given place to the melody of golden harps—when the stars shall have grown dim and gone out in darkness before the effulgence of immortal day.

It is worthy of remark that in the relative position of the cross and the crown, the latter is elevated above the former. The promise to the child of God is prospective with life. In his toils and sufferings he must cast his eye, the eye of a lively faith, upon the object of his hope, and above it he will behold the crown. Does the crown which overhangs the southern cross attract our admiration and awaken enlarged conceptions of its mighty Architect, what will be the Christian's conception of that Architect when he shall behold him no longer through his works, but face to face? What will be his estimate of his crown when he knows that that crown is the eternal and unclouded presence and favor of the Lord God Almighty.

Original.

IMPROVISATION. LACONICS.

BY REV. A. A. LIPSCOMB.

The strongest branches of the tree are nearest to the root, and so the firmest Christian lives closest to the Redeemer.

Every thing has its enemies. The worm destroys the beautiful flower. The promising harvest is blighted by the rust. The cotton-bloom perishes beneath the ravages of the insect. The pathway of the devout Christian is beset by foes, who omit no opportunity, and spare no exertions to defeat his hopes.

I saw a graceful rose bush. The humming bird made low music amid its bloom, and the gay butterfly flitted around its loveliness, but I observed that the bee only extracted honey from it. All men enjoy the Divine mercy, but the Christian only derives blessedness therefrom.

Tall trees bear no fruit. The orchard growth is small.—
Humble spirits glorify God.

The virtues and graces of Christianity should always meet together, just as the noble magnolia exhibits both strength and beauty.

Heaven is the birth-place of music.

Politeness, true and genuine, should be associated with personal christianity. A fine picture should have a handsome frame.

The sailor may relax his attention, and the soldier sometimes lay down his arms; but the devoted Christian must ever watch and pray.

The trade-winds vary, but the gales of the Spirit may waft us continually toward Heaven.

The character of Jesus Christ—the simplicity of sublimity, and the sublimity of simplicity.

AUTUMN.

THE FALL OF THE LEAF.

Oh, there's a beauty in the dying year!
  'Tis sweet at quiet eventide to gaze
  Upon the fading hills, when the dim haze
Hangs like a pall above old Autumn's bier.

These ancient woods! how beautiful in death!
  For see—the vivid green hath left the leaf,
  And brighter hues are there; yet they are brief;
Their pomp will vanish at the cold wind's breath.

There is a breeze amid the leaves; it swells
  Far in the solemn wood-paths, like the peals
  Of music o'er the waters. Hark! it steals
Sweet as the distant sound of evening bells.

It is the voice of Autumn—the low dirge
  Sung mournfully within its ruined halls;
  It stirs the fallen leaves, and sadly falls
On the hushed air like whispers on the surge.

The summer birds have sought a summer shore;
  They lingered till the cold—cold wind went in
  And withered their green homes; their merry din
Is mingling with the rivulet's song no more.

Rich flowers have perished on the silent earth;
  Blossoms of valley and of wood, that gave
  A fragrance to the wind, have found a grave
Upon the scentless turf that gave them birth.

Pale, faded year, thy dying hour hath come;
  Oh, there are crowds that with a joyous brow
  Welcomed thy birth, whose mirthful voices now
Are hushed in the long silence of the tomb.

Original.

THE SISTER'S PORTRAIT.

"Those eyes whence Love diffused his purest light,
  Proud in such beaming orbs his reign to show;
That face with tints of mingled lustre bright,
  Where the rose mantled o'er the living snow;
The rich redundance of that golden hair,
  Bright as the sunbeams of meridian day;
That form so graceful and that hand so fair—
  Where now those treasures? Mouldering into clay!"

Yes, it is too true. That form, those beauties which we admired, which we looked upon with pride, are "mouldering into clay." And yet the portrait, as it hangs in its unadorned loveliness over the piano whose keys yielded sweet music to her slightest touch, recalls the past with a force which almost makes it present bliss. We gaze upon those life-like charms, and drink in the lovely expression of those beaming eyes, till we feel her presence near, and almost fancy we can hold such converse with the unconscious picture as we were wont to hold with the fair being herself, ere she took a farewell of earth and laid her down to die. How the reality comes over us, and memory recalls too vividly the past, till we are constrained to treasure up in our changing hearts her virtues, her unassuming piety, and her filial, sisterly affection.

Elizabeth N—— was one of a large family of brothers and sisters, whose hearts were united in the most endearing bonds Trained up by christian parents, they grew together a family of love, and knew no lack of affectionate interest, no jarring discord, and none of that soaring ambition which so often breaks in upon the family circle with unhallowed restlessness and discontent. Elizabeth was neither the eldest child nor the youngest; but she was one of whom it might truly be said, "to know her was to love her," and those who knew her best were sure to love her most. Wherever we met her, whether engaged in the duties and pleasures of home, or mingling with her youthful companions, many of whom were gay and thoughtless, or amid the variety of characters ever displayed in the School room, in the Sabbath school, the Bible class, or the Sanctuary, Elizabeth was the same gentle, affectionate, sensitive being, whose purity won our love. She was young and fair, and from her eye shone brightly the light of mind; and then the brow above, so pure—so noble, seemed formed for a sculptor's model or a poet's dream. I have often thought when fondly gazing upon her, surely

> "Thine is a face to look upon and pray
> That a pure spirit keep thee."

Otherwise the many allurements spread out before thee by an enticing world may prove an effectual snare. A pure spirit did keep her. The christian's God was her refuge and her strong hold, and from the moment she fixed her trust in Him, He was to her the same "yesterday, to-day, and forever."— She was not one of those joyous, light-hearted beings, who are animated and excited with all that is beautiful, interesting, or bewildering. She was not one day upon the summit of Mount Hope, gazing upon delightful scenes of unfading bliss, and the next, with head bowed down and eyes riveted to the earth, wandering with a slow step in the Valley of Dejection. She was ever calm, thoughtful, and serene, yet cheerful as though filled with the light of undying hope. She was naturally of a slender constitution, and from her earliest infancy was subject to occasional turns of sudden and painful illness; but the Friend of the afflicted seemed ever near to sustain and comfort her.

About a year before Elizabeth's death, her kind and excellent mother, without warning, was taken from this vale of tears to a brighter and better world. The large family, thus deprived of a watchful and affectionate mother, mourned deeply their loss, though they knew it was her eternal gain. At every change, at every step in life, they missed her low, sweet voice and her kind counsel. There was a vacancy in the loved circle as they gathered in social converse or knelt around the domestic altar, which might never again be filled. Death had been there, and had robbed them of a treasure which earth can never replace, impressing them with the uncertainty of all below the skies. The frail Elizabeth received the solemn lesson to her own bosom. A bitter drop of sorrow was mingled in her cup of earthly happiness; a dark shadow was cast upon her pathway of life, and her sensitive spirit told her that now indeed she must begin in earnest

"To act and to suffer, to watch and to pray,"

lest the spoiler should come in an hour when she looked not for him, and too quickly lay her in the tomb. From her feebleness and frequent illness, she clung the more closely to her fond mother, and bitter indeed was the separation; but meekly, though tearfully, she bore the chastening, sometimes almost wishing she too might soon be taken from earth. She struggled to subdue that melancholy so natural to her, which now seemed anew to claim indulgence, and neither in word or tone was there any lack of christian cheerfulness. Yet her loss was great, her trial severe; and from the hour of her bereavement, until she yielded up her own stricken spirit,

"Upon her face there was the tint of grief—
The settled shadow of an inward strife,

> And an unquiet drooping of the eye,
> As if its lid were charged with unshed tears."

At this time, while the "shadows of deep and holy memories were resting like the wing of death upon her brow," this portrait was taken. I seem to fancy, as I gaze upon the speaking countenance, that tear drops are gathering in those beautiful eyes, and the trembling lips are compressed to keep down the rising sigh. So true to nature—so like the sweet Elizabeth herself! How I rejoice that we may retain her likeness, her very image, though she, alas, has departed hence to be here no more. It makes our hearts better while we look upon it and recall her deep-toned piety. It binds our souls in more enduring bonds to remember the purity and devotedness of her sisterly affection. And when we are reminded of her last hour, those dying words which are laid up in the sanctuary of our hearts never to be forgotten, surely we shall be urged onward in the path of duty, never wearying until we meet her in her home on high.

> "Oh, we should cling too close to earth, and love
> Too well its pleasures and delights,
> Were there no shadows on its scene of light,
> No sorrow mingled in its cup of joy."

For several months before her death, though in usual health, Elizabeth seemed daily to receive warning, as if from some invisible power, to hold herself in readiness to yield her trusting spirit up to God. Day after day some new piece of work was finished, some good design accomplished, some last appeal made to those dear to her heart, whom she longed to have serve Christ on earth, and then to unite with her in singing the song of dying love amid the redeemed in heaven. It was well that she did what her hands found to do with all her might and without delay, for the destroying angel stole softly and suddenly upon her in an unsuspected way, and hurried her almost unconsciously into the cold, dark grave. Had she left the work of preparation until a dying hour, as too many have done, it could not have been made, for reason was dethroned; the mind was a chaos of wildness and confusion, until but one lone hour was left, ere she exchanged time for eternity. Only four days before that last hour, she had mingled with her young companions in their accustomed duties and pleasures, feeling as well as usual. But suddenly the destroyer laid upon her his icy hand, and the springs of life began to fail at their fountain. As the delirium increased, she sank rapidly beneath the fatal blow, notwithstanding the faithful exertions of physicians who would fain have kept her from the tomb. In her last hour, reason was kindly restored. Then meekly and trustingly she spoke of hope and brighter days beyond the pass of shadows. She looked earnestly upon the dear ones around her, from whose sorrowing hearts gushed the grief they could not suppress, and prayed fervently for a lasting blessing to descend upon them, for a glorious re-union in the heavenly mansions. Her last earthly breathings arose in prayer for the loved family circle, that no winter's frost might chill their love, no blighting worldly passions break the golden chain that bound them. Serenely she left the world, with a heavenly smile resting upon her countenance. We gaze upon her cherished image, her beautiful portrait, and treasure the memory of her faithfulness, her holy love, the trusting meekness of her last fervent prayer, while

"We travel with a surer step to Heaven!"

SCRAPS.

Outward attacks and troubles rather fix than unsettle the Christian, as tempests from without only serve to root the oak firmer; while an inward canker will gradually rot and decay it.

It is not the will of God to give us more troubles than will bring us to live by faith simply on him; he loves us too well to give us a moment of uneasiness.

Original.

THE DYING ROBBER.

BY MRS. C. H. PUTNAM.

During the period when the cholera raged in Dublin, when "men's hearts were failing them for fear," and all, whose circumstances would permit, had fled from the terrors of the pestilence to the purer air of the country, the following remarkable, but well authenticated events took place.

In one section of the city, peopled principally by the poorer and more degraded class, among whom the ravages of the disease were peculiarly dreadful, there resided a pious clergyman of the Established church, whose sense of duty would not permit him to quit his post, merely because it had become one of fatigue and danger. To the wretched inhabitants of this district, he became a messenger of mercy, administering both to the soul and body, and standing with unwearied kindness by the side of many a sick bed, from which the nearest relatives had been driven by terror or removed by death.— His labors were unremitted, and nothing but the arm of Him, in whose service he was engaged and whose footsteps he was following, could have sustained him under so much exposure and fatigue. One dark, stormy night he had retired at a late hour to seek some repose after having been engaged during the day, in going from house to house, or more properly from garret to garret tending upon the sick; when just as he was about to lie down, a loud knock was heard at the door. His first impulse was not to notice it, so utterly unable did he feel to go forth again upon his work of mercy; but the knock was repeated, till he was obliged to put his head out of the window and ask who was there, and what was wanted. A hoarse rough voice replied, "it is a friend; I want you to go with me to visit my dying father." "But it storms," said the clergyman, "and I must have rest." "For God's sake come with me, sir," said the man "my father is dying, and I cannot return without you. There was something forbidding in the man's voice, which, in spite of the clergyman's familiarity with the worst of the lower classes of men, struck him with a sensation of repugnance and disgust; but the solemn nature of the appeal, and the extreme anxiety with which it was urged, overcame his reluctance, and even his sense of fatigue, and he prepared to comply with the request. When, however, he reached the door, the darkness of the night, the rain, and more than all the haggard looks of the man, almost shook his resolution.

"Where am I to go," said he? "Follow me," said the man, "and I will take you to my father, and return you safe to your dwelling." They went on, the man leading the way, and the minister, with his cloak closely wrapped about him, following behind. They passed through several open streets, but soon turned into dark alleys and narrow passages, strewed with fragments of old buildings—places of which the clergyman had no knowledge, and which he could not have believed were to be found in the city of Dublin. More than once did he stop, declaring that he would go no farther; but the importunity of the man, his rough but solemn energy, and the calm tone of sincerity in which he promised that no evil was intended, and that he should return in safety, would once more re-assure him, and he proceeded. After travelling what appeared to the clergyman to be a great distance, the guide suddenly turned a corner, entered an old ruined building, through which they passed into an open court, and then into another building on the opposite side. As there was no trace of inhabitants in this lonely place, the clergyman again stopped and positively refused to go forward. "How do I know but you intend to murder me," said he to the man. "You have nothing to fear," replied he, "as I live, there shall no evil befal you, and not an hair of your head shall be injured."

Well knowing that if his worst fears were true, resistance was in vain, as he was completely in the power of his companion, he saw no alternative but to follow, trusting in that

THE DYING ROBBER.   105

God, who had shielded him amid the shafts of pestilence and death. They now entered a narrow passage, the clergyman putting one hand against the wall and groping his way in utter darkness, till he found himself descending a winding staircase, at the bottom of which the guide stopped, requesting him to remain a few moments. He then struck against a trapdoor, which opened by a spring, and passed down, but soon returned, bearing in one hand a lantern and in the other a ladder, which he fastened to the opening of the trap door, and motioned the minister to descend. "My last hour has come," thought he "and here, in this region of darkness and crime, must my life be ended by the hand of this ruffian." But the rising fear had scarcely taken possession of his mind, ere it was displaced by better recollections. "Not a sparrow can fall to the ground without my Father," thought he; "and not a weapon formed against me can prosper without his permission;" and, committing himself to the Lord, he followed the guide down the ladder, at the bottom of which was a door which he opened, and they entered a spacious cavern, low, but of great extent; and so far removed from the world above, that it seemed to belong to another region. Here upon pallets of straw, lay stretched out numbers of squalid wretches, past whom the guide hurried him to the furthest corner, where lay an old man evidently in the last stages of cholera. "Here is my father, sir," said he, "and if you can speak a word of comfort to him, do it in the name of heaven." The clergyman approached the dying man, and found him not only agonized with bodily disease, but with the pangs of a guilty conscience. He roused at the sight of the minister and with the last efforts of expiring nature, was about to unburden his mind, when the son interposing, stepped up, and presenting a bible, which the clergyman had laid down when he entered, said; "before you listen to what my father is about to say, you must take an oath upon this book, that you will never, under any circumstances, reveal the place of our retreat." Sensible that resistance or remonstrance was in vain, the clergyman took the oath, and the old man proceeded. It appeared that he was the leader of a band of robbers, who, for years, had infested the city of Dublin, eluding all the vigilance of its police, and committing depredations upon life and property. Here they would probably have remained, bidding defiance to the power of man, had not the arm of God himself reached them in this deep and secret abyss. But it was not cholera alone that had found them out. The Spirit of the living God that searcher of hearts and trier of reins—that omnipotent power which pierces even to the dividing asunder of soul and spirit—that pervades alike hight and depth, length and breadth—that Spirit had touched the heart of this old offender in his hiding place. He related that in one of his visits to the city, which they were in the habit of patrolling during the day for the purpose of marking the spoil to be seized at night, he had passed a church on the Sabbath, the doors of which were open. An impulse which he could not resist had impelled him to enter, and said he, " while I was gazing about, I saw you, sir, in the pulpit, and heard you read from the Bible something about taking the wings of the morning and going up into heaven, and descending down into hell, and that God was in all these places. As soon as I heard these words, I hurried out into the street and began to think, if God is everywhere, he must be in our secret cavern, and sees and knows all our ungodly deeds. I returned disturbed and miserable to this wretched abode, and would gladly have forsaken my evil ways; but though I could not get rid of the words from the book, I dared not even hint to my companions that I desired to do so. In this state, cholera seized me, and with it all the horrors of a dreaded hereafter I entreated to see you, sir, and at the risk of his own life, my son promised to bring you to me."

After listening to the story of the dying man, the clergyman kindly and affectionately spoke to him the words of that gospel which proclaims peace and pardon through the blood of the atonement. He told him of Jesus, who died for sinners, even the chief—that His blood would cleanse the foulest stains— that he cast away none that came to him, not even the dying thief, who hung by him upon the cross. He then kneeled down and commended him to God and the riches of his sovereign grace. When he rose from prayer, the dying man grasped his hand with an almost supernatural energy, saying, "There is hope—I die in peace! Jesus can save," and then expired. The scene was a solemn and awful one, and the clergyman looking round upon the wretched inmates of the place, felt it was a moment to be improved. He opened the sacred volume, which he always carried with him, and read aloud that beautiful passage, "Let him that stole steal no more, but rather let him labor, working with his own hands," etc.— Thus, for the first time, and probably for the last, was that gospel which brings life and immortality to light, preached in those regions of crime and death; and thus, from this second Golgotha, may have been borne to the paradise of God the soul of another DYING THIEF.

The guide now offered to fulfil his promise in taking the clergyman to his home. Leading the way out of the cavern, but in an opposite direction from that by which they had entered, he opened a door into another apartment, which they crossed, and then came to a dark passage which gradually grew lower and narrower, till they were obliged to creep upon their hands and knees, and the clergyman actually found himself passing through one of the common sewers of the city, which had become dry. After some time, they began to breathe the fresh air. The first gleam of morning light broke in upon them, and they emerged into the streets of the city. The guide now bid the clergyman good morning, and was turning away when he said to him, "You surely do not mean to leave me here. I know not where I am, nor which way to go."— Pointing to the spire of a church but a few yards distant, he replied, "That is your own church; there is Baggot street, and you are but a few steps from your dwelling. Remember your oath." Saying this, he was gone before the astonished clergyman could believe it possible that he was really in the midst of his own people, and so near his own abode. The next Sabbath he related from the pulpit the singular events of this night, and the police of the city were immediately upon the alert to discover, if possible, the secret abode of the robbers. But in vain were all their exertions. Though every lane and alley, every ruined building and secret avenue was diligently examined, not a trace could be found of the entrance to the mysterious cavern.

What a striking illustration does this story afford of some of the most prominent and most precious principles of the christian faith. How does it magnify the riches of that grace which has so wonderfully adapted the salvation revealed in the gospel to the extremity of the sinner's case—that the cry of the penitent, even from the lowest depths of crime and wretchedness, can reach the heights of divine mercy, and be answered with words of pardon and peace; which, even in the eleventh hour, proclaims to the vilest of the vile, "that the blood of Jesus Christ cleanseth from all sin." What but the free grace of that gospel, which brings salvation to the guilty and lost, could meet the case of this dying thief? What but the arm of sovereign, everlasting love could have slain the enmity of his heart, burst the iron bonds of sin, making him to taste of its bitterness, while it cleansed him from its defilement, and saved him from its consequences.

But mercy and forgiveness manifested to this "one sinner that repented," is not the only lesson of wisdom which this story teaches. The same God who is "gracious and merciful, pardoning iniquity, transgression, and sin," will by no means clear the guilty. Sinner, dost thou ever reflect how constantly He is about thy path? In vain dost thou seek to hide from him. There is no depth from which his right arm will not bring out his own people to deliver and save them, and from which he will not listen to the sighing of the prisoner, nor any height from which he will not bring down the pride of the wicked to detection and punishment. He will cause a "man's own sin to find him out;" to pursue him to every corner of the earth; to the highest mountain and the deepest cavern; to the haunts of pleasure and to the bed of suffering.

Original.

RURAL DEVOTION.

See Engraving.

BY HENRY M. PARSONS.

In devotion, the soul pours its wants, hopes, fears, guilt or pleasures into the bosom of a heavenly Friend. To do this is the christian's privilege, wherever he may be located and in whatever circumstances placed. But there are seasons and occasions which seem peculiarly designed to awaken gratitude and love towards our Almighty Benefactor.

One of these is represented in the engraving. Summer covers the trees with their loveliest green, and spreads her richest carpet in a valley through which the emigrant family wend their way. The tranquil sky is above, and the gentle breeze wafts the odor of the flower. Forms of beauty, activity, and enjoyment are multiplied around, and naturally lead the soul to their source—the source of all goodness and excellence.

The sire gathers his children around him, unfolds the sacred volume, and reads upon its pages and in the surrounding scene innumerable reasons for praising God. Nor is praise less acceptable because rendered in pastoral simplicity, or incited by the drapery and melody of a temple reared by the hand of Heaven.

Rural life is favorable to devotion. The succession of the seasons and the operation of the laws of nature, are continuous evidences of omnipotence, omniscience, and unmeasured goodness. Though a disposition to regard these changes in the natural world as matters of course may diminish their influence over the current of our thoughts, it does not prevent us from discerning many of the lessons they are intended to impart.— There are numberless voices in the recurring seasons which remind us of our heavenly Father in tones so sweet that we listen unconsciously till our hearts are softened and elevated, and our song of thanksgiving mingles with the hymn of nature. They come to us in the birds of spring—the gentle summer air—the whispering brook and the swollen torrent.

Wherever we ramble in the country, there are countless silent monitors of our indebtedness to God in giving such inexhaustible sources of enjoyment. They speak to us in the valley, the hill, and the mountain, whether their garniture is the lustre of vegetation or the brilliancy of winter's snow.— The very floweret that blushes at our feet, unrivalled by art and emblematical of virtue, bears the impress of a hand divine. The tiniest snow-flake glittering in the moonlight has its errand of kindness, its teaching of God. The dew-drop that sparkles on the rose-bud in the heat of morning, and is transferred to the cloud illumined by the rainbow, tell us no more forcibly that the good of earth will be exchanged for Heaven, than the harvest plain proclaims the goodness of the Deity.— If we are taught thankfulness in the glowing spring time, when the expanding blossoms yield their fragrance, we are reminded of the same duty, when the forest puts on its robe of many colors, and gives its fruits in season.

Rural life is favorable to devotion because of the stillness it affords. Some abstraction from the world is necessary to divest the soul of worldly thoughts. The excitements and business of a residence in town absorb the mind so much as to impede the cultivation of a devotional spirit. In the country, the world, with its inflaming passions, appears in its real insignificance, while the presence of a Supreme Being in His works awakens our reverence, and animates us with higher and nobler purposes, and a truer appreciation of His benevolence. Would we open our ears to the instructions and our eyes to the beauties of nature, we should feel more clearly that "God is love," and oftener would our language at the throne of grace be the language of praise.

In the "Practical Thoughts" of the late Rev. Wm. Nevins, eminent for his attainments in personal holiness, there is an invaluable article entitled, "I must praise more." "Shall all our devotion consist in prayer? Shall we be always thinking of our wants and never of His benefits? always dwelling on what remains to be done, and never thinking of what has already been done for us? always uttering desire and never expressing gratitude? Is this the way to treat a benefactor? It displeases God that we should be always dwelling on our wants as if he never supplied them. How do we know that God is not waiting for us to praise Him for a benefit he has conferred, before he will confer on us that other which we may be now so earnestly desiring of him.

"Christian reader, you complain, perhaps, that your prayer is not heard; suppose you try the efficacy of praise. If you consider the goodness of the Lord, it may be He will consider your wants. There is nothing glorifies God like praise.— 'Whoso offereth praise glorifieth me.' Prayer expresses dependence and desire; but praise is ingenuous. Praise is the employment of heaven. Angels praise. The spirits of the just made perfect praise. We shall not always pray, but we shall ever praise. Let us anticipate the employment of heaven. Let us learn the song now, 'O that men would praise the Lord for His goodness.'"

The Psalmist who was eminently blessed with enlarged conceptions of the wisdom and goodness of God as displayed in nature, abounded in praise. He enjoyed communion with Heaven in his closet, and when surrounded by his retinue of dependents and followers, as well as in the field; and the key of that communion was praise. The christian possesses sweet and cheering peace when his heart goes forth in thanksgiving to Him who delighteth in mercy. How much more abiding would be his joy did he oftener cherish a grateful spirit. How much more ardent would be his desire for a holy preparation for the company of those who sing, "Worthy is the Lamb that was slain, to receive power, and riches, and wisdom, and strength, and honor, and blessing." How much oftener would he feel like David, whose personal distinctions, enjoyments and mercies, so far from strengthening his attachments to earth, only prompted him to exclaim the more earnestly, "I shall be satisfied when I awake in thy likeness."

MANTUA. H.

VIVACE.

1. Child of sin and sorrow, Filled with dismay, Wait not for tomorrow, Yield thee today. Heav'n bids thee come, While yet there's room: Child of sin and sorrow, Hear and obey.

2. Child of sin and sorrow,
Why wilt thou die?
Come, while thou canst borrow
Help from on high:
Grieve not that love,
Which from above,
Child of sin and sorrow,
Would bring thee nigh.